THE GREAT ADVENTURE

THE GREAT ADVENTURE

THEODORE ROOSEVELT

AND THE RISE OF MODERN AMERICA

ALBERT MARRIN

DUTTON CHILDREN'S BOOKS

*This book is dedicated to the memory
of our friend Wally Glassman*

DUTTON CHILDREN'S BOOKS A division of Penguin Young Readers Group
Published by the Penguin Group

Penguin Group (USA) Inc., 375 Hudson Street, New York, New York 10014, U.S.A. • Penguin Group
(Canada), 90 Eglinton Avenue East, Suite 700, Toronto, Ontario, Canada M4P 2Y3 (a division of Pearson
Penguin Canada Inc.) • Penguin Books Ltd, 80 Strand, London WC2R 0RL, England • Penguin Ireland,
25 St Stephen's Green, Dublin 2, Ireland (a division of Penguin Books Ltd) • Penguin Group (Australia),
250 Camberwell Road, Camberwell, Victoria 3124, Australia (a division of Pearson Australia Group Pty
Ltd) • Penguin Books India Pvt Ltd, 11 Community Centre, Panchsheel Park, New Delhi - 110 017, India
• Penguin Group (NZ), 67 Apollo Drive, Rosedale, North Shore 0745, Auckland, New Zealand
(a division of Pearson New Zealand Ltd) • Penguin Books (South Africa) (Pty) Ltd, 24 Sturdee Avenue,
Rosebank, Johannesburg 2196, South Africa • Penguin Books Ltd, Registered Offices: 80 Strand, London
WC2R 0RL, England

The publisher wishes to thank those institutions and individuals who granted permission to reproduce
works, and for their kind cooperation in the realization of this book. Photo credits: Frontispiece and pages
4, 6, 15, 31, 40, 45, 47, 51, 54, 55, 56 (lower right), 57, 64, 66 (upper left), 66 (lower right), 72, 73, 74, 76
(upper left), 76 (lower right), 77, 79, 80, 87, 96, 98, 99, 103, 107 (lower left), 119, 122, 124, 129, 130, 132,
140, 161, 164, 178, 185, 188, 191, 192, 198, 199, 204, 205, 214, 226, courtesy of the Library of Congress;
pages 5, 9, 13, 39, 60, 107 (upper right), 111, 112, 116, 127, 135, 153, 154, 155, 162, 181, 187, courtesy of the
author; pages 14, 16, 18, 19 (lower left), 29, 32, 36, 52, 56 (upper left), 106, 108, 134, 163, 206, 213, 215, 230,
231, courtesy of the Theodore Roosevelt Collection, Harvard College Library; pages 19 (upper right), 136
(lower right), 169, 170, 172 , 232, courtesy of the National Archives; pages 53 and 136 (upper left), courtesy
of the Franklin D. Roosevelt Library Digital Archives; page 68, courtesy of the Museum of the City of New
York, The Byron Collection; page 70 by Horace Taylor, courtesy of *The Verdict*; pages 71 and 128 by Joseph
Keppler, courtesy of *Puck*; page 82, courtesy of the Tamiment Library, New York University; page 156,
courtesy of the Denver Public Library; page 182, by William A. Rogers, and page 202, courtesy of the *New
York Herald*; page 193 by Homer Davenport and page 227 by Morris, courtesy of the *New York Evening Mail*;
page 195, courtesy of *African Game Trails* by Theodore Roosevelt; page 208, courtesy of *Through the Brazilian
Wilderness* by Theodore Roosevelt; page 218 by Ding, courtesy of the *Des Moines Register & Mail*; page 220,
courtesy of Brown Brothers; page 233, courtesy of the New York *World*.

Library of Congress Cataloging-in-Publication Data

Marrin, Albert.
The great adventure: Theodore Roosevelt and the rise of modern America / by Albert Marrin.
—1st ed. p. cm. Includes bibliographical references. ISBN: 978-0-525-47659-7 (hardcover)
1. Roosevelt, Theodore, 1858–1919—Juvenile literature. 2. Presidents—United States—Biography—
Juvenile literature. I. Title. E757.M375 2007 973.91'1092—dc22 [B] 2006035912

Published in the United States by Dutton Children's Books,
a division of Penguin Young Readers Group
345 Hudson Street, New York, New York 10014
www.penguin.com/youngreaders

Designed by Richard Amari   Manufactured in China   First Edition   10 9 8 7 6 5 4 3 2 1

CONTENTS

"It is impossible to win the great prizes of life

without running risks. . . . But life is a great adventure,

and the worst part of all fears is the fear of living."

—Theodore Roosevelt

THE GREAT ADVENTURE

SEVENTEEN COACHES
ALL TRIMMED IN BLACK

Seventeen coaches all trimmed in black
Took McKinley to the graveyard and never brought him back
> *To Buffalo, to Buffalo.*
Seventeen coaches all trimmed in black
Took Roosevelt to the White House and never brought him back
> *To Buffalo, to Buffalo.*

—SONG, 1901

Buffalo, New York, Friday, September 6, 1901. A glorious late-summer afternoon, bright and cloudless. Gentle breezes blowing off Lake Erie gave little relief from the blistering heat. Yet fashionably dressed women wore high-necked dresses with skirts that swept the ground and large feathered hats. Men wore suits, vests, shirts with stiff collars, tightly knotted ties, and straw hats.

For several months, special trains had brought thousands of day visitors to Buffalo, host city to the Pan-American Exposition. People traveled hundreds of miles to glimpse the marvelous future that science promised humanity, perhaps even including space travel. By day, crowds marveled at the machinery displays in the exhibit halls, massive buildings painted in bright pastels. At night, those used to oil lamps for lighting gasped in wonder at a display of electricity, a marvel of the new age, in action.

On this day, thousands sweltered outside the Temple of Music, a large concert hall. Hundreds of others, the lucky first-comers, formed a line to meet William McKinley, twenty-fifth President of the United States. The line moved quickly. Each person shook McKinley's hand for a few seconds, muttered a few polite words, and moved on. After a while, Leon Czolgosz (pronounced *SHOL-gus*), twenty-eight, stood before the president. Like his Polish-immigrant parents, Leon had always struggled for a living. That struggle had so embittered him that it would turn him into a murderer. Before McKinley's bodyguards could react,

Czolgosz drew a pistol and fired twice. The first bullet went wild; the second bullet passed through the president's stomach. Mortally wounded, McKinley died in agony eight days later.

According to the U.S. Constitution, upon the president's death or inability to do his job, the vice president takes over. Czolgosz's bullet cleared the way for a man who was already among the most celebrated figures of his time. Just six weeks shy of his forty-third birthday, Theodore Roosevelt became the youngest man ever to hold the nation's highest office.

The new president was such an imposing figure that seeing him only once left a lifelong impression. Of average height for his day, Roosevelt stood five feet eight inches in his socks and weighed about 180 pounds when he took office. Yet, to anyone seeing him for the first time, he appeared much bigger. Solidly built, he had a thick bull neck and heavy jowls. His muscular arms and chest strained against his clothes, as if about to burst the seams. Roosevelt often invited small boys to punch him in the chest with all their might, wiping away their tears if they hurt their fists.[1]

Roosevelt's blue-gray eyes peered through thick spectacles. He wore his light brown hair close-cropped and parted high and a bit off center; a full mustache of the same color hid his upper lip. His most noticeable feature was his teeth. These appeared like an even row of large white gravestones, thus the nickname "Teethadore." Harry S. Truman, a future president, would recall how, when he was

Shot through a handkerchief. This drawing by an unknown artist depicts President McKinley's assassin at the moment he fired the fatal shot from a small-caliber pistol.

a boy in Independence, Missouri, the presidential train once stopped at the depot. The entire city, said Truman, "wanted to see him grin and show his teeth, which he did." Ads for Sanitol toothpaste showed just a pair of spectacles and a set of teeth; there was no need to identify the subject by name. The post office automatically sent mail addressed with just sketches of teeth and spectacles to the White House.[2]

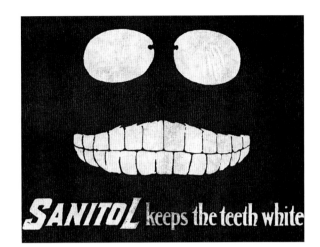
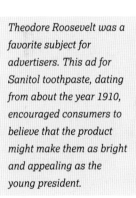

Theodore Roosevelt was a favorite subject for advertisers. This ad for Sanitol toothpaste, dating from about the year 1910, encouraged consumers to believe that the product might make them as bright and appealing as the young president.

Theodore Roosevelt was no ordinary politician. The man had, it seemed, a superhuman zest for living. He wanted to read everything, know everything, and do everything, no matter how dangerous or foolish others might think it. Americans spoke of his "electric quality," of how he radiated energy like a blast furnace. Novelist Henry James called him "a wonderful little machine," with wheels constantly whirring at top speed. This "little machine" squeezed several careers into one lifetime. Besides politics, his chosen career, Roosevelt was a soldier, naturalist, explorer, police-department head, and assistant secretary of the navy. A fiercely competitive sportsman, he boxed, wrestled, swam, rowed, hiked, played tennis, jumped horses, and hunted big game on three continents. A first-rate scholar, too, he spoke three foreign languages and could read three more.[3]

"I am a literary feller," Roosevelt once said of himself. He wrote an estimated eighteen million words for publication and wrote or dictated over 150,000 letters, which often ran to many pages. *The Works of Theodore Roosevelt,* collected in twenty-four volumes, do not contain all of his published writings. He also wrote hundreds of articles, book reviews, and travel accounts for newspapers and magazines. Among his thirty-five books are an *Autobiography* (1913) and serious works of biography, history, travel, and natural history. In 1882, at the age of twenty-four, he published a classic: *The Naval History of the War of 1812.* Though outdated, his *Winning of the West* (1889–96) is still good reading. *The Deer Family* (1902) became the only book ever published by a sitting president. Unlike most presidents before or since, Roosevelt did not trust speech writers; he wrote his own speeches and messages to Congress.[4]

Yet, for all his writing and speech making, Roosevelt seldom revealed his inner self or showed self-insight. He blanked out unpleasant experiences as if

A formal head-and-shoulders portrait of Theodore Roosevelt taken in 1913, shortly after his failed attempt to win election to a second term as president.

they were too painful to remember, or embarrassing for others to know about. His *Autobiography,* for example, is supposedly a candid account of his life. It is not. It says nothing about his first wife or her tragic death. Nor does Roosevelt mention his shattering disappointment as a child over his father's lack of military service during the Civil War.

Roosevelt was a fascinating person—a man of outsize strengths and weaknesses. He had charisma, a gift for connecting with others on an emotional level and winning their hearts through his personality. According to a friend, Lawrence F. Abbott, editor of the *Observer* magazine, "Roosevelt had this magnetic force of personality in a very marked degree. It surrounded him as a kind of nimbus [radiant light] . . . irresistibly drawing to him everyone who came into his presence." Part of that magnetism was, surely, manufactured. Better than any politician of the day, Roosevelt understood the need for having a "good press." To get anything accomplished in a democracy, one must first get elected to public office. Once elected, a politician must get, and keep, public opinion on his side. To do that, Roosevelt cultivated the press with his colorful language, bold deeds, and moral fervor.[5]

There was no wishy-washiness about Roosevelt. As he was definite about everything, you always knew where he stood on important issues. Preaching the "strenuous life," he insisted that people could overcome any hardship if only they had the will to do so. The president was living proof of this. His struggle to overcome asthma, a life-threatening illness, inspired countless sufferers' fight to lead normal lives.[6]

Roosevelt's definiteness, on the one hand a real strength, perhaps also accounts for his less pleasing qualities. "Let us admit, and regret," noted British journalist George Smalley, "that he honestly believes it impossible to differ from him honestly."[7] Since he held firm opinions on nearly every subject under the sun, an honest difference of opinion did not exist for Theodore. Anyone who disagreed with him, he thought, did so not for any legitimate reason, but out of stupidity, dishonesty, or malice.

Roosevelt had a sharp tongue, freely using it to inflict pain on those who displeased him. He relished, an observer noted, "the fun of hating." His remarks sometimes made enemies where, by keeping quiet, or by applying a little soft soap, he might have made allies.

The president's put-downs became legendary. Once Roosevelt lambasted a British diplomat, saying he had "a brain of about eight-guinea-pig power." Of a rival politician Roosevelt said, "Every time he opens his mouth, he subtracts from the sum total of human wisdom." When Oliver Wendell Holmes Jr., a respected Supreme Court justice, disagreed with him, Roosevelt snapped: "I could carve out of a banana a judge with more backbone than that." Indeed, there seemed no end to his stock of insults. A partial list includes: "sissy," "silly," "base," "low," "noxious," "despicable," "deplorable," "contemptible," "swine," "vermin," "skunk," "traitor," "fool," "idiot," "prize jackass," "hypocrite," and "shrill eunuch."[8]

Still, there was more to Theodore Roosevelt than his talents and defects. For reasons that we, and perhaps he himself, cannot always explain, he had a deep understanding of the big issues of his day. That is a special gift, particularly in a political leader. Theodore's talent for understanding the big picture allowed him to become a visionary leader, a president much admired and imitated by generations to come. "The Presidency is not merely an administrative office. That is the least of it. It is preeminently a place of moral leadership," said President Franklin D. Roosevelt (F.D.R.) in 1932. "All of our great presidents were leaders of thought at times when certain historic ideas in the life of the nation had to be clarified." George Washington embodied the idea of federal union, of one nation made up of separate states; Abraham Lincoln fought to preserve the Union and to end slavery. Thomas Jefferson and Andrew Jackson championed democracy, the right of ordinary people to govern themselves through their representatives. "Theodore Roosevelt and [Woodrow] Wilson," F.D.R. continued, "were both moral leaders, each in his own way and for his own time, who used the Presidency as a pulpit. [For] . . . without leadership alert and sensitive to change, we . . . lose our way."[9]

Theodore Roosevelt would have agreed with his distant cousin Franklin, who was a great president in his own right. The first Roosevelt to inhabit the White House called the presidency the "bully pulpit." It was, for him, the ideal place from which to preach his view of the great "historic ideas."

Roosevelt was born into an America undergoing spectacular changes. Triggered by the Industrial Revolution, these changes were a break with the past unlike any in human history before the birth of nuclear weapons, the computer, and the Internet. Throughout the ages, people had made everything they used by hand. Industrialization introduced machinery driven by high-pressure steam or electricity. By grouping machines at central points, called factories, mass production became possible. As industrialization spread, American society changed. Colossal cities arose. Millions of immigrants came from overseas. Skyscrapers, telephones, automobiles, airplanes, mass-produced clothing and food appeared within the space of a single lifetime.

Change is not always easy, pleasant, or peaceful. Often it comes at terrible costs to the innocent, the weak, and the unlucky. The rise of technology brought more goods, but also sharper social inequalities. America became two nations, one of fabulous wealth and luxury, the other of degrading poverty and squalor. An 1893 article in *John Swinton's Paper,* a workers' publication, highlighted the contrasts this way:

> In our busy land, that offers welcome to all mankind, we see the growth of a horde of paupers, beggars, and tramps.
>
> In our land, where all men are said to be born equal, we see the upspringing of a ruling class of millionaires.
>
> In our Congress and our Legislatures, established as agencies of popular power, we see capital holding the reins and running the machine.[10]

When Czolgosz's bullet made Roosevelt president, Theodore had to confront these and other problems—problems we still face in one form or another. The Declaration of Independence and the U.S. Constitution declare all Americans equal under the law, with equal rights and opportunities. Given these "historic ideas," upon which America is based, one might have asked:

Should industry be regulated for the benefit of all citizens equally? If so, who should do it? How?

Could overcrowded cities be made livable? And would the immigrants swarming into them honor American traditions?

How can Americans fight political corruption, the power of money to influence government in favor of the wealthy?

How can we keep our natural resources from being plundered for profit?

The Civil War ended slavery. Should African-Americans have federally protected equal rights, like voting and access to educational opportunities?

Should the nation play a role in world affairs, in keeping with its growing wealth and power? If so, how?

One may quarrel with Theodore Roosevelt's answers to these questions. Still, history has been kind (mostly) to him. For despite his shortcomings, Roosevelt was a man often wiser and more courageous than most, who genuinely sought the public good. That is why, in his lifetime, a 1913 *American Magazine* poll voted

This drawing from about the year 1905 is titled Hello, Teddy! *Most Americans had no idea that Roosevelt regarded the nickname as rude and disrespectful. He was wildly popular with voters, and people used the nickname to show their affection.*

him "the greatest man in the United States." That is also why, during the great economic depression of the 1930s, Franklin D. Roosevelt described him as the greatest man he ever knew. Later, the leading contenders of the 2000 presidential race agreed on little else than dubbing Theodore Roosevelt a hero. George W. Bush placed him among his favorite heroes. Al Gore appealed to voters "whose heroes are Theodore Roosevelt and Abraham Lincoln." Senator John McCain described him as "my ultimate hero."[11]

The modern idea of the presidency began to take shape under Theodore Roosevelt. Today, we think of the president as a kind of ship's captain. It is he who sets the course of our "ship of state" according to his vision of what America should be and where it should go. Naturally, we expect the president to propose a "program" of laws dealing with the country's specific needs.

Before Roosevelt, however, nearly all presidents had a narrow view of their office. The president, Theodore explained in his *Autobiography,* was seen and saw himself as "the servant of Congress rather than of the people." Under our system of government, it was once believed that Congress should take the lead. Congress made the laws, which the president "executed"—enforced. The Supreme Court decided if the laws squared with the Constitution.[12]

Despite resistance from within his own Republican Party, Roosevelt increased the president's power, proposing new laws and insisting that he play a key role in setting the national agenda. "My belief," he explained, "was that it was not only [the president's] right, but his duty to do anything that the needs of the Nation demanded unless such action was forbidden by the Constitution or by the laws. . . . [Thus] I did and caused to be done many things not previously done by the President. . . . In other words, I acted for the public welfare. I acted for the common well-being of all our people. . . . And I always finally acted as my conscience and common sense bade me act."[13]

At home, Theodore Roosevelt established the principle that the federal government should be an active force for good. Led by the president, it must tackle the problems born of the industrial age. Abroad, he recognized that America could no longer find safety behind its two oceans. Like it or not, the nation's wealth and power made it a player in world affairs. It must do its "duty," join other "enlightened and civilized" nations in preserving order, if necessary by force. "Aggressive fighting for the right," he insisted, "is the noblest sport the world affords."[14]

The presidency has been called "the splendid agony," an office that left its holders careworn and exhausted. Speaking for himself, Theodore Roosevelt would have disagreed with this strongly. From beginning to end, he enjoyed being president. He enjoyed it not only for the power, but also for the opportunity to serve the nation. The office energized Roosevelt, challenging him to do his best. "It is a wonderful privilege," he told his son Kermit, "to have been given the chance to do this work."[15]

The president had reason to be proud. His legacy includes a Nobel Prize, the first ever won by an American, for negotiating an end to a war between Russia and Japan. It includes laws to regulate big business, laws to guarantee the purity of our food and drugs, national parks, and millions of acres of land set aside to protect our natural heritage. His legacy also includes the Panama Canal and the most powerful navy on earth, second only to Britain's Royal Navy. Although Theodore Roosevelt died nearly a century ago, in a sense we still live in the America he helped to shape.

1

A BOY OF OLD MANHATTAN

A boy of old Manhattan,
A boy like you and I,
Once watched its towers rising
Until they spanned the sky.
—MORRIS ABEL BEER'S TRIBUTE TO
THEODORE ROOSEVELT, C. 1902

October 27, 1858, was an unseasonably cold day in New York City. Visitors to the four-story brownstone house at 28 East Twentieth Street stood shivering on the doorstep until a busy servant heard the brass door knocker and let them in. Upstairs, Martha Roosevelt rested after giving birth to a "sweet and pretty" boy named Theodore, after his father.[1]

Theodore Roosevelt Jr. was a seventh-generation Knickerbocker, a member of one of New York's oldest families. In 1644, Claes Martenzen van Rosenvelt left his native Holland for New Amsterdam, then a tidy village huddled at the southern tip of Manhattan Island. The name Rosenvelt means "Field of Roses," although what this particular family had to do with roses is a mystery. Anyhow, twenty years after Claes arrived, the duke of York landed with an English army, and New Amsterdam became New York.

Claes seems to have been more interested in money than in war or politics. He, his sons, and grandsons never shied away from hard work. Their efforts brought them success in the form of money and property. Over the generations, they took brides from equally hardworking and successful families, whatever their European origins. Thus, the youngest Roosevelt claimed Dutch, Scottish, English, Welsh, Irish, and German ancestors. As president, he would boast, "I am partly Jewish, too!"[2]

Theodore's grandfather, Cornelius Van Schaak Roosevelt—C.V.S. for short—was among the "richest of the rich" men in New York City, in 1858 one of its ten millionaires. C.V.S.'s wealth came from several sources. He sold hardware, imported plate glass, traded stocks, and served as a bank director. Yet the bulk of his fortune came from Manhattan real estate: commercial buildings, warehouses, docks, vacant lands. As each of his five sons came of age, C.V.S. made him a partner in one of his businesses. When a son married, he gave the newlyweds a house within walking distance of his own home, a mansion set on a whole square block bordering Union Square.[3]

With a population of over 800,000 people, New York had a wild "go-aheadness," a hectic pace. "New York is certainly altogether the most bustling, cheerful, lifeful, restless city I have yet seen in the United States," an English lady wrote. "Nothing and nobody seem to stand still for half a moment in New York." Just a few steps from baby Theodore's home lay Broadway, the city's main thoroughfare and the heart of its business district. Hours before sunrise, and long after sunset, horse-drawn vehicles streamed along the cobblestoned road. Heavy goods wagons rumbled noisily, jostling stagecoaches and private carriages. Red-and-yellow streetcars, called omnibuses, carried up to thirty passengers, packed into each vehicle like "live timber." Drivers raced these "insane vehicles," narrowly avoiding collisions and making pedestrians leap out of the way.[4]

Broadway, about the year 1860, two years before Theodore Roosevelt's birth. The future president's house was just a few blocks away, within easy walking distance of New York City's main business district.

Soon after its newest member began to toddle, the Roosevelt family began calling him "Teedie," pronounced *T.D.* Teedie was his parents' second child. Sister Anna was three years older than he. Known as "Bamie" (from *bambina,* Italian for "little girl"), this "little Atlas" was a

The former Martha Bullock, nicknamed "Mittie," was one of the great beauties of her day. Her eldest son, Theodore, loved her but did not consider her strong-willed and decisive, qualities he admired in his father.

smart, serious, and loving older sister. Handsome, high-strung Elliott, or "Ellie," was born in 1860. Sister Corinne—"Conie"—arrived the following year. A bright, adventurous child, Conie liked to "turn cartwheels and stand on her head."[5]

Their mother was the former Martha Bullock of Roswell, Georgia. Called "Mittie" by relatives and close friends, Martha's family owned cotton plantations and slaves. Her skin was fair and her hair jet-black. Admirers thought Mittie one of New York's most beautiful women. Speaking in a mellow Southern drawl, she entertained her children with fairy tales and stories about the "black folks" back home. Yet she was a disorganized person, barely able to run a household even with servants to do everyday chores. Fearing the tiniest speck of dirt, she always bathed twice— once to wash, then to rinse. "No dirt," said a friend, "ever stopped near her." Mittie seemed so helpless that, as her children grew, they took to calling her "Motherkins," "Mother-ling," and "Muffie."[6]

Nobody would have called her husband "Fatherkins." There was nothing delicate about Theodore Roosevelt Sr. Nicknamed "Thee," he was a big, robust man with a square jaw, brown hair, full beard, and brilliant blue eyes. A person of boundless energy, he enjoyed dancing all night and driving his carriage so fast that his manservant might fall out when he took a tight turn. Thee influenced his children more than anyone else. They adored him. "My father . . . was the best man I ever knew," said his firstborn son. "He combined strength and courage with gentleness, tenderness, and great unselfishness. He would not tolerate in us children selfishness or cruelty, idleness, cowardice, or untruthfulness. . . . He never physically punished me but once, but he was the only man of whom I was ever really afraid." Thee once spanked Theodore Jr. for biting Bamie's arm.[7]

Teedie's father described himself as a man with "a troublesome conscience." Not that he had wronged anyone. Heaven forbid! Thee meant that he could not bear to see another person suffering without feeling he must help. As head of C.V.S.'s glass-importing firm, Thee became wealthy in his own right. Spending freely, he liked to have the best things money could buy. Yet he also believed there was more to life than making money and living well. We have duties to others, Thee taught his children, and the wealthier we are, the greater our duties.[8]

Thee took a special interest in New York's "street rats," homeless orphan boys or boys cast out by poor parents unable to care for them. Sleeping under piers along the waterfront, the boys survived on the pennies they earned from selling newspapers. To give them a square meal and a decent place to stay, Thee founded

Nicknamed "Thee," Theodore Roosevelt Sr. was a warm, generous man with, it was said, "a heart of gold." Throughout his life, Theodore Jr. took his father as a role model.

the Newsboys' Lodging House. He spent every Sunday evening with the newsboys, listening to their concerns and giving them advice. Thee also was one of the founders of the Children's Aid Society to aid needy youngsters, and the New York Orthopedic Hospital to treat those with bone diseases. Wealthy friends knew what to expect when this kindly man had "that look" in his eyes. "All right, Theodore, how much is it this time?" they'd ask, reaching for their checkbooks.[9]

When visiting his charities, Thee often took his own children along, to fire their sense of duty toward the less fortunate. He called it *noblesse oblige,* a French term for the obligations that go along with, and justify having, great wealth and high social rank. The idea of *noblesse oblige* helped shape young Theodore's view of the world. Later, as a political leader, he saw things not only in terms of any specific problem, but also in moral terms. For Roosevelt, any decision he took had to be morally "correct." There were no in-betweens, no grays, for him—only whites and blacks, goods and evils. He always felt as if his father were standing beside him, judging his actions by the absolute standards of his, Thee's, "troublesome conscience." Theodore Jr. would always try to "do my duty as a clean and

Theodore Roosevelt wore a dress and a girl's hat in his first formal photograph. It was customary in the nineteenth century for young upper-class boys to wear girl's clothing to show that they were under the control of the elder women in their family.

decent man."[10] Others, however, might accuse him of hypocrisy, of using "morality" as a mask for doing some very nasty things.

In about April 1861, Teedie had his first picture taken in a shop on Broadway. When we see that photo today, it may seem odd that the future president is wearing a dress. Yet this was not unusual for upper-class boys in the 1800s. When worn by a boy, a dress symbolized the child's dependence upon women; boys usually got their first pair of pants around the age of five. Family photos show that, when Theodore became a father himself, his sons wore dresses, too.

In November 1860, just five months before Teedie had his first picture taken, Abraham Lincoln was elected president. Fearing he would abolish slavery, eleven Southern states seceded, leaving the Union to form a separate nation called the Confederate States of America. On April 12, 1861, Confederate gunners fired on Fort Sumter, a Union position in the harbor of Charleston, South Carolina. So began the Civil War, the most terrible conflict in American history.

War fever swept the loyal states of the North and West. In New York City, it seemed that a flag hung from every window. At a mass meeting in Union Square, six blocks from Teedie's front door, crowds chanted death to Confederate traitors. Soldiers marched up Broadway to the sound of throbbing drums, blaring bugles, and thunderous cheers. The loudest cheers were for the Zouaves, soldiers dressed "Turkish-style" in red shirts and baggy pants with colorful sashes. Fashionable parents dressed their sons as Zouaves. "The very children have become tainted with the military epidemic," a visitor reported, "and little toddling Zouaves, three and four, strut, armed to the teeth, at their nurses' apron strings." Little Theodore also wore a Zouave uniform. "Are me a soldier laddie too?" he would ask. Told yes, he stood up straight, as a soldier should.[11]

Just as slavery divided the nation, so it divided the Roosevelt family. Mittie favored the Confederacy and praised slavery. Having grown up among enslaved black people, she thought slavery natural, as much a part of reality as sunrise and sunset. At birth, her parents had given her a girl named Toy for her very own. Also called Mittie's "little black shadow," Toy slept on the floor at the foot of her bed, available for errands at any hour. When Mittie grew up and was engaged to Thee, her mother sold four slaves to pay for their wedding. The slave stories Mittie told her own children were not always pleasant. Sometimes she scared them with tales of slaves driven insane by abuse, or their murder by her relatives, masters enraged at some offense.[12]

Her husband also saw nothing wrong with slavery. Enslaved African-Americans, said Thee, were "perfectly happy" to be white people's property. How he knew this is a mystery. Nevertheless, he agreed with President Lincoln that Southerners had no right to leave the Union, whatever their grievances. Making war on the Union was illegal and immoral.[13]

Nearly all of Mittie's male relatives fought in the Confederate armies. Two of her brothers, Irvine and James Bulloch, joined its navy. When Lincoln blockaded rebel seaports, Mittie's brothers organized a squadron of fast ships to smuggle supplies from Europe and to capture Union merchantmen on the high seas. Mittie aided their efforts by collecting money, clothing, and medicine from Southern sympathizers in New York. While picnicking with the children in Central Park, she met Confederate agents, telling them where they might pick up the supplies.[14]

Teedie sided with his father. Once, while saying his evening prayers, he became enraged about the war. Loudly he begged God to "grind the Southern troops to powder." Mittie laughed, but warned him not to say such hurtful things again. Some of those Southern troops were family![15]

Meanwhile, Thee's "troublesome conscience" told him to enlist in the Union Army. Mittie objected strongly, and loudly. It would "kill her," she moaned, to know that her husband was fighting her kinsmen. So, rather than enlist or wait to be drafted, for a thousand dollars Thee hired Abraham Graf, a recent German immigrant, to fight in his place. This was perfectly legal. Using their influence in Washington, D.C., rich people had persuaded Congress to let them avoid serving by hiring substitutes. Poor Graf died of fever in a Union hospital in Maryland.[16]

The huge parades, flashy uniforms, and rousing speeches left their mark on

little Teedie. He did not just admire soldiers. He worshiped them. The idea of war as noble, exciting, and grown-up helped shape his character. For him, courage—the readiness to sacrifice one's life in a noble cause, a *moral* cause—defined a man. Yet his beloved father was not playing a man's part, not doing his duty. That "failure" seems to have angered the child. He never showed his anger openly, perhaps was not even conscious of it, but it was there nevertheless. A half century after the Civil War, in his *Autobiography*, Theodore did not mention his father's lack of military service. He did, however, explain why he felt he had to serve in the Spanish-American War. "I had always felt that if there were a serious war I wished to be in a position to explain to *my* children why I did take part in it, and not why I did not take part in it." In 1917, when America entered World War I, he practically forced his sons to join the army and seek the most dangerous service in the front lines. Doing anything less, he said, would have made them "slackers." Yet, as we will see, this did not mean that Roosevelt loved war for itself, that he was always eager to fight rather than negotiate. His actions as president showed a man willing to use the "big stick"—force—but who preferred using reason and persuasion, if possible.

Thee did more for the Union cause as a civilian than he could have as a fighting man. With their breadwinner in the army, countless families could not make ends meet. Forced to find work, many wives were still unable to feed their children. In New York, for example, police reports cited babies dying of starvation. Soldiers seldom sent money home. On payday, there was too much temptation to drink or gamble away the twelve dollars they received each month. Teedie's father helped persuade Congress to create an Allotment Commission, headed by himself. Commissioners visited army camps,

Theodore Roosevelt in 1865, at the age of seven. He has graduated to knickers — short, loose-fitting trousers gathered just below the knee. He is also wearing high-buttoned shoes, thought to correct "weak ankles." Notice also that he still has the girl's hat worn in his first photograph.

persuading soldiers to allow them to deduct part of their pay each month, the money to go to their families.[17]

Thee often went to the White House on commission business. "Honest Abe" saw Mr. Roosevelt as a man much like himself—a strong, gentle person who despised war. Mary Lincoln, the first lady, took to him at once. She asked Thee to join her on long carriage rides, even took him shopping for bonnets. Thee also befriended John Hay, the president's young private secretary, who once stayed a month with the Roosevelt family in New York. Hay discussed books with the children and told them stories about the leading men of the day, particularly the president. Teedie adored Lincoln and soaked up Hay's stories. Forty years later, Hay became President Roosevelt's secretary of state.[18]

On April 24, 1865, a photographer snapped a picture of Union Square. Lincoln had died of an assassin's bullet nine days earlier, and his flag-draped coffin passed through the square on its way to burial in Springfield, Illinois, his hometown. The picture shows two small figures in a window of a mansion draped with flags. They are six-year-old Theodore and his brother, Elliott, age five.

Thee's wartime duties kept him away from home for months at a time, so that Mittie had to deal with the children's health problems alone. They were a sickly lot. Bamie wore a special harness to correct her curved spine, caused, perhaps, by a birth defect. Ellie suffered attacks of "nerves," possibly due to epilepsy. Conie had bouts of asthma, usually mild. Teedie was the most frail of all the Roosevelt children. Constant headaches, fevers, stomach cramps, and diarrhea plagued him. Yet, miserable as these ailments made him, they did not threaten his life. Asthma did.

The disease first struck in June

ABOVE: *Abraham Lincoln about the year 1860. He would soon grow a beard at the suggestion of a young girl, who thought it would make him look less ugly.*

LEFT: *Theodore and his brother, Elliott, view President Lincoln's funeral from a second-floor window overlooking Union Square, New York City, April 25, 1865.*

1862, worsening throughout the Civil War years and afterward. Asthma is terrifying for an adult, let alone for a child. An allergic reaction usually triggers an attack. It begins with a sudden swelling of the bronchial tubes, the twin branches of the windpipe that carry air to the lungs. The chest tightens and a wheezing cough develops, making sleep impossible except in a sitting position. A person having an asthma attack has to fight for every breath. It feels like drowning, and looks like it, too, for the sufferer may turn blue from a shortage of oxygen.

"The asthma," as Teedie called it, made his childhood a constant struggle. "I was rather a sickly, rather timid little boy . . . nervous and self-conscious," he recalled years later. Often an attack brought horrible nightmares. In one nightmare, which came repeatedly, the devil carried the screaming child away. In another nightmare, a snarling werewolf crouched at the foot of his bed, ready to spring at his throat. Even certain words terrified Teedie, because their very sound seemed so menacing. One Sunday, in church, the minister spoke about "zeal"—enthusiasm. Theodore did not know what the word meant, but it scared him. For weeks afterward, he imagined that a monster he called "the Zeal" crouched in the shadows of the church, ready to pounce on him, just like the asthma.[19]

No effective asthma medicine existed at the time. Desperate to relieve patients' suffering, doctors used bizarre "treatments." These included electrical shocks, laudenum (opium dissolved in wine), whiskey, enemas, drawing blood with leeches, and a dried plant commonly used in rat poison.[20]

Thee spared his son from this stuff. He took him to the best doctors in New York, who prescribed coffee and cigars! They thought that the caffeine in strong black coffee, drunk at the outset of an attack, might halt coughing spasms. Cigar smoke, inhaled deeply, supposedly had the same effect, yet no sane doctor would recommend it today.

When things were at their worst, Teedie could count on his father's love and support. Night after night, Thee walked the floor with the child in his arms, comforting him until the attack passed. On some cold nights, he bundled Teedie into his carriage and sped through the streets, forcing air into his lungs. Years later, Teedie told a friend what his father's care had meant: "The thought of him now and always has been a sense of comfort. I could breathe, I could sleep, when he had me in his arms. My father—he got me breath, he got me lungs, strength—life."[21]

Like other wealthy New Yorkers, the Roosevelts did not send their children to public schools. These were for the "common" people, they felt, and would "coarsen" their children. Until she married, Mittie's younger sister, Anna, served as the family's tutor. It was Aunt Annie who taught Teedie to read, a blessing for the ailing youngster. When reading, he took an unusual position; he stood on one leg, with the other leg raised, like a stork.[22]

Little Theodore had the run of his parents' sizable library and was free to read whatever he pleased. Books became more than sources of amusement and information. They became an escape, however brief, from the clutches of illness, allowing his imagination to range across time and distance. His favorite subjects were geography, travel, and natural history. But nothing thrilled him more than stories about heroes, men like Daniel Boone and Davy Crockett. "I had," he recalled years later, "great admiration for men who were fearless and could hold their own in the world, and I had a great desire to be like them."[23]

Early one morning, Mittie sent him to a market to buy strawberries for breakfast. As he walked along Broadway, he saw the body of a seal laid out on a board outside a shop. Now seven, he had read about seals in books. But this was a real seal. It was killed, the shopkeeper said, in New York Harbor. The impression the seal made on Theodore was overpowering. In his *Autobiography,* he told how "that seal filled me with every possible feeling of romance and adventure." Theodore could not get it out of his mind. Day after day he returned to look at it, to measure it, to describe it in his notebook. As it slowly rotted away, the shopkeeper gave him the skull. Theodore's father had been a founder of the world-famous American Museum of Natural History. Now the little boy started his own private collection, and called it the Roosevelt Museum of Natural History. It grew steadily, reaching a thousand specimens by the time he turned eleven.[24]

Theodore also collected living specimens, which he caught himself or bought from dealers. At age nine, he wrote a scientific paper, his first, entitled "Natural History on Insects." Although another boy had given him information about "beetlles" and the like, Theodore declared that "mostly I have gained their habbits from ofserv-a-tion." Despite the spelling errors, his observations of insects are remarkably accurate for one so young. Equally important, the paper showed a "scientific spirit," a willingness to learn for oneself how creatures actually looked and behaved.[25]

Theodore kept his animals close by. Meeting the elegant Mrs. Hamilton Fish, a friend of his mother's, on an omnibus, he politely lifted his hat. Instantly, "several frogs leaped gaily to the floor." There was no telling when dinner guests might find a snake wriggling in a crystal water pitcher or a snapping turtle tied to a sink leg. A mouse once peeked out of a piece of Dutch cheese as guests passed it around the dinner table. Later, Mittie found a litter of field mice Theodore kept in the icebox. "The loss to Science, the loss to Science," he groaned as she threw them out.[26]

Of all the seasons, Theodore liked summer best. Luckily for him, his family always spent their summers in the country. New York summers are awful. In the era before air-conditioning, searing heat and stifling humidity killed hundreds of people each year. Diseases like polio, typhus, and cholera claimed hundreds of lives, too. Those who could afford to summer elsewhere escaped the city until the fall. In certain neighborhoods, you could walk for miles and see nothing but houses with boarded-up doors and windows. The only sound was that of the patrolman on his beat, tapping his nightstick against the iron railing as he passed. At first, the Roosevelts stayed in hotels in upstate New York. But in 1868, they spent the first of many summers in a large house Thee rented with his brothers in Oyster Bay, Long Island. During those summers at Tranquility, the house's name, Theodore roamed the woods, collecting birds' feathers and listening to their calls. So began his lifelong passion for ornithology, the study of birds.

The children expected to return to Tranquility each summer. Their father, however, had other plans for the summer of 1869. The family, he announced, would make the "Grand Tour." A kind of finishing school for upper-class Americans, the Grand Tour involved an entire year traveling around Europe, seeing sites, learning languages, and generally "improving" oneself in a place considered more cultured and sophisticated than the United States. The children were not thrilled with Thee's plan. A year without pony rides and exploring the woods of Long Island! A year of railroad stations, stagecoaches, and hotel rooms! Nevertheless, when Theodore was ten and a half, on May 12, 1869, the family sailed from New York aboard the steamer *Scotia*. After sightseeing in England, the family went to France, Switzerland, Germany, and Italy. As tourists, the Roosevelts were always in a rush. They felt as if they must keep to a set time-table, lest the world end. They visited so many churches, palaces, museums, monuments, and "places of interest" that they lost count.

Theodore was never well for more than a week or so. Asthma still stole his breath, to the point of making him unable to blow out a candle. During severe attacks, his father gave him the usual cups of black coffee to drink. Once, he told his diary, "I sat up for 4 successive hours and Papa made me smoke a cigar." He could not wait to go home. On May 25, 1870, after more than a year of traveling, he rushed to the ship's rail and shouted, "New York!!! Hip! Hurrah!"[27]

Theodore was still a skinny, pale, timid child. His family considered him a weakling. Yet something *was* different after Europe. Theodore's father, once so protective, had grown increasingly annoyed at having to change his plans whenever the youngster got sick. Finally, he decided the time had come for a serious father-and-son talk. For Thee, that talk was really about two things: an admission of defeat and a confrontation. He had tried everything to help the boy, and failed. So had the best doctors in New York. Enough was enough! There seemed just one way to go. If Theodore hoped to lead a normal life, he must conquer "the asthma" by himself. In other words, the youngster must cure himself through willpower and courage.

"Theodore," his father declared, "you have the mind but you do not have the body, and without the help of the body the mind cannot go as far as it should. You must *make* your body. It is hard drudgery to make one's body, but I know you will do it."

His sister Corinne tells what happened next. Theodore accepted his father's challenge. "Looking up, throwing back his head . . . with a flash of those white teeth . . . he said, *I'll make my body.*" This was more than a promise to the father Theodore adored—and feared. It was a promise to himself, which he must keep for his own self-respect.[28]

Thee enrolled his son in a gymnasium run by John Wood, a professional trainer. Under Wood's guidance, Theodore did push-ups, lifted weights, and worked out on a machine designed to expand the chest and improve breathing. At home, he trained on a second-floor porch equipped with bodybuilding equipment. Slowly, the boy grew stronger, at least by his standards.

After a serious asthma attack, Thee sent Theodore to Maine to join some friends on a camping trip. The boy, thirteen years old at the time, shared a stagecoach with two rowdy youngsters of about his own age. Teasing him mercilessly, the boys dared Theodore to fight. At first, he ignored their taunts. Finally, his temper aroused, he struck out with his fists. But his fists might just as well have been balls of cotton, for all the damage they did. Laughing, the boys showed that just one of them could handle Theodore "with easy contempt," controlling him without hurting him while keeping him from doing any damage in return. After this incident, Theodore felt like a pushover. He was a sissy in his own eyes. The word *sissy* took on special meaning for him. As an adult, the word seems to have reminded him of what he had once been—weak and vulnerable. As if to convince himself that he was no longer like this, he called men he considered weak "sissies."[29]

Humiliated, Theodore asked his father for boxing lessons. John Long, an ex-prizefighter, became the boy's coach. Now, besides his bodybuilding exercises, Theodore spent hours at the punching bag and in the ring with Long, practicing boxing moves. Long hit his pupil often and hard, but not hard enough to break anything. Learning to box was painful, yet, in time, something inside the boy clicked. Of course he feared getting hurt. However, he also learned to control his fear, and by so doing to overcome it. It was all a matter of attitude. "There were all kinds of things of which I was afraid of at first," he would write, "but by acting as if I was not afraid I gradually ceased to be afraid." In this way, the youngster found his courage. This was a life-shaping lesson. To the end of his days, Theodore was known for his fearlessness and devotion to physical fitness.[30]

Theodore had other breakthroughs that would also help him find success. The first grew out of his desire to add birds to his natural-history collection. To encourage the boy to spend more time outdoors, his father gave him a rifle. Still, though he blasted away furiously, Theodore missed even targets nearby. An eye test revealed that he was nearsighted and needed spectacles. Almost magically, the spectacles "opened an entirely new world to me," he recalled. Until then, neither Theodore nor his family realized he had a vision problem. "I had no idea how beautiful the world was until I got those spectacles . . . [because] I could not see and yet was wholly ignorant that I was not seeing."[31]

Now that he could see properly, Theodore was much more successful with his hunting and his collection of birds grew. Thee took his son to John G. Bell's taxidermy shop on Broadway. Mr. Bell, an expert "stuffer," taught Theodore to skin, preserve, and mount the specimens he shot. Allowing Theodore to do his own stuffing, however, involved a great deal of confidence on his parents' part. Taxidermists kept skins from rotting by brushing them with liquefied arsenic, a deadly poison that smells like burned almonds. Theodore's parents considered him a responsible youngster—so much so that they trusted him to be careful with arsenic, which Thee probably bought for Theodore from a druggist's shop.[32]

Besides, his interest in taxidermy was not uncommon among upper-class young-sters at this time. Like foreign travel, collecting birds and other small creatures, particularly butterflies, was seen as an "improving" activity. Theodore's distant cousin Franklin D. Roosevelt collected birds, too, although his parents paid a professional taxidermist to preserve them.

By age fourteen, everything came together for Theodore. Reading, body-building, boxing, shooting, taxidermy: all combined to turn a gawky weakling into a self-confident teenager. While he never totally conquered asthma, the attacks became less severe over time. Theodore's general health also improved. Moreover, his battle for health taught him a priceless lesson. Young Theodore realized that he was the master of his destiny. Pain? Fatigue? Illness? Fear? They would not rule him. Instead, he forced himself to resist any weakness in himself and in others. Life was for living. It held endless possibilities. Push ahead! Fight on! Never surrender! Although Theodore gave this advice as a mature man, it is rooted in his boyhood struggles: "Get action, do things; be sane, don't fritter away your time; create, act."[33]

In October 1872, a few days before Theodore turned fourteen, the family sailed from New York on a new foreign adventure. This time its destination was the Middle East, particularly Egypt. Traveling by donkey in the desert near the city of Cairo, they visited the Sphinx, a gigantic statue with a lion's body and a woman's head. Another time, they climbed to the top of the Great Pyramid through a low, narrow passage filled with dust and screeching bats. But the high-light of their trip was a two-month journey on a houseboat up the Nile River. Thee hired the vessel, crew, and servants for $2,000, a fabulous sum, roughly four times the yearly income of an average American family.[34]

Theodore marveled at the ancient temples they visited ashore. He gazed up at giant statues of pharaohs who had ruled Egypt thousands of years earlier. Still, for Theodore, these wonders of the ancient world did not compare to hunting wildlife with his new shotgun, a gift from Thee. The Nile Valley is a flyway, or aerial highway, for migrating birds. It was paradise for the young ornithologist. He collected and mounted two hundred exotic birds: cranes, herons, egrets, ibises. In years to come, he would shoot more dangerous game, such as grizzly bear, wolf, buffalo, lion, and elephant. Eventually, some of these animals were used to "decorate" his Long Island home. Others were given to the American Museum of Natural History. Theodore, a friend would note, "wants to be killing something all the time." For him, hunting was about more than collecting specimens for study. It met deep emotional needs. Through hunting, as with physical exercise, Theodore proved to himself that he could meet any challenge, overcome any limitation. It seemed to prove that he was no sissy, but a *man*.[35]

From Egypt, the family toured Palestine and Syria, sailed across the Mediterranean Sea to Greece, then went by train to Germany. While Mittie and Bamie, now seventeen, continued touring, for five months Theodore, Elliott, and Corinne, ages fourteen, twelve, and eleven, lived with families in Dresden, a beautiful German city dating from the Middle Ages. Meanwhile, Thee returned to New York City to oversee the completion of their new home, a mansion at 6 West Fifty-seventh Street, just off Fifth Avenue. As New York's poor immigrants crowded into older neighborhoods downtown, the wealthy were moving uptown, turning Fifth Avenue into the most fashionable street in America. Thee could easily afford the move. His father, C.V.S., had died in 1871, leaving Thee over a million dollars.

In Germany, Theodore and Elliott stayed with the family of Dr. Minkwitz, an official in the Dresden city government. The Minkwitzes' eldest daughter, Fräulein Anna, taught the boys French and German. Especially German. Although Minkwitz family members knew English, they spoke only German to their young guests, even if the boys did not understand a word. The idea was to familiarize them with the sound and flow of the language. Before long, the boys began to speak, even to think, in German. Theodore kept up his physical exercises, boxing with local boys. "If you offered rewards for bloody noses," he proudly wrote his father, "you would spend a fortune on me alone."[36]

The youngster's passion for taxidermy, however, shocked his hosts. There was no telling when he might pull a dead bat from his pocket, for stuffing, he'd explain. Worse, he kept arsenic in his room. "My scientific pursuits cause the family a good deal of consternation," Theodore reported. "My arsenic was confiscated and my mice thrown . . . out of the window." Nevertheless, he enjoyed his stay in Dresden. Before they left for home, Fräulein Anna told Mittie not to worry about Theodore's future. She thought him brilliant. Surely he would become a professor, "or, who knows, he may become even President of the United States."[37]

What *would* he become? That question often arose in Theodore's mind after his return to New York in November 1873. Whatever career path the youngster chose, he must first graduate college—that was certain. Thee had attended Harvard College. He wanted his son to enter Harvard in the fall of 1876. That left less than three years to prepare for the entrance exams. While this may seem like a long time, it was not. Theodore had not gone to high school, and home study had left wide gaps in his knowledge. Yes, because of his interests and travel, Theodore knew a lot about science, history, and geography. His French was good, his German excellent. He could also get by in Italian. Yet, he recalled, he was "lamentably weak in Latin and Greek and mathematics." So Thee hired Arthur H. Cutler, an expert in preparing boys for college. For eight hours a day, six days a week, Cutler kept Theodore at his studies. When the time came, he breezed through the exams.[38]

Theodore enrolled in Harvard in September 1876, a month before his eighteenth birthday. A college education was rare at this time, reserved for the privileged. When Theodore was young, only one American in five thousand attended college. Harvard, the nation's first college, had 821 students. Located in the village of Cambridge, Massachusetts, it consisted of a few buildings in Harvard Yard, a place of wide lawns and graveled paths. Its student body, all male and all white, came almost entirely from upper-class Protestant families in nearby Boston. Harvard had only three Roman Catholic students. It had no blacks, no Jews, no foreigners, and no Boston Irish.[39] These Roman Catholics, the decendants of Irish immigrants who had settled in Boston in the 1840s, were considered "inferior" by the Protestant majority.

While it was difficult to get into Harvard, once you did, you could get by with little effort. One did not attend Harvard to prepare for a career. Making a comfortable living was not a problem for a Harvard man; he could always enter the family business, live off inherited wealth, or study for a profession like medicine or law after graduation. At Harvard, America's future leaders came together to get to know one another. Today, we would call it "networking," gaining a group of powerful friends and allies that would be helpful in later life. A Harvard man cultivated an upper-class "style"; that is, a distinct accent (the "Harvard drawl") and bearing (the "Harvard swing"). He wore English-cut clothes, carried a walking stick, and parted his hair in the middle. He cared much about sports: rowing, running, football, tennis, boxing, wrestling. Those who took their studies seriously were called "digs," because of their annoying habit of digging into books more than was "seemly." A poem titled "Ode to Indifference" captures the students' attitude:

> We ask but time to drift,
> We deem it narrow-minded to excel.
> We call the man fanatic who applies
> His life to one grand purpose till he dies.
> Enthusiasm sees one side, one fact;
> We try to see all sides but not to act. . . .
> We long to sit with newspapers unfurled,
> Indifferent spectators of the world.[40]

Theodore had only contempt for most Harvard men. A first-class snob, he considered few of them the "gentleman-sort." The New Yorker grumbled about "how few have come here with any idea of getting an education." Even worse, in his eyes, they were "ignorant of all that men had ever thought and hoped." Science, poetry, novels, and history left them cold. To put it another way, Theodore had nothing in common with his schoolmates.[41]

Harvard freshmen could not choose their courses. Instead, they took a required program: mathematics, physics, chemistry, Latin, Greek, German. Although Theodore earned high grades, these came easily, for he never worked up to his full capacity. Years later, he admitted that he had coasted through college. Theodore found his professors, all scholars in their fields, drab and uncreative. Sadly, they never inspired him to work with the same energy his bodybuilding and boxing coaches demanded, and he did not find college a challenge. "There was very little in my actual studies which helped me in later life," he would recall.[42]

Fellow students were not impressed by Theodore, either. By the time he enrolled at Harvard, he had reached his full height of five feet eight inches, and weighed 124 pounds. Surely, his years of exercise had made him stronger than he would have been without them. Yet he was scrawny, a "youth in the kindergarten stage of physical development," as a classmate described him after seeing him in the gymnasium. His eyes squinted through thick spectacles. A shrill, high-pitched voice grated on people's nerves. His laughter was an "ungreased squeak."[43]

At eighteen, Theodore had none of the personal magnetism for which he would later become famous. Schoolmates described him as "a campus freak," "half-crazy" and "different," an "eccentric" who kept dead birds and live snakes in his room. He did not walk across Harvard Yard, as others did; he bounded across it. A true "dig," he once sat before a fireplace so absorbed in a book that only his smoking shoes broke his concentration. Having never been in a class with others before, he saw professors as personal tutors. Whenever an idea popped into his mind, he interrupted the lecture, a most irritating habit. "Now look here, Roosevelt, let me talk!" a professor snapped. "I'm running this course."[44]

Theodore missed his family during his first year away from home. Everyone wrote to him, and he to them, often. Above all, he knew that he was loved. "I do not think there is a fellow in College who has a family who love him as much as you all do me," he wrote Thee. "I am *sure* that there is no one who has a Father who is also his best and most intimate friend, as you are mine."[45]

Theodore may have loved his family all the more because he made so few friends at Harvard. "Most of his classmates simply did not like him," one recalled years after they graduated. Only Henry Minot, who left at the end of his freshman year, shared Theodore's interest in birds. As the result of a collecting trip to the Adirondack Mountains, they issued a four-page pamphlet, "The Summer Birds of the Adirondacks in Franklin County, N.Y.," Theodore's first publication.[46]

While classmates did not like him, they gradually grew to accept him. It helped that he tried to fit in. Theodore became an editor of the *Harvard Advocate,* a student newspaper. He reached out, joining social clubs, picking up expressions like "by Jove" and "dear old boy," and going in for athletics. By Harvard standards, he was merely an average boxer.

Roosevelt as a Harvard oarsman. Fellow students thought the future president "eccentric," a strange person with strange ways, like collecting and stuffing dead animals.

But he had "moxie," a popular term for courage. Theodore also displayed good sportsmanship. After taking a drubbing in the ring, he would praise his opponent's skill.

One day, fellow student Richard Welling invited him to go ice skating. Welling soon regretted leaving his cozy room. It was bitterly cold. Fierce winds sent them careening across the ice, their "arms waving like windmills in a gale." Welling wanted to quit, but felt he should not make the first move. Theodore surely felt the cold as keenly as his companion. But he put on a brave face and refused to give in to discomfort. Welling recalled:

> . . . when any sane man would have voted to go home, as the afternoon's sport was clearly a flop, Roosevelt was exclaiming, "Isn't this bully!"—and the harder it blew, and the more we skated, the more often I had to hear, "Isn't this bully!" . . . Never in college was my own grit so put to the test, and yet I would not be the first to suggest "home." Nearly three hours passed before Roosevelt finally said: "It's too dark to skate any more. . . ." I recall my numbed fingers grasping the key to my room and unable to make a turn in the lock. That afternoon of so-called sport made me realize Roosevelt's amazing vitality.

Bully! was a favorite expression. If Roosevelt really liked something, he used it instead of *excellent, wonderful,* or *great.*[47]

Theodore had begun to adjust to Harvard. In his sophomore year, he chose some elective courses: botany, anatomy, geology. By then, however, things were going badly at home. In December 1877, his father suddenly collapsed. The diagnosis, cancer of the stomach, was a death sentence. With final exams drawing near, the family decided not to tell Theodore how serious things were. A few weeks later, an urgent telegram called him home. Thee, "mad with pain," was rapidly slipping away. Only large doses of opium relieved his pain for a few minutes. As news of his condition spread, poor people gathered outside the Roosevelt house on Fifty-seventh Street. These, too, were family. Boys from the Newsboys' Lodging House sat on the stone steps, beside little Italian girls from a Sunday-school class he taught. They sat quietly, respectfully, awaiting the end. Thee died on February 9, 1878, at the age of forty-seven, several hours before his namesake arrived. Now there was only one Theodore Roosevelt.[48]

Theodore was heartbroken, and felt as if a dark cloud enclosed him. "Oh Father, Father, how bitterly I miss you, mourn you and long for you," he wrote in his diary. Yet Theodore still felt his father's presence. During a church service at Oyster Bay, he believed he saw Thee. "I could see him sitting in the corner of the pew as distinctly as if he were alive. . . . Oh, I feel so sad when I think of the word 'never.'" Living or dead, Theodore felt his father would always be with him in spirit. He was there, President Roosevelt would say many years later, blessing his son on the first night he slept in the White House.[49]

A young woman helped Theodore recover from his grief. He met her in October 1878, a week before he turned twenty. A classmate, Dick Saltonstall, had invited him to his home at Chestnut Hill, a Boston suburb. Dick's cousin Alice Hathaway Lee, seventeen, lived next door with her wealthy parents, whose fortune came from banking.

Alice Lee, photographed sometime between 1880 and 1884. The moment TR saw the Boston socialite, he fell madly in love with her.

A beauty, visitors described Alice as "radiant," "flowerlike," "an enchanting creature." Cheerful and "full of life," she was tall and athletic, with delicate features, long blond curls, and blue-gray eyes. Theodore fell in love the instant he saw her. "See that girl?" he told a friend. "I am going to marry her, she won't have me, but I am going to have her." He was right on each count.[50]

So began a one-sided courtship. Theodore came on strong—too strong. Eager to please, he wrote Alice nearly every day. He brought her parents gifts, drank tea with them, and played up to their youngest daughter, Alice's sister. He took Alice on long walks. She liked him, but only as a friend. When he tried to show affection, she kept her distance. When he proposed marriage, she did not say yes or no, but changed the subject.

Oh, the misery! "I have been pretty

nearly crazy," the suitor wrote. Wretched, he spent sleepless nights wandering the woods near Cambridge alone. Once he threatened suicide if Alice would not have him. Fearing she would run off with a rival, he bought a pair of dueling pistols. Theodore would die, or kill, for Alice. Yet, if his struggle with asthma had taught him anything, it was persistence. She finally gave in. On January 25, 1880, the young woman he called his "darling little sunshine" accepted Theodore's marriage proposal.[51]

Her acceptance raised that old question: What would he become? Money was not a problem at this time. Theodore could easily support Alice and the large family he hoped to have with her. His share of his father's fortune, $125,000, made him financially independent. Invested wisely, it would earn $8,000 a year, three times the salary of any of his professors. It would guarantee Theodore a comfortable life without having to take a job. The dollars in his pockets bought more, and so were worth more, than our dollars today. As a result of inflation, $125,000 in 1880 would be worth $2,475,192 in 2005.[52]

Theodore felt his career choices were limited. Business held no interest for him. He would have liked a career in biology. However, colleges in America and Europe taught this strictly as a laboratory science. Instead of outdoor fieldwork, biologists relied on detailed measurements made on the dissecting table and microscopic examination of specimens. This sort of minute, indoor study was not for Theodore. He saw himself as a field naturalist, one who observed animal behavior in the wild. Alice gave him no encouragement, either. Beautiful and charming as she was, she knew little about science, and cared less. During a visit to a zoo, for example, she saw male lions. Their manes puzzled her. Probably thinking of fashionably groomed poodles, she astonished Theodore by asking who had shaved the rest of their bodies![53]

Theodore would always love natural history. But it would have to be a hobby, one of many interests, not his career. As graduation and marriage drew near, he made his choice. "I am going to try to help the cause of better government in New York City; I don't know exactly how," he told a friend, historian William Roscoe Thayer.[54] In short, he would become a politician. America was changing—and not always for the best. Like his father, Theodore's "troublesome conscience" would not let him sit idly on the sidelines. In the rough-and-tumble of politics, *there* he would "get action."

On June 30, 1880, Theodore graduated twenty-second in a class of 170. Before the big day, he visited the college doctor for a checkup. The good news was that he had gained twelve pounds since entering Harvard. The bad news was that years of asthma attacks and too-strenuous exercise had weakened his heart. To avoid further damage, the doctor advised him to live quietly. No dashing upstairs. No hunting trips. No excitement. Rest a lot.

Theodore rebelled. He had defeated asthma—mostly. He had "made" his body. Whatever happened, he *would* lead a strenuous life. "Doctor," he said, "I am going to do all the things you tell me not to do. If I've got to live the sort of life you have described, I don't care how short it is." Until the year of his death, he kept the doctor's warning secret from everyone.[55]

The couple married on October 27, 1880, the groom's twenty-second birthday.

2

THE LIFE OF EFFORT

The life that is worth living, and the only life that is worth living, is the life of effort, the life of effort to attain what is worth striving for.

—THEODORE ROOSEVELT

Marriage was all Theodore expected it to be. Alice had put aside her reserve and was now as openly in love with him as he was with her. Always eager to please her dearest "Teddykins," she was his "Sunshine," his "little pink wife," a "teasing, laughing, pretty witch." For their honeymoon, they went to Switzerland, where he climbed mountains in defiance of doctor's orders. Upon their return to America, they moved into the Fifty-seventh Street house with his mother, brother, and sisters.[1]

Theodore decided that becoming a lawyer would help him promote good government in New York, a cause that had been dear to his father's heart. Lawyers, he believed, had special knowledge, invaluable in defending the innocent and fighting corruption. So, early each morning he kissed Alice good-bye and walked three miles downtown, at top speed, to the Columbia University law school near the tip of Manhattan Island. After class, on the return walk, he might stop at the Astor Library at Forty-second Street and Fifth Avenue. There he worked on a book he had begun writing at Harvard, a history of the naval side of the War of 1812.

As Theodore learned more about the legal profession, he became disenchanted. His father had been a man of strong moral principle. "Take care of your morals, your health next and finally your studies," Thee said when his son began college. Now, when he compared Thee's principles with the teachings in the law books and the classroom, he saw problems. Morality is always about doing the right thing, about justice. In contrast, the law he studied was open to interpretation, and thus to abuse. Lawyers, especially for big corporations, often twisted the law to benefit their clients whether or not the client was in the right or wrong.

Theodore could not see himself as a morally ambiguous legal finagler. So, toward the end of his second year, he left Columbia to follow another career: politics.[2]

Theodore began by dropping into Morton Hall, his district Republican Party club. Becoming a Republican came naturally to him. After all, this had been Abraham Lincoln's party, opponents of slavery and defenders of the Union. By contrast, Democrats, even in the North, had defended slavery and disunion. Moreover, New York City Democrats were the party of Tammany Hall, a corrupt political organization that fleeced taxpayers in countless ways.

Morton Hall itself was a large, drafty room over a saloon on East Fifty-ninth Street. Furnished with rickety tables and splintery chairs, it smelled of sawdust, sweat, and cigars. Brass spittoons, or spitting pots, stood at strategic locations, but tobacco chewers often missed, squirting yellow spit patches on the floor. Most evenings, men out to make their fortunes—saloon keepers, shop owners, small-time lawyers—came to play cards and talk politics. At first, they gave Theodore the cold shoulder. With his expensive clothes and upper-class bearing, he was an outsider, a "swell." Unfazed, Theodore took their distrust as just another obstacle to overcome. He joined the discussions, smoked, and took a hand at poker—even put up with vulgar jokes. Gradually, club members accepted him.[3]

His family, however, disapproved. Men of Theodore's dignified background did not "go into" politics, the Roosevelt family sniffed. Politics were "low." In New York, political professions were the domain of poor Irish and German immigrants. Knickerbockers had nothing in common with their "sort." Well-off gentlemen did good deeds on their own, avoiding public life and politics, which Thee had called "a dirty business." His son agreed; politics *was* often dirty—disgustingly dirty, full of bribery, dishonesty, and corruption. Yet Theodore vowed he would not sit on the sidelines or, like his father, do justice as he saw the chance. Instead he would face "evil" with the same courage he summoned up to face an opponent's fists in the ring. *Noblesse oblige,* he would use politics—government—to make a better world.[4]

His opportunity came sooner than expected. Joe Murray, an influential Republican with a shady past, decided that Roosevelt was the perfect nominee for a seat in the New York State Assembly, the lower house of the state legislature. At twenty-three, Theodore seemed the ideal candidate—intelligent, wealthy, energetic, well connected.

Would Mr. Roosevelt care to run for that seat? Murray asked.

Why, yes, he would.

Since the young Roosevelt knew nothing about campaigning, Murray suggested that the candidate tour "Saloon Row" on the West Side, along Sixth Avenue. When a saloon owner griped about saloon taxes, Theodore replied that saloon taxes were too low; he would double them. Murray gasped. This was definitely *not* the way to run for office. Rather than let Theodore put his foot in his mouth again, he changed the strategy. Murray sent club members to campaign for Roosevelt in the working-class district. Meanwhile, the candidate worked the

"silk-stocking crowd," his wealthy neighbors, talking in general terms about the need for "good government." As election day drew near, Tammany Hall hired thugs to terrorize Republican voters. Theodore countered by getting the Columbia College football, boxing, and wrestling teams to guard the polls. Roosevelt won in a landslide, 3,502 votes to 1,528. In all, he would serve three one-year terms in the state assembly.[5]

In January 1882, Assemblyman Roosevelt took his seat in the state legislature in Albany. As long as the legislature was in session, Theodore lived alone in rented rooms; his wife and family, who had not accompanied him, stayed in New York City. On weekends, he returned by train to be with them. Most legislators left Albany on weekends to be with their families at home.

It seemed that Theodore's family had been right about politics. Albany hardly seemed the place for a Knickerbocker gentleman. The brainpower of fellow Republicans, Roosevelt snobbishly noted, "about equals that of an average balloon."

But compared to the Democrats, they were geniuses. Showing an anti-immigrant bias typical of the Knickerbockers, Theodore considered the Irish Democrats the worst of the lot. "The average Catholic Irishman of the first generation, as represented in this Assembly," Roosevelt said with a sneer, "is a low, venal, corrupt and unintelligent brute." He described their leader, ex-prizefighter "Big John" MacManus, of Tammany Hall, as a drunken, red-faced "unutterably coarse and low brute."[6]

The newcomer saw the assembly as a den of thieves, "a cesspool of iniquity." Most members, he believed, had anything but "troublesome consciences." They had gone into politics not to serve the people, but to collect "boodle"—graft money. "Boodlers" worked in various ways. Some simply sold their votes to the highest bidder. The more sophisticated ones proposed bills threatening a corporation's interests. Not that they wanted their bills to become law. Instead, they wanted the corporation to pay for withdrawing the law from consideration. Former assembly members also served as lobbyists. Hired by corporations, lobbyists "worked the lobbies"; that is, the waiting areas outside the assembly and senate chambers. Lobbyists used money to persuade legislators to sponsor or oppose certain legislation.[7]

The name Theodore comes from Theodoros, Greek for "Gift of God." In Theodore Roosevelt's case, assemblymen believed the Almighty's gift was a living, breathing joke sent to amuse them. "Who's the dude?," the fancy dresser, they asked one another the first time he appeared in the assembly. "His teeth seemed to be all over his face," a member recalled. He parted his hair in the middle and had long, bushy sideburns. He wore skintight pants and a morning coat, or cutaway jacket with tails that nearly reached his shoes. In one hand he held a silk hat, in the other a gold-headed cane. Whenever he wanted to make a point, he cried in a grating, high-pitched tone: "Mister Spee-kar! Mister Spee-kar!" Members called him "the exquisite Mr. Roosevelt," "Jane Dandy," and "Young Squirt."[8]

That "squirt" was no pushover, they soon learned. When John J. Costello, a Tammany bigwig, called Theodore a "Mamma's boy," Roosevelt knocked Costello down. As Costello tried to get up, Theodore knocked him down again. Then he told the bloodied fellow to wash his face and watch his words. Another time, Big John MacManus and his cronies thought it might be fun to humiliate Theodore. "By God! MacManus," the intended victim hissed. "I hear you are going to toss me in a blanket. By God, if you try anything like that, I'll kick you, I'll bite you, I'll kick you in the balls, I'll do anything to you—you'd better leave me alone." Big John took the hint.[9]

Theodore found it was one thing to win respect with his fists; the Tammany men were tough customers, having risen in politics through their shrewdness, ruthlessness, and brawls in the saloons and party club rooms of New York City. Clearly, Theodore could not beat anyone into accepting his ideas about reform. Yet Roosevelt was a fast learner. That quality astonished Isaac Hunt, an early political ally. Hunt described his friend's first term in the New York State Assembly:

> He made me think of a growing child. You know how you take a child and in a day or two their whole character will change. They will take on new strength and new ideas, and you can see them growing right up. . . . He would leave Albany Friday afternoon and he would come back Monday night and you would see the changes that had taken place. . . . New ideas had taken possession of him. He would run up against somebody and he got a new perspective. . . . He would be entirely changed, just like a child.[10]

Gradually, Theodore learned a vital lesson about politics in a democracy. Politics is, above all, the art of compromise: of settling differences by making mutual concessions. If people were angels, and we lived in an ideal world, compromise would be unnecessary; everyone would do the right thing automatically. In the real world, however, different people have different ideas of right, different needs, different interests. What is good for one group may harm another. Moreover, selfishness is a human quality. Whether we like it or not, people often think only of themselves. The politician may *know* he is right. Roosevelt certainly did. Still, to get anything done, he must accept others opinions and goals, and work from there.

As he settled into work in the legislature, Theodore began to realize this. He told a friend, newsman Jacob Riis:

> I looked the ground over and made up my mind that there were several other excellent people there [in the assembly], with honest opinions of the right, even though they differed from me. I turned in to help them, and they turned

to and gave me a hand. And so we were able to get things done. We did not agree in all things, but we did in some, and those we pulled at together. That was my first lesson in real politics. . . . [One] must work, if he would be of use, with men as they are. As long as the good in them overbalances the evil . . . work with them for the best that can be obtained.[11]

His privileged upbringing had sheltered Theodore from the harsh realities faced by working people. He knew poverty was widespread in American cities, yet it was not something he had seen up close, let alone felt deep in his soul. Like so many of his social class at this time, he believed poverty was a matter of individual character, nobody's fault but the sufferer's. "I grew into manhood thoroughly imbued with the feeling that a man must be respected for what he made of himself," Theodore explained in his *Autobiography*. "But I had also, consciously or unconsciously, been taught that . . . pretty much the whole duty of the man lay in his making the best of himself. . . ."[12] Poverty, then, was due to the individual's lack of intelligence, drive, and effort, not to social conditions. Therefore, Theodore, as a legislator, objected to organized labor.

Samuel Gompers helped create the American Federation of Labor, the most powerful alliance of trade unions the nation had ever seen.

Trade unions and strikes, he felt, unfairly penalized employers, who had earned their success in the rough-and-tumble of free competition. He also opposed pay increases for police, firefighters, and other city workers, saying these put too heavy a burden on taxpayers.[13]

Roosevelt, however, balanced his notion of rugged individualism with his ideas of morality and *noblesse oblige.* These gave him an uncompromising hatred of exploitation. No one, Theodore insisted, had a right—*ever*—to take unfair advantage of another person. Doing so was simply immoral, he believed.

As Theodore learned more about social problems like poverty, his ideas broadened. But as we shall see, changes in his thinking came slowly, over decades. His first lesson came from a short, squat English-born Jew named Samuel Gompers, soon to become America's foremost labor leader. In 1882, during Theodore's second term in the assembly, Gompers headed the Cigarmakers' Union. Since union members worked under dreadful conditions, Gompers proposed a law barring cigar manufacturing in New York

"The Cigar Makers", by Jacob Riis. A pioneer in using photography to stir public interest in social reform, Riis captured this scene in a home workshop located in a New York City tenement.

City tenements as a health hazard. Theodore refused to believe that conditions such as Gompers described could exist in America. Well, the union chief replied, if you don't believe me, come see for yourself!

Gompers took Roosevelt into some New York City tenements. Theodore was shocked at what he saw. Years later he wrote: "I have always remembered one room in which two families were living. There were several children, three men and two women in this room. The tobacco was stowed about everywhere, alongside foul bedding, and in a corner there were scraps of food. The men, women and children in this room worked by day and far into the evening, and they slept and ate there." This visit convinced him that, whatever he had been taught about the causes of poverty, common sense and human decency demanded an end to cigar making in tenements. Thanks to his support, the legislature passed the proposed law. However, the courts declared it unconstitutional because it violated the principle of free contract, under which a person could refuse to work if they disliked their wages or working conditions.[14] Although his first effort to improve the lot of poor workers wasn't successful, TR would continue to broaden his thinking and work on their behalf throughout his life.

Turning from working conditions to fighting corruption, Roosevelt targeted Judge Theodore R. Westbrook of the New York State Supreme Court. His Honor took bribes from a millionaire named Jay Gould. Gould was a frail little man who counted among his holdings the Western Union Telegraph Company and 10 percent of America's railroads. In 1882, Gould's business shenanigans won him the Manhattan Elevated Railway, a profitable mass transportation company. When opponents of the deal went to court, Judge Westbrook ruled in Gould's favor—for a price.

Both political parties resisted Roosevelt's demand for an investigation. However, the public outcry caused by articles about the bribe in the *New York Times* and the *New York Herald* forced them to summon the Judiciary Committee to investigate. In reply, Gould dug into his bag of tricks. A Gould agent offered Roosevelt a million dollars, in cash, to stop his attacks, thereby halting the investigation. When bribery failed, Gould's private detectives searched for "dirt" in Roosevelt's private life. When they found nothing, they tried blackmail. One night, a woman "tripped" on the sidewalk in front of Roosevelt. After helping her to her feet, she asked him to take her home. Suspicious, he put her in a cab and sent her away. It was a setup, Roosevelt later learned. Gould's men had hoped to use her to involve him in a sex scandal. In the end, cash in the right hands cleared Gould and Westbrook of wrongdoing in the eyes of the Judiciary Committee.[15]

Though Gould got away with his crimes, the campaign against corruption made Roosevelt a celebrity. During his second term, the assembly Republicans voted him minority leader, the youngest man ever to hold that post. Newspaper reporters, fascinated by Theodore's oddball ways and crusading zeal, featured him in their articles. Governor Grover Cleveland, an anti-Tammany Democrat, saw him as an ally. Known for his unshakable honesty, Cleveland had fought corruption all of his political life.

In 1883, Congress passed the Pendleton Act to reform the civil service. Until then, nearly all federal jobs fell under the "spoils system." Upon winning control of Congress, the victorious party usually fired workers appointed by the previous administration. It then gave their jobs—the "spoils," or prizes, of victory—to party loyalists as a reward for their support. This, in turn, often led to the appointment of unfit or dishonest men to important posts. The Pendleton Act replaced the spoils system with the merit system, where jobs and promotions went to the highest scorers in competitive examinations. Governor Cleveland wanted a similar law for New York State. When the measure got tied up in political maneuvering, Roosevelt helped break the logjam. That victory helped Cleveland win the presidency. In time, President McKinley would repay Roosevelt's support.[16]

A rising star in state politics, Theodore's career was going splendidly. Better yet, in the summer of 1883, while vacationing at Oyster Bay, Alice announced that they were going to be parents. Thrilled at the news, Theodore bought 155 acres of land on a hilltop overlooking Long Island Sound. Then he hired an architect to draw up plans for a twelve-bedroom house, for, he said, he liked large families. In his wife's honor, he called the place Leeholm, after her maiden name Lee.[17]

The new legislative session began at the end of the summer. As usual, Theodore stayed in Albany during the week, returning home on weekends. The morning of Wednesday, February 13, 1884, found him in the assembly chamber. He knew his mother, Mittie, was running a high fever from some sort of infection. Alice, however, seemed fine. As business began, a telegram arrived. Good news! Late Tuesday night, his wife had given birth to a baby girl, also named Alice. Mother and daughter were well. Before long, a second telegram arrived. We do not know what it said. All we know is that a panicky Theodore caught the next train for New York City.

Toward midnight, Elliott met him at the front door of 6 West Fifty-seventh Street. "There is a curse on this house," said his brother grimly. "Mother is dying, and Alice is dying too." Doctors had diagnosed Mittie's illness as typhoid fever, a disease caused by bacteria found in impure food and water. All her precautions against dirt had not protected her from nature's invisible killers. She died early the next morning. Alice had nephritis, a deadly kidney aliment. As the poisons accumulated in her body, she became delirious, dying in her husband's arms that afternoon.[18]

In his diary for February 14, 1884, the widower drew a large cross. Beneath it he wrote: "The light has gone out of my life." That was no exaggeration. In the days following the double funeral, Theodore went about in a daze. Overcome by shock, despair, and anger, Theodore seemed as if he might lose his mind.[19]

To keep his sanity, he forced himself to forget his loss. From the day Alice died, apparently, Theodore never spoke of her. One of his biographers, Edmund Morris, notes that Roosevelt destroyed the written traces of their life together. With only four exceptions, he burned their love letters. Photographs of Alice were torn from their cardboard frames. Bamie, his sister, arranged to sell the Roosevelt family home and divide the money with her sister and brothers. Theodore's autobiography never mentions his first wife, the beautiful young woman who was taken from him at the age of twenty-two.[20]

In his grief, Theodore practically abandoned the new Alice, his infant daughter. Unable to speak her name, he called his daughter "Baby Lee." Sent to live with Bamie, the child seldom saw her father. Her aunt cared for her, telling her about her mother in heaven. Bamie, for her part, had her hands full. Not only was she caring for a child, she had to deal with her younger brother, Elliott, who had made a mess of his life. A family friend recalled that he "drank like fish and ran after the ladies"; he would also become a drug addict. On October 11, 1884, his wife, Anna, gave birth to a girl. In time, their daughter, Eleanor Roosevelt, would become the most famous woman in America.[21]

What next for Theodore? He did not know. One thing was certain: he would not run for a fourth term in the assembly. When the legislative session ended in June, he left Albany. Yet he did not leave politics completely.

Eighteen-eighty-four was a presidential election year. The Democrats easily chose Grover Cleveland as their candidate. Republicans, however, had a serious problem. The leading contender at their Chicago nominating convention was James G. Blaine, of Maine. Blaine was an out-and-out crook who used his post as Speaker of the House of Representatives to enrich himself. Meanwhile, the nation learned that Cleveland, a bachelor, had fathered a son with a Buffalo widow.

Theodore attended the Republican convention. He despised Blaine and liked Cleveland, an honest politician, despite the scandal. When Blaine won the nomination, Roosevelt vowed to sit out the election campaign. During the convention, however, he met Henry Cabot Lodge of Massachusetts. Lodge was a fellow Harvard man, a shrewd politician, and an able historian. They clicked immediately, becoming lifelong friends. Lodge argued that party should come before personality. No reformer could hope to bring change by himself, Lodge said. To be effective, even a genius needs a party behind him. By supporting Blaine, Lodge argued, Roosevelt would show his party loyalty, earning its loyalty in return. Roosevelt agreed, but supported Blaine without enthusiasm.[22]

During the campaign, gleeful Democrats chanted: "Blaine, Blaine, James G. Blaine, continental liar from the state of Maine." Republicans attacked Cleveland over his illegitimate child, shouting "Ma, ma, where's my pa?" Yet the Democrats had the last laugh. As the returns rolled in, they bellowed:

> Ma, ma, where's my pa?
> Gone to the White House, ha, ha, ha.

Grover Cleveland became the first Democrat to win the presidency since before the Civil War.

Theodore had done his duty to his party, but its candidate had lost. Now he felt exhausted, emotionally and physically. The widower needed to get away from the familiar, to pull himself together, to take his bearings. Groping for a way to rebuild his life, he boarded a train bound for the Dakota Territory.

No stranger to the West, Theodore had left Alice early in her pregnancy to hunt buffalo in the Dakota Territory. Someone had told Theodore that he must act quickly if he wanted to shoot a buffalo. The lumbering beasts, which had once roamed the Great Plains by the millions, were under constant attack by white men. They would probably vanish before too long.

While Alice remained in New York, Theodore arrived at "Little Misery," as locals pronounced the town's name, Little Missouri. It lay on the bank of Little Missouri River in what is today southwestern North Dakota. Native Americans called this area *Mako Shika,* "bad land," translated by whites as Bad Lands. A desolate area, the Bad Lands are a jumble of buttes, rocky hills rising sharply from the surrounding country, their slopes covered with stunted pines and cedars. Over the ages, wind and rain, heat and frost, have carved the buttes into weird shapes. Strewn along their bases, one can still find dinosaur bones weathered out of the hillsides. The Bad Lands area also has wide prairies carpeted by grass and wildflowers. To Theodore, this was "hero country," a land worthy of the strongest and bravest. "Here," he would say, "the romance of my life began."[23]

The hunting trip began badly. Theodore and Joe Ferris, his hired guide, slept on the ground. It rained. The ground turned to mud, froze, unfroze, and went back to mud. They were cold, wet, and hungry. Sighting a buffalo, the last of a recently slaughtered herd, they gave chase on horseback, but lost it. Yet the New Yorker enjoyed every moment of the chase. "Isn't this bully!" he would shout. "By Godfrey, but this is fun!" Finally, after two weeks, he shot a buffalo. Wild with joy, he stomped around the carcass, his teeth gleaming, whooping and hollering in his version of an Indian victory dance. Theodore was so excited by his Bad Lands experience that he decided to invest in ranching. Before heading home, he put up $14,000 for his own herd of cattle. Joe Ferris and his brother, Sylvane, agreed to pasture the herd on their Maltese Cross Ranch, in what is today the Bad Lands of North Dakota.[24]

Returning to the ranch after Alice's death, Theodore invested another $26,000 in cattle. The Maltese Cross was a working ranch. Forty miles to the north, he built Elkhorn Ranch, just a large cabin where he could escape from the world. But he owned no land. None

Theodore Roosevelt armed to the teeth, in his tailor-made hunting suit, 1885. Although he loved animals and studied them all his life, TR was also an avid hunter.

of the ranchers in this area did. The Bad Lands was public domain, the property of the United States government. Until sold to settlers, the land was "open range"; that is, anyone could start a ranch and graze cattle on it without charge.

Ranching was more than a way of making money for Theodore. It was a kind of therapy, a way of learning to deal with his grief. Whenever he chose, he retreated to the Elkhorn Ranch. With no one around for miles, he read, made his own meals, and rode his favorite horse, Manitou. These rides were special. He would set out across the plains alone, with no fixed destination or idea of how far he would go. Sometimes he rode for days, stopping only to rest Manitou, eat some beans and jerky (dried beef), and sleep. Now and then, he drove his spurs into the horse's side, making him gallop. Speed! How good it felt! Galloping on his horse, Theodore seemed able to forget his sadness for a while. "Black care," he explained, "rarely sits behind a rider whose pace is fast enough."[25]

New acquaintances at the ranch found Theodore strange, as usual. Hired hands on the Maltese Cross thought him a play rancher. For starters, he wore eyeglasses, rare things in the West then, thus the nickname Four Eyes. Cowboys also called him "tenderfoot," "punkin-lily," and "goo-goo," all of which mean they considered Roosevelt a softie. He took it all in stride. Respect, he knew, did not come out of thin air. It must be earned. So he set out to earn the cowboys' respect by becoming one of them.

Roosevelt asked their advice, learned their ways, and worked as hard as any of them. On his first cattle roundup, he called in his Harvard accent: "Hasten forward quickly there!" Everyone who heard him roared with laughter. It became a ranch joke, and cowboys began ordering one another around with, "Hasten forward quickly there!"[26]

Yet the joke was soon tinged with affection. For what Roosevelt lacked in experience, he made up for with determination. The boss never whined, never complained, never shirked. When an ornery bronco threw him, he climbed on again—and again—until the horse saw things his way. He herded cattle all day under the broiling sun, rode night guard, roped steers, and branded calves. During dry spells, when immense grass fires rolled across the plains, he pitched in to help fight the flames. Cowboys would shoot a steer, split it in half along the backbone, and drag it along the fire's edge, using the blood to control its direction. Years later, he reminisced about his experiences:

> We worked under the scorching midsummer sun, when the wide plains shimmered and wavered in the heat; and we knew the freezing misery of riding night guard around the cattle in the late fall roundup. In the soft springtime the stars were glorious in our eyes each night before we fell asleep; and in the winter we rode through blinding blizzards, when the driven snow-dust burnt our eyes. . . . We knew toil and hardship and hunger and thirst; and we saw men die violent deaths as they worked among the horses and cattle, or fought evil feuds with one another; but we felt the beat of hardy life in our veins, and ours was the glory of work and the joy of living.[27]

The New Yorker proved himself in yet another way. Cowboys expected a man to stand up for "hisself"; that is, to defend his honor and his property. Well, one night a bully noticed Roosevelt eating alone at a saloon table. "Four Eyes is going to treat," he bellowed, drawing two six-shooters. Roosevelt tried to ignore the threat, but it was impossible. Clearly, he must give in, branding himself a coward, or risk getting shot. In the instant it took to decide, he sized up the fellow with his boxer's eye.

"Well, if I've got to, I've got to," he muttered, rising from the table. A right to the jaw did the rest. Down went the bully, guns blazing, striking the corner of the bar with his head. When he awoke, he boarded the next train for parts unknown. Another time, Roosevelt confronted a Texan who had threatened to shoot him

TR as a Dakota rancher, 1885. Cowboys called him "Four Eyes," because he wore eyeglasses, but they meant no disrespect. He worked as hard as any hired hand and put down more than one bully with his fists.

over some cattle dispute. "You're talking like an ass!" Roosevelt snapped, patting the pistol at his side. "Put up or shut up! Fight now, or be friends!" The Texan shook his hand. Before long, cowboys changed his nickname from Four Eyes to Old Four Eyes. In that violent place, where death often came quickly, it was an honor to be know as "old."[28]

Roosevelt's experiences inspired his creativity. In all, he would write three books about his Western life: *Hunting Trips of a Ranchman* (1884), *Ranch Life and the Hunting Trail* (1888), and *The Wilderness Hunter* (1893). A keen observer of nature, his descriptions of animals, ranging from skunks and snakes to buffalo and grizzlies, have an almost poetic beauty. Moreover, he helped shape the modern image of the cowboy. Until the 1880s, Easterners viewed cowboys as mounted tramps, failures at everything but swearing, drinking, and fighting. Roosevelt portrayed them as loyal, honest (usually), and hardworking. Cowboys loved him for it.

In later years, Roosevelt said that had he not once lived among cowboys, he would never have become president. Perhaps. What is certain is that his stay in the Bad Lands was a turning point in his life. Ranching renewed Theodore's self-confidence. Each day, he measured himself—tested himself—against rugged men with deep suntans and callused hands. Yet measure up he did, becoming a man among men. Moreover, his Western writings reminded the public that, in Roosevelt, it had a tough, resourceful outdoorsman as well as a writer and thinker.

Hard work in the open changed Roosevelt physically, too. Every few months, he would return to New York to check on baby Alice. Upon meeting him, people who had known him all his life gasped in amazement. Gone was the scrawny dandy with the squeaky voice. In his place stood a bronzed he-man, "one hundred and fifty pounds [of] clear bone, muscle, and grit," with a bull neck, broad shoulders, and a barrel chest. When Roosevelt spoke now, it was in a voice "hearty and strong enough to drive oxen."[29]

Ladies welcomed the change.

In September 1885, a servant let Roosevelt into his sister Bamie's house on Madison Avenue. As he climbed the stairs to the parlor, he met Edith Kermit Carow, twenty-four, coming in the opposite direction. They had known each other since childhood, when they were next-door neighbors and she played house with his sisters. Four-year-old Edith had stood at the window with Theodore and

Elliott, watching Lincoln's funeral procession in Union Square. When she burst into tears at the sad scene, the boys locked her in a closet.[30]

As they grew up, Edith and Theodore found they had much in common. They liked the same things, spending hours together reciting poetry, reading aloud, and discussing books. In time, they became more than just friends; both families assumed they would eventually marry. During his first two years at Harvard, Theodore missed "her Ladyship" desperately. Compared to the local women, Edith was prettier, smarter, and more mature, he thought. However, in the summer of 1878, while he was still struggling to get over his father's death, something came between them. While they never explained what it was, Edith said he had "not been nice." Soon afterward, Theodore fell for Alice Lee.[31]

Meeting again at Bamie's, they realized they still had feelings for each other, which soon ripened into love. "You know all about me, darling," she wrote. "I love you with all the passion of a girl who has never loved before." Since Edith's father had recently died after losing his fortune, she had planned to move with her mother and sister to England, where they could live more cheaply. Now Edith changed her plans. Within six weeks of their meeting, she accepted Theodore's marriage proposal. After helping her family settle in London, he would join her there for the wedding.[32]

Meanwhile, the Republicans asked Roosevelt to run in the upcoming election for mayor of New York City. Not that they thought he had any hope of winning, even as "the cowboy candidate," who had once battled corruption in the state legislature. The party, never strong in this Democratic fortress, needed a sacrificial lamb, a warm body to show that it was participating in the contest. Knowing this, Roosevelt agreed to run anyhow, mainly to find a way back into politics. Edith was about to become his wife, and Theodore decided he could not ask a sophisticated New York lady to rough it on a cattle ranch.

There were two leading contenders in the mayoral race. Abram Hewitt, the Democrat, was a businessman who had been friendly with Roosevelt's father. Henry George, an accountant, ran with the backing of the trade unions, pledging to end poverty by putting a heavy tax on all land sales. "Respectable" New Yorkers, or well-off people with houses and bank accounts, saw George's proposal as a threat. Fearing a split in the anti-George vote, even loyal Republicans supported Hewitt. They thought it would be better to let a Democrat win than risk letting George win by voting for any other candidate. Roosevelt came in last. Just days after the election, he sailed for London and married Edith in England on December 2, 1886.

During their honeymoon, word came of a disaster in America. The tragedy is still called the "Die-up of '87." Late in January, massive blizzards rolled across the Great Plains. One rancher reported that the snow "was like a tornado of pure white dust or very fine sand, icy cold, and stinging like a whiplash." Cattle stood belly-deep in snow, their eyelids frozen shut, icicles dangling from their muzzles, starving because dried grass lay buried under the snow. Ranchers lost between 40 and 90 percent of their livestock. Hundreds of small outfits went bankrupt. Roosevelt lost $50,000, nearly his entire investment, in what he called the "smash-up." From then on, he returned to Elkhorn Ranch only for brief hunting trips.[33]

The newlyweds settled at Oyster Bay. Out of consideration for Edith, "Theodore changed the name of the estate from Leeholm to Sagamore Hill, after Sagamore Mohannis, an old-time Indian chief. No matter where they happened to sleep, even if it was the White House, Sagamore Hill would always be the Roosevelts' real home. Their love grew stronger at Sagamore Hill. "I love you all the time in my thoughts and think of our honeymoon days, and remember them all one by one, hour by hour," Edith wrote years afterward. Theodore felt the same way. Many years later, in 1915, he told how they would sit by the great fireplace: "We sit and read, and she looks so pretty and charming that now and then I have to get up and make love to her—which is rather absurd on the part of a gouty old man."[34]

It is said that behind every great man stands a great woman. In Theodore Roosevelt's case, that woman was his second wife. Along with his love for her went, perhaps, a little fear, too. If so, it was a healthy fear. Edith was "cool" in the best meaning of the term. She had sound common sense; Theodore told friends he was married to "the sanest women he has ever known." Edith sensed when her husband was about to go off track or make a fool of himself by saying too much. Before he did, she would say "Now, Theodore!" in a special tone she used at such times. "Why Ee-die," he would stammer, "I was only going to say . . ." She could also handle money better than he. Their income came from interest on the money Theodore had inherited from his father and whatever he had made by investing the inheritance on his own. With money tight after the Bad Lands disaster, Edith took over the family finances. She kept the checkbook, paying all the household bills. Since Theodore never knew how much he spent, she gave him a daily allowance (usually twenty dollars). He would never write of Edith as his "pink little wife," as he had of Alice.[35]

Edith returned from Europe pregnant with their first child. Little Alice now came to live at Sagamore Hill. Although Theodore never mentioned her mother, he had become relaxed enough to call his daughter by name. Alice helped him discover his natural gift of playfulness with children. Each morning, for the ride to the breakfast table, she climbed on Papa's back, crying, "Now pig! Now pig!" Alice's brother Theodore Jr. (Ted) was born in September 1887; she called him "a howling polly parrot" who "eats Mama" when Edith nursed him. Four other children arrived within a decade: Kermit (1889), Ethel (1891), Archie (1894), and Quentin (1897).[36]

The children's education began at home, with lessons in reading and writing from both parents. Yet, unlike their parents, the new generation of Roosevelts attended public

TR's second wife, Edith Kermit Carow, in 1905. Smart and practical, Edith also knew how to tame her husband's exuberant spirits.

elementary schools, unusual for upper-class children at this time, and later went on to private high schools. Most important, their parents did not believe that children should be seen but not heard. They expected their children to talk—a lot. Meals were verbal brawls, where ideas and information flew back and forth, with everyone having to contribute. In this way, the children learned how to take a position and defend it with facts and logic. When guests came, the youngsters sat with the adults, contributing to the conversation as best they could.

Sound minds need sound bodies, Theodore believed. Using his own struggle for health as the model, he demanded that his children face pain and discomfort without complaining. "I would rather one of them should die than have them grow up weaklings," he often said. Above all, young Roosevelts must show courage. If one of his boys refused to stand up to a bully, Father promised "to thrash him until I had some degree of manhood in him." When, for example, a boy threw apples at Ethel, he ordered Ted to fight him, although the bully was bigger.[37] Roosevelt did not expect Ethel to fight. She knew how to defend herself verbally or, if need be, call upon her brothers for help.

Physical activity was built into the family routine. Theodore encouraged "scrambles," vigorous horseplay, and took the children on overnight camping trips; before turning in, he gathered them around the campfire for a bloodcurdling ghost story. As they grew, he insisted that the boys take up team sports like football, threatening to "disinherit" any son who did not try his best. Everybody went swimming. Alice liked to swim, but diving terrified her. Even so, Father insisted. She recalled as an adult: "I can still see my father at Sagamore shouting at me from the water, 'Dive, Alicy, dive.' And there I was trembling on the bank saying through tears, 'Yes, Father,' to this sea monster who was flailing away in the water, peering nearsightedly at me without glasses and with his mustache glistening wet in the sunlight. It was pathetic."[38] The scene might have been "pathetic," but the children seem not to have resented their father's demeanor. He loved them deeply—that they knew. If he made demands, it was probably for their own good. Besides, most activities were just plain fun.

While Theodore's niece Eleanor could not swim, when he ordered her to jump off the dock, she obeyed—and came up gasping for air. Eleanor would do anything to please her uncle, for she knew he adored her. Tall and gawky, with protruding teeth, she was shy and self-conscious. Between 1892 and 1894, she lost both parents, her mother to diphtheria, her father to alcoholism and drug addiction. After that, Eleanor, who lived with her grandmother, often

In a photo that may have been taken by Edith, TR plays with a group of young cousins at Sagamore Hill, 1894. His own children, Alice and Theodore Jr., are in the foreground.

visited Sagamore Hill. The moment she arrived, Uncle Theodore would hug her so tightly it felt as if the buttons of her dress would pop. Although Aunt Edith pitied the orphan, she saw something special in her. "Poor little soul, she is very plain," Edith wrote. "Her mouth and teeth have no future. But the ugly duckling may turn out to be a swan."[39]

Roosevelt's chance to get back into politics came in 1888. That year, the Republicans chose Benjamin Harrison, a former Union general, to challenge Grover Cleveland for the presidency. During the campaign, Roosevelt volunteered to give speeches for Harrison. When he won, Harrison named Roosevelt to the U.S. Civil Service Commission. The job paid $3,500 a year, not a large sum for someone of Roosevelt's background, but it helped Edith pay the bills of the growing family more easily. Renting a house for the family in Washington, in addition to the upkeep of Sagamore Hill, put an added strain on the budget. Sometimes money became so tight that, to save a few pennies, Edith made the family's tooth powder out of ground fish bones.

Eleanor Roosevelt at fifteen, in 1899. TR loved his niece as if she were his own daughter.

Created under the Pendleton Act of 1883, the Civil Service Commission enforced the merit system in the appointment of many, but not all, federal workers. Theodore was one of three commissioners, all equal in power, but the others quietly accepted his leadership. Roosevelt stormed into the commission offices, bursting with energy and ideas for reform. As always, his sense of fairness, of rewarding people for honest hard work, drove him forward. "Every day I went to the office," a fellow commissioner recalled, "it was as to an entertainment. I knew something was sure to turn up to make our work worthwhile, with him there."[40]

Roosevelt operated on two fronts at once. For starters, he demanded that examinations identify the best person for a specific job. Existing exams, he found, tested irrelevant book learning rather than practical, job-related skills. He ordered the exams revised, to make them more realistic and useful in selecting the best person for the job. The border patrol, for example, arrested rustlers caught smuggling stolen Texas cattle into Mexico. So, instead of testing candidates'

Grover Cleveland in 1888. Although TR was a Republican, Cleveland, the first Democratic president elected after the Civil War, saw him as an ally in the cause of civil service reform.

spelling, Roosevelt developed a test that measured their ability to ride, shoot, and read cattle brands.[41]

At the same time, Roosevelt attacked corruption in the Post Office Department. While the department head appointed local postmasters, the merit system supposedly protected clerks, letter sorters, and carriers. It did not! John Wanamaker, the postmaster general, was also the leading Republican fund-raiser. Soon after taking office, he fired thirty thousand postmasters nationwide, replacing them with Republican loyalists. In many post offices, including some in the president's home state of Ohio, postmasters "suggested" that workers donate to the party. A refusal meant losing any chance of promotion, even dismissal on trumped-up charges. When Roosevelt told Wanamaker of the scandal, he did nothing. President Harrison backed his fund-raiser.

Harrison planned to dump Roosevelt for blowing the whistle on corruption, but the Democrats got rid of Harrison first. In the election of 1892, President Harrison, a Republican, faced the Democrat's Grover Cleveland a second time. Bitter over Harrison's do-nothing attitude toward post office corruption, in private Roosevelt called him "the little runt of a President." Still, as a good party man, Theodore swallowed his anger and campaigned for the Republican nominee. In the landslide that followed, the Democrats recaptured the presidency and took control of Congress. Roosevelt expected to lose his job. Yet President Cleveland, grateful for his help in civil service reform in New York, asked him to stay on.[42]

For the next two years, Roosevelt fought corruption in the Bureau of Indian Affairs, the agency in charge of running Indian reservations nationwide. For years, bureau officials had cheated Native Americans, selling government-issued rations for their own profit, while those in their charge went hungry. Roosevelt fired scores of bureau officials, replacing them with honest men. In addition, he converted twenty-six thousand federal jobs from patronage to merit selection, and ended sex discrimination in federal employment by allowing women to compete for positions equally with men. By 1894, Theodore had been in Washington for six years. Although proud of his achievements, he felt that he had done all he could for civil-service reform. So, when New York's new mayor, Republican businessman William L. Strong, asked him to head the four-man Board of Police Commissioners, he leaped at the offer. It paid $5,000 a year. The family moved back to Sagamore Hill, while Theodore lived in a small rented apartment in Manhattan during the workweek.

Roosevelt had no illusions about his position or conditions in his hometown. The Big Apple's "finest," as its police officers are known, have always had a few rotten apples. In the 1890s, however, rotten apples came in bushels.

The rot went from top to bottom. Police Chief Thomas Byrnes, the highest-ranking uniformed officer, had grown wealthy from bribes; he had $350,000 in cash and an estate in Ireland. Precinct captains bought their positions from Tammany politicians for as much as $15,000. Captains, in turn, sold patrolmen's jobs for $300. The patrolman then reimbursed himself by taking bribes from neighborhood criminals. Many officers charged a weekly fee in exchange for ignoring gambling parlors, opium dens, and houses of prostitution. Even ragged street kids knew the score. For them, the policeman's copper badge stood for crime and corruption. "What are pennies made of?" one would ask. "Dirty copper," the other would reply.

Mulberry Street was the heart of the Lower East Side, one of New York City's poorest crime-ridden neighborhoods.

Armed with a new technology—the camera—the Danish immigrant named Jacob Riis exposed the city's dark side as never before. Riis was a reporter for the *Evening Sun.* He had a tiny office on Mulberry Street opposite number 300, police headquarters. It was the worst street of the city's worst neighborhood, the Lower East Side.

ABOVE: *Theodore Roosevelt in his second-floor office in Police Headquarters, 300 Mulberry Street.*

RIGHT: *Known as "Street Arabs," New York's homeless children did not go to school, ate whatever they could beg or steal, and slept in doorways and under bridges. Jacob Riis took this picture on Mulberry Street about the year 1889.*

Riis shot it all. His photos, now in the Museum of the City of New York, document the filthy alleys and crowded tenements. Through his camera's eye we see "Bandit's Roost," an alley where life was cheap, nasty, and short. We see mounds of garbage, children playing beside dead horses, and homeless children called "street Arabs" sleeping in doorways.

Riis's 1890 book, *How the Other Half Lives,* is a classic in American photojournalism. The book was an overnight bestseller. Along with many well-off Americans, Roosevelt read it, too. One day, soon after the book's publication, he came by the author's office. Finding that Riis was out, Theodore left his card with a scribbled note: "I have read your book and I have come to help." Riis later recalled, "I loved him from the first day I saw him."[43]

"Hello, Jake," the new commissioner shouted to Riis, who was sitting on a chair outside his stuffy office. Beckoning the reporter to follow him into police headquarters, Roosevelt bounded up the rickety stairs to the second floor, trailed by the reporter. It was May 8, 1895, Roosevelt's first day on the job. Suddenly Roosevelt wheeled about and asked: "What do we do first?"[44]

The reporter briefed him thoroughly. Watch out for Chief Byrnes, a crook who, given the chance, will stab you in the back. Trust inspector so-and-so; he is a good cop, if a bit too free with his fists. For starters, though, let me show you the Lower East Side as nobody else can. While Samuel Gompers had taken Roosevelt to a few cigar makers' homes, Riis gave New York's new police commissioner the grand tour. On these excursions, Roosevelt explained, "I get a glimpse of the real life of the swarming millions." Miniature worlds crowded into two square miles. These worlds had different names: Little Italy, Poletown, Jewtown, Germantown, Chinatown. One might walk in these places for hours without hearing a word or seeing a sign in English. Yet the misery needed no words. Roosevelt saw it all, and smelled it everywhere.[45] It was just as Riis had described in *How the Other Half Lives*—the dirt, the overcrowding, the hunger, the destruction of the human spirit. Theodore vowed to help the poor. If he could not give them food and shelter, at least, as police commissioner, he could see that the police served them honestly.

Everyone knew the commissioner's motto: "Woe to the policeman who exposes himself to the taint of corruption." At first, the corrupt snickered, thinking nobody could touch them. They soon changed their tune. Like others before them, policemen learned that Roosevelt never bluffed. He started at the top. Calling Chief Byrnes into his office, he shut the door. Byrnes must have gotten an offer he dared not refuse, for he resigned imme-

diately. Byrnes was lucky; he had powerful political friends, so Roosevelt may have decided to get rid of him without fuss rather than antagonize them. Other thieves with badges were not so lucky. In all, Roosevelt fired two hundred officers for dishonesty and incompetence.[46]

He and Riis prowled the streets after midnight. Pity the poor copper they found "cooping"—sleeping at his post. Awakened by a jab in the ribs, the first thing he saw was a gleaming row of large white teeth. Report to my office today, Roosevelt would growl. Once, he saw a patrolman drinking beer in front of a

Jacob Riis photographed Mullen's Alley in 1888 or 1889. Also known as "Bandit's Roost," the place was a notorious hangout for thieves and cutthroats.

saloon. The fellow ran away, but the commissioner caught him. Newsmen loved these funny, adventurous exploits. Roosevelt was "good copy," they said, meaning a good, entertaining story. On an otherwise dull day, you could count on him for a colorful headline. Readers became fascinated by his teeth. They imagined officers standing before the commissioner's desk, hypnotized by his teeth. According to one report, those grinders seemed to say: "Tell the truth to your Commissioner, or he'll bite your head off." Peddlers sold tin whistles called "Teddy's Teeth," which citizens blew at patrolmen who seemed to shirk their duty.[47] Those who did not know Roosevelt personally often called him "Teddy," though he resented the nickname as "rude" and "impertinent." His family never used it, nor did anyone who knew him well.

Leadership, however, is more than forcing people to follow orders. To succeed, a leader must motivate others to *want* to do the right thing. Roosevelt appealed to his men's "better selves," to their pride and decency. Merit became the rule, as did civil-service examinations replacing bribes. The commissioner rewarded courage. Officers who risked their lives in the line of duty, like the one who dove into the East River to save a drowning woman, won medals and promotions. Thanks to Roosevelt, the police reclaimed their honor, truly becoming New York's Finest. Afterward, a captain explained it this way:

> He put new morale into the Force. . . . No man was afraid to do his duty while Roosevelt was commissioner, because he knew that the commissioner was behind him. The crooks were afraid of the cops—and the cops were not afraid of the crooks. All the decent, manly fellows on the Force loved this strenuous master who led them. He was human. You could talk to him. . . . He had an open door for any member of the Force. Every man who really tried to do right or, having gone crooked, reformed and showed he was trying to do right, always received a fair chance. He detested cowardice and shirking . . . but he always stuck to the man who proved he was doing or trying to do his job. . . . I guess that nine-tenths of the men that's ever come in contact with Theodore Roosevelt are better and squarer men because of it.[48]

Reading this would have made Thee proud of his son. Merit, honesty, decency—these were the very values he had tried to instill in all his children. Within months of taking charge, Roosevelt had created America's first modern police department, a model for the rest of the country. To train officers properly, he founded the Police Academy. By installing telephones in local station houses, he improved communications. He created "flying squads" of officers on bicycles to speed to crime scenes. To identify criminals, he introduced a rogues' gallery of photographs and fingerprinting, a method pioneered in England.[49]

Public safety was his main concern. Once a clergyman came from Germany to "preach a crusade against the Jews." Fearing violence, Jewish community leaders begged Roosevelt to keep him from speaking. Instead, he made the preacher look ridiculous by assigning forty Jewish policemen to guard him as he spoke. Roosevelt had a lifelong horror of disorder, of anything that threatened to unravel the fabric of society. Whoever caused disorder—rabble-rousers, criminals, strikers, drunks, rowdies—he would crush them without mercy, in what today we might call "police brutality." "No decent citizen had anything to fear from the police," he recalled. "But we constantly encouraged the police to prove that the violent criminal . . . was himself in grave jeopardy." To quell disorder, Roosevelt urged his men to use their clubs freely. If clubs failed, let them use their pistols. And let them shoot to kill.[50]

One problem gave Commissioner Roosevelt more trouble than anything else. A state law banned saloons from selling liquor on Sundays. Yet the law was a dead letter. Wealthy New Yorkers did not drink in saloons, but in private clubs and fine hotels. City saloons, some fifteen thousand of them, served working people. True, drunkenness often led to violence, broken homes, and mental illness. However, for countless people, especially men, saloons were also centers of social life. The neighborhood saloon allowed them to flee the crowded tenements for a few hours. Workers met friends there, shared job leads, and held union meetings. Saloons also provided services, like free newspapers and toilets. For many, then, the Sunday closing law was a hardship and an outrage. Saloon keepers agreed. Each Sunday, they closed their front doors, while doing a roaring business through their back doors.

No drinker himself, Roosevelt knew the ravages of alcohol; it had destroyed his brother. Yet he did not favor closing saloons on Sundays or any other day. If people wanted to drink themselves stupid, he said, that was their business. However, there were more important issues at stake, and Theodore felt he must enforce the law even though he disagreed with it. Overlooking any lawbreaking, even "a singularly foolish law," bred contempt for all law and led to disorder, he insisted. Moreover, the Sunday closing law fed corruption, as saloon keepers bought protection from the police, while refusal to pay led to a raid and a fine. Roosevelt felt he must act. "The police used the partial . . . enforcement of the law as a means of collecting blackmail," he explained. "I was only enforcing honestly a law that had hitherto been enforced dishonestly."[51]

Despite his good intentions, a storm of resentment swept the city. Saloon keepers, Tammany politicians, and decent citizens deprived of their Sunday "snort" denounced Roosevelt as a tyrant. Cartoonists portrayed him as the bulldog of the "Mulberry Street Zoo." Protesters in a section of the city called Germantown carried a banner reading SEND THE POLICE CZAR TO RUSSIA. This was a terrible insult, since Russia's current czar (emperor), Nicholas II, was an ignorant bigot.[52]

Death threats poured into Roosevelt's office. Once, a postal worker discovered a letter bomb addressed to the commissioner. After that, he told a friend, a package containing an "infernal machine," or bomb, arrived at headquarters. "They put an infernal machine in my office the other day wound up to kill me; the boys discovered it in time and saved me. . . . There are gunmen in this city that would kill me . . . for $100, and there are many that would put up the money, but bad men are miserable cowards. I am not afraid of one of them. . . ."[53] And why should he be afraid, he who had faced down drunken cowboys waving six-shooters?

The crackdown continued. Clearly, by refusing to give in to the public's demands, Roosevelt had made himself, not lawbreaking, the issue. Yet an honest man could do nothing else, he thought. Gradually his frustration grew. He became bitter. "The people who had demanded honesty, but

Theodore Roosevelt, the ever-watchful "guard dog," stands ready to enforce the law against selling liquor on Sunday.

who did not like to pay for it by the loss of illegal pleasure, joined the openly dishonest in attacking us," he wrote years later.[54]

Another election saved the day for Roosevelt. In June 1896, the Republicans nominated William McKinley to run for president against the Democratic candidate, William Jennings Bryan of Nebraska. Known as the "Boy Orator," Bryan, thirty-six, could fire up a crowd like nobody else with his cries for social justice. Ever loyal to his party, Roosevelt campaigned for McKinley. Wherever Bryan gave his most rousing speeches, Roosevelt turned up like clockwork a day or so later. Whipping himself into a frenzy, he revealed his darker side, unfairly calling the Democrat a "silly and wicked" champion of mob rule. McKinley trounced his opponent. As a reward, he appointed Theodore assistant secretary of the navy.[55]

In April 1897, Roosevelt returned to Washington and left his problems as New York's police commissioner behind. Let us leave him there for now, since we cannot go any further without first learning more about his America. In certain ways, Roosevelt's story is that of the forces shaping the country during his lifetime. Historians call those forces the Industrial Revolution.

3

A THUNDERING EXPRESS TRAIN

*The old nations of the earth creep on at a snail's pace; the Republic thunders past with the
rush of the express.*

—ANDREW CARNEGIE, 1886

Theodore Roosevelt grew to manhood in a nation that was already the wonder
of the world. Groping for ways to describe America, foreign visitors used words
like *dynamic* and *colossal, stupendous* and *miraculous.* These did not seem like exag-
gerations. Its people moved about faster, farther, and in larger numbers than
anywhere else. Each year its farms and factories set records, producing more food
and manufactured goods than any nation in history. More people enjoyed a
higher standard of living than anywhere else, including the most advanced
nations like England and Germany. Yet, in many ways, America was also a
troubled land, one of both astonishing promise and heartbreak.

Once it had been a nation of vast distances, of small farms and small towns.
Most artisans, or craftspeople, worked for themselves, with their own hands and
tools in their own shops. Whatever they made—cloth, paper, furniture, ironware,
whiskey, wagons—they sold locally. Thus, with hard work and luck, a person
of humble origins might overcome poverty. That is what Roosevelt's hero,
Abraham Lincoln, meant when he said everyone deserved "the right to rise," to
go as far as ambition and talent could take them.[1]

Yet, at the very time Lincoln spoke, the Industrial Revolution was replacing
the artisan's labor with machinery. The change had begun in Europe a decade
before the Revolutionary War, spreading to America within a generation. Because running water turned the wheels that drove the early machines, owners
built their factories beside inland streams and rivers. These were tiny affairs, for
labor was scarce; at most, factories employed a few dozen local people, usually
farmers out to make extra money. Owners and hired help saw themselves as

equals. Often they worked side by side, called one another by their first name, and ate together during breaks.

The Civil War (1861–65) marked a turning point for America. That conflict did more than end slavery and preserve the Union. In Robert E. Lee and Stonewall Jackson, the Confederacy had brilliant generals. But the Union had the bulk of the nation's productive capacity. New inventions, particularly the steam engine, were already making factories more efficient. Streams often dried up in summer and froze in winter, forcing the nation's first factories to shut down for part of the year. The steam engine, however, furnished a different kind of power. Originally used in America in 1807 on boats, inventors adapted the steam engine to industry. No longer dependent on running water for power, factories sprang up in many Northern cities. With their larger populations, cities guaranteed a regular, low-wage workforce. As factories grew in size, their output vastly increased. That enabled the Union to produce more guns, more clothing—more *everything*—than its opponent, whose wealth depended on agriculture rather than on manufacturing.

The Civil War was a bonanza of opportunity and wealth for the ambitious. Some men, called "robber barons," became masters of the shady, get-rich-quick scheme. Robber barons speculated in the stock market, buying heavily to drive prices up, then quietly selling out, bankrupting ordinary investors. Taking advantage of the military's needs, the early robber barons were manufacturers who got their start by selling the Union Navy leaky cargo ships. Union soldiers got cardboard boots and defective rifles. After the war, a host of newcomers, honest and otherwise, entered the business world. These were flush times, full of opportunity, when America became the workshop of the world.

America owed much of its success to its railroads. Until they appeared in the 1820s, moving people and goods overland was slow and expensive, as roads were hardly more than paths through forests. The federal government saw the "iron horse," or steam locomotive, as crucial to binding the nation together. Starting with the Civil War, to enable the Union to move troops and goods, Congress and state legislatures spurred railroad construction with generous cash and land bonuses for each mile of track laid. The results were spectacular. From 30,000 miles of track in 1860, the mileage leaped to 164,000 by 1890, and to 193,000 by 1900, greater than Europe and South America combined.[2]

Railroads were the first big business. They enabled Americans to master an immense continent, opening the land to settlement and its natural resources to exploitation. As railroads sold some of their lands, towns arose beside the tracks to serve settlers' needs. Settlers came to town to buy manufactured goods, brought by trains, and to sell their produce, which trains carried to market. Railroads created a national market, so that products like Theodore Roosevelt's cattle found their way to dining room tables thousands of miles from the Dakota Bad Lands.

The national market encouraged entrepreneurs, those who organize and operate business ventures. Let's say a company made a new product that appealed to consumers. Immediately, others rushed into the field, eager to cash in, too. Before long, the field became crowded, forcing companies to compete for customers by lowering prices. Everyone was supposed to benefit, and they did, at least for a time. Manufacturers made profits. Workers found jobs. Consumers paid less. Manufacturers opened plants and hired more workers. The economy grew.

Yet the good times could not last forever; they never do. After a while, companies began producing more than consumers needed. As unsold goods piled up in warehouses, prices and profits fell. Every decade or so, the country had

After becoming fabulously wealthy by making cheap, high-quality steel, Andrew Carnegie gave most of his fortune to charity.

a depression, a sharp economic downturn, triggering massive business shutdowns and unemployment. Competition, then, became wasteful and costly. Some entrepreneurs realized that, to prosper, they must limit competition by creating monopolies. In a monopoly, a person or a group controls the production or sale of a raw material, finished product, or service. Three Americans created near-perfect monopolies in their industries, making them the wealthiest men in the country. Like Theodore Roosevelt Sr., each hired a substitute to serve in the Union Army for him during the Civil War.

Andrew Carnegie was a poor Scottish immigrant who rose to become a branch manager for the Pennsylvania Railroad. That experience convinced him that railroads could not expand without ever more steel for tracks. Stronger than iron, steel is made by burning away the carbon impurities found naturally in iron and adding various minerals to harden the metal. Although people had made steel for thousands of years, the difficulty in reaching very high temperatures limited output to small batches at a time. However, in 1856, an English inventor, Henry Bessemer, found that the oxygen in a jet of air forced through molten iron quickly burned away the carbon. When the Civil War ended, Carnegie quit his job and invested his savings in making steel the Bessemer way.

Although others did the same, they lacked his business savvy. Rather than buying any raw materials from others, giving them a profit, the Scotsman cut costs by creating an industrial family to serve his Carnegie Steel Company. To supply its steel mills with raw materials, Carnegie bought iron mines, coal mines, railroad lines, and cargo ships. Cost-cutting led to price-cutting; his price for steel fell by half, from forty to twenty dollars a ton. Vastly increased sales more than made up for the lower per-ton price. Unable to keep up, competitors folded, making Carnegie ruler of an empire of steel. In time, he became the world's largest producer of steel. Besides railroad track, Carnegie steel was used to build bridges, form the skeletons of the first skyscrapers, and went into the precision machinery that made these marvels possible.

Oil—petroleum—was as vital to industrial growth as steel. Before Thomas A. Edison's invention of the electric lightbulb, oil refined into kerosene replaced candles and whale-oil lamps for indoor lighting. Oil is also the ideal lubricant. In all machinery, friction produces heat where metal parts move against one another. Oil reduces friction, preventing breakdowns and prolonging a machine's useful life. Only later, with the coming of the internal combustion engine and the automobile, did gasoline, originally a waste product of oil refining, power motor vehicles.

Before John D. Rockefeller came on the scene, the oil industry was a wild brawl. The son of a traveling salesman, Rockefeller believed that success in oil lay not in drilling for it, but in refining it and getting it to market cheaply. In 1863, as the Civil War raged, he and four partners built a refinery in Cleveland, Ohio. Meanwhile, Rockefeller secretly got railroads to give rebates, or givebacks, on freight charges, by offering them a guaranteed amount of his business. This was legal at the time. Since competitors paid regular rates to ship their oil, they could not beat his Standard Oil Company's prices. Next, Rockefeller created the "trust," a group of companies united by him to monopolize the oil industry. Rockefeller used his monopoly to control not only oil fields, but everything needed to produce, refine, and get oil to market: rail lines; chemical plants; iron mines, for

ABOVE: *Oil tycoon John D. Rockefeller. At the beginning of the twentieth century, his Standard Oil Company had a near-monopoly of the American oil industry.*

RIGHT: *Nicknamed "Jupiter" after the Roman god, J. P. Morgan ruled the world of American finance, providing the money and credit business needed to expand.*

barrels; tanker ships. By the 1890s, Standard Oil ruled over 90 percent of the oil business, making Rockefeller the first American to have a personal fortune of a billion dollars. Giant sugar, meatpacking, aluminum, tobacco, and life-insurance companies soon copied his model, creating trusts in their industries.

Money is the lifeblood of economic growth. After the Civil War, many businessmen wanted to buy the latest machinery to expand production and, in that way, increase their profits. That took lots of cash, which few had. Their need created yet another type of business: investment banking. Unlike ordinary bankers, investment bankers did not take deposits or make loans. Instead, they were go-betweens who dealt in investment opportunities. In return for a hefty fee, and a share of a company's stock and profits, they brought borrowers and lenders together.

John Pierpont Morgan—"J.P." for short—ruled the investment banking world. Born into a wealthy New York family, Morgan had a ferocious personality, which some compared to a jungle animal's. His blazing eyes seemed to hold people in a vise, boring into them as if reading their innermost thoughts. Even strong men became timid under his gaze. The sight of his nose, a swollen red knob, the result of a skin disease, made children burst into tears. Like Carnegie and Rockefeller, Morgan hated the "wastefulness" of competition. Using his financial muscle, he came to dominate America's leading industries: railroads, shipping, farm machinery, electrical power. A haughty man, he was called "Jupiter" by his rivals, after the king of the Roman gods. Like the god, Morgan's very words were "I command!"

During this time, the gap between the rich and everyone else grew steadily. Census figures gathered by the federal government every ten years tell the story. The 1890 census showed that the richest 1 percent of families, some 630,000 individuals, earned over $50,000 a year and owned 51 percent of the nation's property. A decade later, 0.35 percent of the population, or 250,000 individuals, owned 75 percent of the property, which did not leave much for everyone else. America's wealthiest got their money from their own firms, directorships in other firms, and investments in stocks and bonds. There were no federal income taxes until 1913, so they kept nearly every dollar they earned.[3]

How to justify such wealth? An 1859 book, *On the Origin of Species* by the pioneer English naturalist Charles Darwin, offered one popular way to explain it. Darwin held that all forms of life evolve, or develop, through the law of struggle. Life, he said, is a struggle where only animals and plants able to adjust to changes in their environment survive; those that cannot adjust die out. Although Darwin did not apply the law of struggle to human society, others did. Called Social Darwinists, they insisted that nature guarantees progress through endless conflict, in which "superior" people prosper and the "inferior" go under. As Rockefeller put it, the growth of a giant trust like Standard Oil "is merely a survival of the fittest." Taking over or eliminating rivals "is merely the working out of a law of nature and a law of God." A devout Baptist, the oil tycoon found it most comforting to know that the Lord favored him.[4]

A few wealthy men felt obliged to use their money to help others. Despite his ruthlessness in business, John D. Rockefeller funded medical research and educational projects. J. P. Morgan supported museums and the Morgan Library, the world's finest private collection of rare books. Andrew Carnegie, however, outspent everyone. During the last eighteen years of life, the steel king gave nearly $350 million to libraries, universities, and other "worthy causes," as he called them. Yet many American millionaires, of whom there were 4,074 in 1896, used their wealth less for the public good than to support a lavish lifestyle.[5]

"How lovely the earth is! I wonder if Heaven will be more beautiful," said a New York millionaire. Well might he wonder about heaven; for people like him already lived in a kind of earthly paradise. Leaders of industry enjoyed a lifestyle rivaling that of the old European nobility. While not nobles by birth, American millionaires saw themselves as self-made "steel barons, coal lords, dukes of wheat and beef." For them, a lavish lifestyle proved that they had arrived, that they were somebody. It showed their superiority and, they imagined, brought the respect from others that they deserved.[6]

The wealthy traveled in elegant carriages, sleek yachts, and private railroad cars, complete with velvet seats and crystal chandeliers. When the automobile appeared after 1901, they "motored" in gleaming vehicles driven by uniformed chauffeurs. Millionaires lived in grand imitations of European palaces and mansions. Hordes of servants—butlers, cooks, maids, nannies, gardeners, grooms, secretaries—kept things running smoothly. Into their grand houses they poured treasures imported from Europe, such as antique furniture, rare carpets, fine wines, leather-bound books, and paintings by old masters. Without batting an eyelash, some plunked down $200,000 for a bed, $75,000 for opera glasses, and $65,000 for a dressing table. To show off his good taste, a "copper king" bought an entire art museum. In their wills, "rich ninnies," as critics called them, left more money to aging dogs than to charity. A pet monkey had its own room and a butler to attend to its every need.[7]

Millionaires gave banquets where guests, crowned with laurel like ancient kings, literally burned money; that is, they lit cigars with flaming hundred-dollar bills. In 1897, a depression year, New York banker Bradley Martin and his wife spent $350,000 on a gala ball. Bradley's brother, who disapproved, described the affair:

The interior of the Waldorf Astoria Hotel was transformed into a replica

Bankers holding cigars and wearing vine-leaf crowns partying in a New York hotel, 1897. With little government regulation and no federal taxes on incomes, big business could do pretty much as it pleased.

[of the French palace] of Versailles and rare tapestries, beautiful flowers, and countless lights made an effective background for the wonderful gowns and their wearers. I do not think that there has ever been a greater display of jewels before or since; in many cases the diamond buttons worn by the men represented thousands of dollars and the value of the historic gems worn by the women baffles description. My sister-in-law['s] . . . gold embroidered gown was trimmed with pearls and precious stones. Bradley, as [King] Louis XIV, wore a court suit of brocade. . . . The suit of inlaid gold armor worn by Mr. Belmont was valued at ten thousand dollars.[8]

Great wealth also bought political power. As early as 1828, President Andrew Jackson urged Americans not to take democracy for granted. Jackson thought that rule by the people might easily become a plutocracy, rule by the wealthy few. Within sixty years, Jackson's worst fears seemed about to come true. Although Americans still elected their representatives, in reality wealthy special interests controlled lawmakers. Not surprisingly, the wealthy wished to protect and enlarge their fortunes, and to do so they freely manipulated the government. All too often, however, they had no sense of public duty, no feeling of responsibility to anything other than their own desires. William H. Vanderbilt, owner of the New York Central Railroad, was brutally honest about this. Asked if he felt he had a duty to the public, he snarled, "The public be damned!"[9]

Men such as Vanderbilt did not look to government to solve problems. The best government is the one that governs the least, they insisted. Government should keep order, protect private property, and defend against foreign enemies. It should not regulate the economy, as that would limit a citizen's God-given right to make money. Moreover, the hard world of business taught many wealthy men that "money talks," that everyone has his price. For enough money, the wealthy thought they could get the government to do whatever they wanted. E. H. Harriman, president of the Union Pacific Railroad, boasted he could spread money around so that it shouted. An associate reported: "Whenever it was necessary, he could buy . . . Senators and Congressmen or State Legislators to protect his interests, and when necessary he could buy the Judiciary. These were his own words."[10]

Headquartered in Wall Street, New York's financial district, the alliance of money and politics infected all levels of government. Senators led the list of

Titled "The Trust Giant's Point of View," this cartoon by Horace Taylor appeared in The Verdict *magazine on January 22, 1900. "What a funny little government," says John D. Rockefeller, who contributed heavily to the election campaigns of senators and representatives.*

offenders. Since the modern idea of conflict of interest—a conflict between the private interests and official duties of a public official—was unknown then, senators freely promoted their own business interests. "The U.S. Senate represented corruption," recalled newsman Lincoln Steffens, Theodore Roosevelt's friend since his days as police commissioner. "It was a chamber of traitors, and we used to talk about the treason of the Senate." Until 1913, state legislatures, not state voters, elected senators. By paying the going price, about $60,000, a candidate's backers bribed key legislators, then owned the senator. In this way, "railroad senators" defended the railroads, "textile senators" proposed laws favorable to cloth manufacturers, and so on. Judges went along, too. Often recruited from the ranks of corporation lawyers, judges were called by a critic "political henchmen who have . . . twisted the law for the protection of the favored few."[11]

Each census taken between 1880 and 1910 reported a population rise of not less than 20 percent. Part of this dramatic increase was due to American-born people starting families of their own. The bulk, however, represented the flood of immigrants that reached American shores, over 8.8 million in the decade 1901–10. Before 1880, what people called "the old immigrants" came from Northern and Western European countries: Great Britain, Germany, Holland, Scandinavia. After 1880, "the new immigrants" came from Southern and Eastern European countries: Italy, Greece, Russia, Poland, Hungary, Romania, Serbia. By 1910, one in three Americans had been born outside the country, or had at least one foreign-born parent.[12]

Like earlier immigrants, these newcomers saw their adopted land as a haven. For so many, Europe was a prison without bars, because they did not feel they could rise above the station in which they were born. Most of those who left it were fleeing something: poverty, forced military service, religious bigotry. Among the latter, the largest number were Jews. Anti-Semitism was widespread, particularly in Russia, where it was the official policy of the government. Russian Jews could not live in most places, own land, or follow many trades. In bad economic times, Russia's rulers directed popular anger away from themselves and toward the Jews. Pogroms—government-approved riots—swept Russia, claiming hundreds of Jewish lives. At such times, the entire population of small Jewish towns, called "shtetls," fled Russia together. "Sympathy for Russia?" a fugitive doctor asked. "It is impossible . . . that a Jew should regret leaving Russia."[13]

Joseph Keppler's cartoon, "Bosses of the Senate," appeared in Puck, a humor magazine, around the year 1900. With the great trusts standing over them, senators clearly cared more for the interests of a wealthy few than for the American people as a whole.

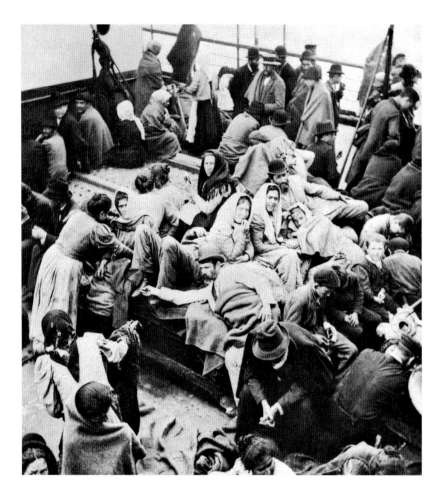

Huddled masses yearning to be free. In this 1905 photo, steerage passengers enjoy the fresh air on deck as their ship approaches Ellis Island in New York Harbor.

Coming to America at the beginning of the twentieth century was easier than it had ever been. Crossing the Atlantic Ocean in a sailing ship used to take three to seven weeks, depending on the weather, and might cost one's entire savings. By 1903, however, steamships had revolutionized ocean travel. In that year, the voyage from the German port of Hamburg to New York took six to twelve days. The cheapest passenger quarters were in the steerage, the section near the ship's rudder, and cost $33.50. Though fast and cheap, the ocean crossing could be an awful experience. First-time sea travelers described the steerage as "hell afloat." One recalled:

We were all herded together in a dark, filthy compartment in the steerage. . . . Wooden bunks had been put up in two tiers. . . . Seasickness broke out among us. Hundreds of people had vomiting fits. . . . As all were crossing the ocean for the first time, they thought their end had come. The confusion of cries became unbearable. . . . I wanted to escape from that inferno but no sooner had I thrust my head forward from the lower bunk than someone above me vomited straight upon my head. I wiped the vomit away, dragged myself onto the deck, leaned against the railing and vomited my share into the sea, and lay down half-dead upon the deck.[14]

Most immigrants landed in New York. The Statue of Liberty, unveiled in 1886, was the first landmark they saw as they entered the harbor. For some, the city was their final destination. "Although in America, it is not American. New York is

New York, and nothing else," an English traveler wrote. It was a metropolis, a world city, a melting pot where people of all backgrounds lived, worked, played, and intermarried. For many other immigrants, however, it was the "Golden Door," the entryway to the vast continent that lay beyond. From New York, a network of railroads sped them to distant manufacturing centers, cities of belching smokestacks and factories hungry for cheap, unskilled labor.[15]

It was soon clear that America's real genius lay in its ability to change millions of foreign immigrants into loyal, productive citizens. The Industrial Revolution enabled middle-class Americans, and not just millionaires, to live better than anywhere on Earth. Such people, usually men, served industry as managers, accountants, architects, lawyers, chemists, engineers, and a host of other occupations. Middle-class family income ranged from about $1,000 a year to about $3,500. Owning their own homes, such families employed a housekeeper, and could afford to let their children finish high school and go to college.[16] As for the working class, the "aristocrats of labor," highly skilled men who earned as much as $900 a year, stood at the high end of the scale. They could own a small house, even a piano, and afford to let their children finish grade school. Upon graduation, their sons usually became apprentices—learners—in their father's trade. Girls were usually married by the age of seventeen.

Yet middle- and working-class prosperity does not tell the whole story. According to the 1900 census, three-fourths of all Americans lived in poverty, defined as having a family income of $553 a year or less. The majority, unskilled workers of all sorts, averaged only $286 a year. Experts calculated that a family needed between $650 and $800 a year to cover basic needs: food, clothing, housing, fuel, medical attention.[17]

Ellis Island in 1905, by Lewis Hine. Having passed their medical inspections, a mother and her children prepare to board the ferry that will take them to the mainland and their new life in America.

Although wives earned less than husbands for doing the same jobs, many poor families needed the women's earnings to make ends meet. Children of both sexes worked, too. The census showed that nearly 1.8 million children under sixteen worked. In some Southern cotton mills, six- and seven-year-olds worked up to thirteen hours a day. Other children worked in "sweatshops," small urban factories infamous for low wages, long hours, and unhealthy conditions. Yet, in a sense, they were lucky, for they at least got regular wages. "Pieceworkers" did not. Under this system, employers paid entire families according to the number of items or pieces they made, usually in their tenement apartments. For example, small children sewed clothing, assembled cardboard boxes, and made artificial flowers. Youngsters often quit grade school to work, and many never set foot in a classroom at all.

Many children born into poor families had to work rather than go to school. The girl in this photograph by Lewis Hine is working in a mill, producing cotton thread.

Normally, workers spent ten to twelve hours a day on the job, although some put in longer hours; miners worked up to eighteen hours a day. The "weekend" as we know it did not exist a century ago. Even bosses worked Saturday. Yet, unlike them, workers could not afford to get sick or hurt. America had more industrial accidents than any other country. About 500,000 workers had serious accidents, and 30,000 died, on the job each year. By contrast, in 2002, 5,535 Americans died by work-related injuries and diseases. When a worker in Roosevelt's time was hurt, well, tough luck! There was no such thing as a safety net, no health insurance, no old-age pensions, no Social Security or Medicare. Helping the needy was the responsibility of private charities and churches. Government hardly played a role in citizens' daily lives. Nor should it, most politicians and their business backers argued. President Grover Cleveland explained: "Though the people support the Government, the Government should not support the people."[18]

When thinking about the Civil War, some wondered if slavery, its main cause, had been so bad after all. Once black people had been human property without human rights. Yet slaves were costly "investments," so owners usually provided a minimum of life's necessities—food, clothing, and shelter. Industrial workers could not expect even that. Although supposedly free, they had little control over their lives. True, if they did not like a job, they could quit. But then what? Starve? Often they saw themselves as "wage slaves," doomed to never-ending toil, but enjoying none of the fruits of their labor. "We wiped out slavery and . . . began a system of white wage slavery worse than the first," said Mary Lease, a Kansas reformer. "Wall Street owns the country. . . . The great common people of this country are slaves, and monopoly is the master." Such anger, such desperation among the working poor might at any moment plunge America into the horrors of revolution.[19]

Large-scale trouble began the year after Theodore Roosevelt entered Harvard. Claiming reduced earnings, in July 1877, the Baltimore & Ohio Railroad cut wages. But the company still paid high dividends—or share of profits—to its stockholders. Protesting the wage cuts, workers in West Virginia struck, walking off the job and bringing B&O trains to a halt. In retaliation, B&O directors persuaded the governor to call out National Guard troops to prevent violence. That only made matters worse. Curses flew. Rocks flew. Then bullets flew. Before long, workers on other rail lines joined in the first nationwide strike in American history. Shouting "wage and revenge," they tore up tracks and wrecked machine shops; hundreds of locomotives, boxcars, and passenger coaches burned. Federal troops finally broke the strike, but not before as many as two hundred people lost their lives.[20]

New immigrants brought new ideas from Europe, where poor workers were also suffering under the effects of the Industrial Revolution and harsh working conditions. Among these ideas, anarchism was the most extreme—and the most frightening. Anarchists believed that people are born free, but that governments and laws are oppressive. Therefore, it followed, people must abolish the state, replacing it by a society where all work voluntarily for the welfare of each. Most anarchists thought this would happen peacefully, once humanity saw the truth. A

minority, however, had no faith in education and goodwill to bring change. Calling themselves "anarchists of the deed," they insisted that force alone could bring justice. President McKinley's assassin, Leon Czolgosz, was an anarchist of the deed.

Czolgosz used a pistol, but most violent anarchists believed justice grew out of a stick of dynamite. European governments strictly regulated explosives. At $1.75 a pound, however, dynamite in the United States was easy to find. Any adult American could buy it in a hardware store. Anarchists called dynamite the "great equalizer" and the "people's friend." An anarchist newspaper said: "Dynamite, of all good stuff, this is the stuff. Stuff several pounds of this sublime stuff into an inch pipe (gas or water pipe), plug up the ends, insert a cap with a fuse attached, place this in the immediate neighborhood of a lot of rich loafers who live by the sweat of other people's brows, and light the fuse. A most cheerful and gratifying result will follow."[21]

Citizens of Chicago found nothing cheerful about dynamite. On May 4, 1886, anarchists gathered in Haymarket Square to protest the police's killing of two strikers outside a factory. In case of trouble, those who called the rally hung up posters asking their followers to bring guns. The rally went peacefully until the end, when police tried to clear the square. Suddenly someone, never identified, threw a bomb into their ranks. After the explosion, the police regrouped and shot into the crowd. Although several protesters may have shot back, eyewitnesses

claimed that, in the confusion, officers shot their own comrades. The police had eight dead and seventy wounded. Nobody knows how many protesters died; the number may be as high as fifteen.

Panic swept the nation. Overnight, terrified citizens expected to be killed by anarchist bombs. Outraged, the normally calm *New York Times* demanded that hangmen cure the foreign "disease" of anarchism. The Chicago police arrested eight anarchists. At their trial, the prosecutor admitted that he had no evidence linking the accused to either the bombing or shooting. But since anarchist ideas had supposedly "inspired" the phantom bomber, he insisted they were equally guilty. A jury of businessmen agreed. Four anarchists went to the gallows, and one committed suicide in jail. Calling their deaths "judicial murder," even workers who rejected anarchism honored the "Haymarket martyrs." Illinois' German-born governor John Peter Altgeld later pardoned the remaining three, sentenced to life imprisonment, since not a shred of evidence pointed to their guilt. To commemorate their comrades' deaths, the labor movement made May 1 a day honoring workers worldwide.

During the great railroad strike of 1877, strikers fought pitched battles with soldiers. This picture of riots in Chicago is from Michael J. Schaack's 1899 book, Anarchy and Anarchists: A History of the Red Terror and the Social Revolution in America and Europe.

The Haymarket tragedy was a wake-up call for law-abiding, well-off people. Although Americans condemned terrorism like the Haymarket bombing, they also demanded that big business not act as if it were a law unto itself. Congress responded to the outcry by passing two laws. With the Interstate Commerce Act of 1887, for the first time an industry, the railroads, came under government regulation. The act banned rebates, creating the Interstate Commerce Commission (ICC) to ensure "reasonable and fair" charges on freight carried from one state to another. In 1890, the Sherman Antitrust Act became the first government effort to curb unfair competition and monopolies. Unfortunately, both measures had loopholes wide enough for corporation lawyers to drive a train through.

A depression in the early 1890s made matters worse. It began with America's first big business, as one in four railroads went bankrupt. When railroad building halted, steel orders fell. Demand for manufactured goods slowed, ruining dozens of producers. Borrowers could not repay their loans, forcing nearly five hundred banks to close their doors. In some cities, unemployment among industrial workers reached 25 percent before the depression ended in 1897. Jobless men became wanderers. Leaving home, they hitched rides on freight trains, hiding in boxcars and scrounging for food. Americans knew those who "hit the road" by different names. Hobos were respectable men forced to travel to find work, while tramps traveled but would not work.

The depression brought out Andrew Carnegie's nasty side. While he gave millions to favored charities, he showed little charity toward his employees. Always keen to cut costs, he turned his attention to the giant steelworks at Homestead, Pennsylvania. When it came to safety, this place had an evil reputation. Asked how workers fared there, a Catholic priest said, "Oh, that is a slaughterhouse; they kill them there every day." Loads falling from overhead cranes crushed men to death. Workers falling from slippery catwalks vanished into cauldrons of bubbling steel.[22]

In his drive for longer hours and lower wages, Carnegie decided to destroy the steelworkers' union. Unions had begun to spring up in every major industry after the Civil War. Their demands for higher wages and better working conditions, such as shorter hours and safety equipment, were deeply resented by employers. Employers felt that they, and they alone, should decide how they ran their businesses. Besides, meeting workers' demands would cut into profits. Thus, employers had no qualms about using force to prevent the formation of unions, or to crush unions that had already gained a foothold in their plants.

Andrew Carnegie was a fervent "union-buster." But he did not want to dirty his own hands in breaking the steelworkers' union; he paid others to do that for him. After giving the task to his second-in-command, Henry Clay Frick, Carnegie left for his castle in Scotland. Frick took a hard line, trying to provoke the union into striking. When it finally did, he brought in strike-breakers, or "scabs," to replace union workers, and three hundred private guards from the Pinkerton Detective Agency to protect them. With their reputation for brutality, when the "Pinkertons" broke a strike, they usually left behind a trail of dead union men. This time, however, they found their would-

be victims armed and ready for a fight. After the smoke cleared on the morning of July 6, 1892, nine strikers and seven Pinkertons had died in a furious gun battle. A few days later, the Russian-born anarchist Alexander Berkman shot Frick, but not fatally. Now protected by the Pennsylvania national guard, strike-breakers operated the Homestead works, destroying the union. There would be no effective steelworkers' union for another forty years.

By 1894, groups of unemployed threatened to march on Washington to demand government help. The largest group, numbering about five hundred, was Coxey's Army. Its leader, Jacob Coxey, an Ohio businessman, had a plan to end the depression through a massive federal road-building program. Today, the federal government routinely stimulates the economy with building projects, tax cuts, and other measures to put money into people's pockets. Back then, however, Coxey's proposal seemed too extreme. When the army reached the U.S. Capitol on May 1, the police sent it packing and arrested its "general" for walking on the grass.[23]

An artist's conception of the Homestead Steel Strike depicts strikers and their families confronting strike-breakers. The drawing appeared in Frank Leslie's Weekly, *a popular illustrated magazine of the time.*

No sooner had Coxey's Army scattered than the Pullman Strike began. The Pullman Palace Car Company manufactured railroad sleeping cars in its Chicago plant. Like other companies, during the depression it cut costs by cutting wages and firing workers. On May 11, the remaining workers struck against further wage cuts and for guarantees of job security. The company had the upper hand, and its directors expected an easy victory. Instead, the American Railway Union (ARU) voted to help the Pullman workers. This was serious, for the ARU represented every skill needed to operate a railroad: engineers, firemen, brakemen, switchmen, mechanics, conductors. Instantly, a Chicago labor dispute became a national crisis.

Eugene V. Debs, thirty-nine, led the ARU. "Gene," as folks called him, inspired deep emotions. Very tall and very lean, bald as an egg, with sparking blue eyes, he drank more whiskey than a man should. Yet nature had been generous to him. Smart and sensitive, he had a magical gift for speaking. When Gene Debs denounced injustice, his words raised goose bumps, for they had the ring of

During the 1894 Pullman Strike, President Cleveland backed the railroad owners, ordering troops to escort the trains and protect "scabs," men hired to replace strikers. Many workers saw soldiers as "mercenaries," thugs hired to oppress workers. This drawing appeared in Harper's Weekly *on July 21, 1894.*

divine anger. Like Theodore Roosevelt, Debs also had a magnetic personality. People loved him, because they sensed that he loved them. "I have a heart for others and that is why I am in this work," he would say. Poet James Whitcomb Riley wrote:

> Go search the earth from end to end
> And where's a better all-round friend
> Than Gene Debs—a man that stands
> And jest holds out his hands
> As warm a heart as ever beat
> Betwixt here and the Mercy Seat.[24]

When Pullman refused to negotiate, Debs raised the stakes. At his urging, ARU members refused to handle trains hauling Pullman cars, a challenge to the railroads themselves. The Pullman Company directors accepted the challenge and raised the stakes, hiring scabs and coupling mail cars to trains with Pullman cars. That move drew the federal government into the dispute. Rain or shine, peace or war, the mail must go through! To see that it did, President Cleveland put soldiers aboard trains run by scabs. History repeated itself. As in the railroad strike of 1877, the army made things worse. Railroad traffic halted nationwide. Strikers tipped over idle trains, built barricades across tracks, and sawed through the supports of railway bridges. A striker tossed his baby, wrapped in the Stars and Stripes, into the path of an oncoming train; it stopped in time. For their part, soldiers fired at strikers from moving trains. In Chicago, they shot twelve strikers dead.

Government lawyers found a bloodless way to end the walkout. The Sherman Antitrust Act had made it illegal for companies to restrict trade across state borders. Corporation lawyers argued that the law applied to unions as well. Federal judges agreed, and issued injunctions against the strike, orders forbidding a party to do a certain thing. Not only did these "paper bullets" ban interference with the mail, they threatened those who tried to persuade others to stay on strike with fines and imprisonment. In other words, injunctions curbed freedom of speech, a basic right under the U.S. Constitution. For speaking freely, a judge might send a citizen to jail without a trial. Gene Debs went to jail. The strike collapsed. Pullman won total victory.

Freed from the burden of running a union, jail gave Debs time to think things through. The federal government, Congress, and the courts all sided with business against labor. Unions seemed powerless to change things, while anarchist violence only bred more violent crackdowns. Debs decided the way out lay in another idea brought by European immigrants. Democratic socialism offered the hope of changing society by a peaceful revolution. Through free elections, socialists might win control of the government, abolishing child labor and making other reforms. They would also take over America's chief industries, running them not for private profit, but for the benefit of society—thus the term *socialism*. Debs entered jail as a union chief and left as a socialist leader. Soon after his release, Debs helped organize the American Socialist Party, and would run as its presidential candidate four times.

Eugene Debs makes a point. Debs, a forceful and eloquent speaker, formed the American Railway Union (ARU) in 1893 to demand higher wages and better working conditions for railroad employees.

Whether the nation enjoyed prosperity or suffered in a depression, African-Americans were always the last hired and the first fired. The Civil War had ended slavery, but failed to answer a key question: How can blacks and whites live together fairly and peacefully? We have still not answered that question entirely.

Republicans led the effort to safeguard the former slaves' freedom. They sponsored the Fourteenth Amendment to the Constitution (1868), which made onetime slaves, called freedmen, American citizens. The Fifteenth Amendment (1870) declared that no state could prevent a citizen from voting for reasons of race or color. Finally, the Civil Rights Act of 1875 declared every citizen entitled to "full and equal" use of public facilities such as trains, hotels, restaurants, and theaters. Protected by the Constitution, and by federal occupation troops, freedmen made great strides in the South. Black newspapers and political clubs flourished. Black voters elected blacks to offices in local and state governments, and to Congress. But it did not last. The North, busy with its own industrial development, lost interest in the freedmen. In 1877, the year of the great railroad strike, the last federal troops left the South.

While accepting military defeat, most Southerners rejected any notion of black equality. Apparently, they had two reasons for this attitude. The first was money. As before the Civil War, the South remained a farming region, specializing in cotton growing. To keep profits high, planters needed low-wage labor. However, the source of that labor, former slaves, wanted decent wages. The second reason, equally powerful, was social. In the Old South, white skin had always been a badge of honor and privilege; even the poorest white might look down on the slave, who had no rights at all. Although the Constitution now declared blacks equal, racist whites meant to force African-Americans back into their "proper," lowly, place. The departure of the federal troops left blacks in the South to the mercy of foes who would show no mercy.

In a democracy, voting is the chief means of protecting one's rights. A voter elects lawmakers that are pledged to defend the voter's rights. No wonder African-Americans held the right to vote as sacred, precious as their freedom itself. Indeed, they knew they could not have the one without the other. "The ballot," explained William Sinclair, a black doctor and author, "is the citadel of the colored man's safety; the guarantor of his liberty; the protector of his rights. With the ballot the negro is a man; an American among Americans. Without the ballot he is a serf, less than a slave; a thing."[25]

Even though blacks had the constitutional right to vote, Southern state legislators used various methods to deny them the vote. Laws requiring payment of a "poll tax" of two dollars before voting discouraged poor blacks; it was a large sum to a struggling laborer. Some states required would-be voters to pass a *literacy test.* The test consisted of reading and then explaining a paragraph to an election official, who could disqualify even educated blacks. For white illiterates, however, states applied the *grandfather clause.* This allowed a person to vote merely if his father or grandfather had voted in 1867, the year before the Fifteenth Amendment took effect. Thus, in one Southern state after another, the numbers of black voters fell to practically zero. When blacks turned to the U.S. Supreme Court for help, they got a brush-off instead. In 1883, it effectively repealed the Fifteenth Amendment, ruling that the states alone set voting qualifications.

Unable to defend themselves with the vote, blacks fell victim to segregation, or forced racial separation. Segregation was something new in the South. Before the Civil War, slavery made it all but impossible to keep the races apart; they mingled constantly in cotton fields, in slaveholders' homes, and in town workshops. Now that blacks were free, Southerners used segregation to keep them "in their place"—quiet, obedient, submissive.

Southern legislatures passed hundreds of so-called Jim Crow laws, another name for segregation. From cradle to grave, Jim Crow governed African-Americans in their daily lives. Black doctors or midwives delivered black babies only. Black patients lay in black hospital wards, tended by black nurses. Black children went to black schools staffed by black teachers. In court, blacks took the oath on black-only Bibles. If found guilty (by white juries), blacks went to all-black prisons. Public facilities had "Whites Only" and "Colored" signs. Railroad cars and streetcars had black-only sections in the rear, but black riders had to give their seats to whites if asked. A black barber could not touch a white person's hair, and vice versa. Jobs had colors, too. "Black" jobs, like digging ditches and hauling garbage, were heavy and dirty. In death, blacks went to their rest in all-black cemeteries.[26]

In 1896, the Supreme Court gave its blessing to Jim Crow. In that year, it handed down its infamous ruling in *Plessy v. Ferguson,* a challenge to a Louisiana law requiring segregation on railroads. By a vote of eight to one, the justices said that segregation was legal, provided both races got equal treatment, making "separate but equal" the law of the land. Justice John Marshall Harlan, the only Southerner on the High Court and a former slaveholder, disagreed with the majority's decision. Harlan explained:

Our Constitution is color-blind, and neither knows nor tolerates classes among citizens. . . . We boast of the freedom enjoyed by our people above all other peoples. But it is difficult to reconcile that boast with a state of the law which, practically, puts the brand of servitude and degradation upon a large class of our fellow citizens, our equals before the law. The thin guise of "equal" accommodations for passengers in railway coaches will not mislead any one, nor atone for the wrong this day done.

The Supreme Court would not overturn *Plessy v. Ferguson* until the *Brown v. Board of Education* case in 1954.[27]

Racism was the chief justification for segregation. Called "man's most dangerous myth," racism is the belief that certain peoples are naturally, and forever, inferior to others. In the nineteenth century, even educated whites condemned African-Americans in crude, offensive terms. "Niggers," said J. P. Morgan, "are lazy, ignorant, and unprogressive." Many, Harvard professors among them, thought blacks had smaller brains than whites, and thus lacked a white person's ability to learn. Some medical doctors argued that education would harm blacks. By packing in more knowledge than they could hold, education would supposedly enlarge the front part of their brains, making it impossible for them to walk without tipping over! Racists accused black men of "animality," having a superstrong sexual drive that made them "lust" after white women.[28]

Segregation, however, rested less on court decisions or scientific theory than on terrorism; that is, the use, or threatened use, of violence to inspire fear. For generations, lynching was the chief form of racist terrorism in America. *Lynch* comes from the name of Charles Lynch, a Virginia judge during the Revolutionary War. His Honor was famous for having British loyalists whipped, fined, and imprisoned without trial. Afterward, *Lynch-law* came to mean murder by a mob in the name of justice. We call this an oxymoron, or a combination of contradictory words. *Lynch-law* is as much an oxymoron as *deafening silence.*

The numbers tell a chilling story. Between 1885 and 1900, lynch mobs murdered 2,404 Americans; that is, roughly one every two days. The mobs were always white, and their victims nearly always black men; mobs also lynched several black women. Usually, after the police made an arrest, the mob snatched its victim from jail; sometimes it grabbed him in his own home, off the street, or coming out of church. Local newspapers might announce a lynching days in advance, proof that the murderers planned their actions carefully. Attracted by the forthcoming carnival of death, crowds gathered around the "lynching tree," a local landmark. Spectators came from hundreds of miles away by special low-fare trains. None of this could have happened without police cooperation, or at the very least without lawmen looking the other way.[29]

As the crowd cheered and vendors sold refreshments, men lifted the bound victim to a noose dangling from a tree, tied it around his neck, and let him drop. Most victims did not die immediately, but after several minutes of suffocating in agony. Yet, by lynching standards, hanging victims got off "easily." Others found death a release from prolonged torture. Take Sam Hose, accused of shooting his employer. On April 24, 1899, the *New York Tribune* reported from Georgia:

> In the presence of nearly 2,000 people, who sent aloft yells of defiance and shouts of joy, Sam Hose . . . was burned at the stake in the public road. . . . Before the torch was applied to the pyre, the Negro was deprived of his ears, fingers and other portions of his body. . . . Before the body was cool, it was cut to pieces, the bones were crushed into small bits and . . . disposed of as souvenirs. The Negro's heart was cut in several pieces, as was also his liver. Those unable to obtain the ghastly relics directly, paid more fortunate possessors extravagant sums for them. Small pieces of bone went for 25 cents and a bit of the liver, crisply cooked, for 10 cents.

Amateur photographers took pictures of the grisly scene and crazed mob, which they made into postcards. Sold locally, these horrific pictures then circulated nationwide, so that nobody could say they did not know about lynching. Often the pictures showed lynchers themselves, grinning and pointing to their victims, big smiles on their faces.[30]

Mobs lynched blacks for any reason they chose. Most often, mob leaders claimed, they gave "justice" to black men who had raped white women. We cannot know if lynch victims really were rapists, for they never had their day in court. Other reasons for lynching would fill pages of small type. These included trying to register to vote, arguing with a white man, threatening to sue a white man, testifying in court against a white, "frightening" a white woman by not getting out of her way fast enough on the sidewalk, "glaring" at a white, and showing "disrespect" for whites. Racist politicians known as "fire-eaters" built careers by defending lynching. For example, "Pitchfork" Ben Tillman, a senator from South Carolina, boasted about terrorizing blacks. "We stuffed ballot boxes. We shot them. We are not ashamed of it," he said. "To hell with the Constitution," if it stood in the way of lynching.[31]

Ida B. Wells crusaded against lynching. Born into slavery, after the Civil War she attended a school for freedmen, becoming a teacher. Also interested in journalism, in 1891 she moved to Memphis, Tennessee, where she helped found the newspaper *Free Speech*. When a mob lynched a friend of hers for daring to run a successful grocery store, this heroic woman attacked lynching in an editorial. Within days, a mob destroyed the newspaper office and threatened to lynch her. Fleeing to New York, she spoke out against lynching in a pamphlet, "A Red Record" (1895), and in a book, *Lynching and the Excuse for It* (1901). Wells approached lynching as a social scientist would. She began by gathering evidence: newspaper accounts, printed records, reports by white private detectives she hired to interview Southern blacks. Then she analyzed the evidence and drew her conclusions.

Ida B. Wells's 1892 book, Southern Horrors: Lynch Law in All Its Phases, proved that lynching had nothing to do with justice but was a racist device for controlling black people by terrorizing them.

Wells questioned the rape charge, arguing that white men raped vastly more black women than the other way around.[32] Whatever the excuse, Wells decided that lynching was Jim Crow's supreme weapon. Segregation aimed at keeping black people down, as near to slaves as possible, doing the dirty work without complaint. Leading Southern politicians like James K. Vardaman admitted as much. The Mississippi senator declared that the black had only one role to play in American life: "That of a menial. That is what God designed him for and the white people will see to it that God's design is carried out." Lynching—terrorism pure and simple—would keep black Americans in line.[33]

Often it had just that effect. For generations, fear of lynching hung like a thundercloud over African-Americans. Lynching was a reality of black life, an ever-present danger. Although not every black person would have lost a loved one this way, all knew about those who had. There was no telling when an innocent glance or remark might summon a lynch mob. Novelist Richard Wright (born in 1908) recalled his childhood in Mississippi this way: "I had never in my life been abused by whites, but I had already become as conditioned to their existence as though I had been the victim of a thousand lynchings."[34]

Such was Theodore Roosevelt's world. In 1897, as he took up his duties as assistant secretary of the navy, America was changing rapidly. No one knew where those changes might lead. At home, mansions and tenements, privilege and oppression, promise and despair, existed side by side as never before. Abroad, America stood on the verge of world power. Although Roosevelt did not know it, he would soon be in charge of shaping the nation's course.

4 FOLLOWING THE DRUM: FROM BATTLEFIELD TO WHITE HOUSE

Cowboys or doughboys,
We'll follow his drum, boys,
Who never said, "Go, boys!"
But always said, "Come, boys!"

—ARTHUR GUITERMAN, 1898

Newsmen Jacob Riis and Lincoln Steffens burst into the commissioner's office at police headquarters. A rumor had been floating around, saying that their friend might make a bid for the presidency. Would he? They wanted to get the story straight from the horse's mouth. What they got instead was a towering temper tantrum.

Roosevelt sprang out of his chair as if the seat were red-hot. With teeth bared and fists clenched, Theodore on the warpath was terrible to behold. "Don't you dare ask me that," he shouted at Riis, his eyes bulging with rage. "Don't put such ideas in my head." The frightened newsman cowered, expecting God knows what to strike him.

Suddenly Roosevelt must have remembered that Riis was a loyal friend. Struggling to regain his composure, he put his arm over Riis's shoulder. Slowly, choosing his words carefully, he explained how it was. "I must be wanting to be president. Every young man does. But I won't let myself think of it; I must not, because if I do, I will begin to work for it, I'll be careful, calculating, cautious in word and act, and so—I'll beat myself. See?"[1]

Roosevelt had campaigned for presidents, had seen them up close. Always a fierce competitor, he must have compared himself to them; it would have been only natural. In his mind, he probably saw himself as at least their equal in intelligence and ability. So why shouldn't he be a president? Not only would it confirm his manhood in his own eyes, it would put him in a position to tackle the great problems of the day—to tackle them with the same determination that he knew his father, with his "troublesome conscience," would have wished him to.

Yet wanting the presidency is very different from having a plan to attain it. Already Roosevelt was gaining a national reputation and, he hoped, time would open great opportunities for him. Until then, he must be himself, doing what came naturally rather than calculating every move in detail. Although he could not have known it that day in Mulberry Street, his road to the presidency lay across a battlefield. It would be a Cuban battlefield, as Americans sought to fulfill what many thought was their national destiny.

That destiny was bound up with imperialism. Nearly as old as recorded history, imperialism refers to a country's gaining control of another people by taking their territory and setting up colonies. The first major European societies, ancient Greece and Rome, were empires that colonized large stretches of Europe, the Mediterranean, and the Middle East. Centuries later, Spain followed up the discoveries of Christopher Columbus by conquering an empire in the Caribbean, South and Central America, and the Philippine Islands. Before long, other nations joined the assault on the New World. Portugal seized Brazil. France took Canada. Great Britain founded colonies in what later became the United States. During the Industrial Revolution, imperialism spread worldwide. Needing raw materials like oil and rubber, and markets for their manufactured goods, Europeans carved out colonies in Asia and Africa.

As America industrialized, foreign trade grew in importance to its economy. To prosper, it, like Europe, needed access to raw materials from abroad and from overseas markets. This, in turn, required a merchant marine protected by a powerful fleet of warships—battleships, cruisers, destroyers. America had once been a naval power. During the Civil War, the Union built 626 warships to choke off enemy trade, an effort that proved largely successful. In the economic boom that followed the Civil War, Americans abandoned their navy, because doing so made sense at the time. Navies are expensive to build and maintain. Since the nation had no foreign enemies, it broke up nearly all of its warships for scrap or allowed them to rot at anchor. President Chester A. Arthur made a case for allowing this to happen in his 1883 message to Congress. "It is no part of our policy," he said, "to create and maintain a navy able to cope with that of the other great powers of the world."[2]

The U.S. Navy's rebirth began on the pages of books. As President Arthur spoke, public opinion was already shifting, thanks in part to Theodore Roosevelt. While still at Harvard, we recall, he had begun writing about warfare at sea. Published in 1882, his *Naval History of the War of 1812* seems more like an adventure novel than a work of serious history. Packed with colorful characters and pounding action, Theodore's book was loved by the reading public. The Naval War College at Newport, Rhode Island, embraced it as a textbook for training officers. For in writing this study, Roosevelt had folded the action stories around a central message: America must have a first-class navy to defend its growing overseas trade.

One of Roosevelt's fans was Captain (later Admiral) Alfred Thayer Mahan, a professor at the Naval War College. A seaman who easily became seasick, Mahan wrote scores of articles and several important books on naval history and strategy. Although he had done extensive research, like all writers Mahan borrowed facts and ideas from others. In his most famous work, *The Influence of Seapower upon History,* he expanded Roosevelt's case for a modern navy.

The captain claimed that no people had ever remained great or prosperous without command of the sea. America was no exception to that rule. With its dynamic economy, a time must come when its factories would produce far more than consumers could use at home. When that time came, America would have to sell the surplus overseas, against foreign competition. Foreigners, however, would try desperately to keep Americans out of their imperial markets, by force if necessary.

To survive in a world of cutthroat competition, Mahan insisted that the nation needed three things. The first was a battle fleet to protect its merchant ships and coastal cities, prime targets in a war. Enemy warships would try to blockade harbors and bombard them with their guns. Second, the nation needed overseas bases for repairing and refueling its warships. Finally, with two coastlines to defend, the nation must build a canal across Central America to shorten the distance between its Atlantic and Pacific seaports.

Congress, persuaded by Mahan's arguments, voted to spend money expanding the navy. Between 1890 and 1897, six battleships joined the fleet: the U.S.S. *Maine, Texas, Oregon, Indiana, Massachusetts,* and *Iowa.* Armed with big guns, these man-made sea monsters were the fleet's heavy hitters. Known as "capital ships," because of their great cost (over $3 million each) and power, they were marvels of modern engineering. Built entirely of steel—Carnegie steel—and powered by steam engines, they carried their heaviest guns in rotating turrets. Smaller vessels, like cruisers and destroyers, had lighter guns and torpedoes. All would soon see action, urged on by the assistant secretary of the navy.

Those who knew Roosevelt thought his ideas on war were "odd." To a friend, Judge William Howard Taft, he had "the spirit of the old berserkers," Viking warriors who worked themselves into a frenzy while fighting. When the behavior of a foreign government annoyed him, Roosevelt would bluster, "The country needs a war." In a minor quarrel with England, he urged war. Stunned by the remark, Senator Mark Hanna, of Ohio, snorted, "You're crazy, Roosevelt!" Give him the chance, Hanna added, and "we'd be fighting half the world."[3]

His ideas about war probably came from two sources. As we know, the Civil War deeply affected the frail child. Little Teedie idolized soldiers, heroes in a just cause, while resenting his father for not serving at the front. Nothing, the child vowed, would ever make *him* shirk a patriotic duty. Scientific study later convinced Theodore that nations, like individuals, competed and struggled for their existence. Thus, war was the ultimate test of a people's strength, character, and resolve. From his point of view, war brought out the best in people: loyalty, patriotism, courage, self-sacrifice.

No other American leader ever praised war more forcefully, and more publicly, than Theodore Roosevelt. The man loved war, wished for war, and yearned to prove his manhood in a war. In a June 1897 speech at the Naval War College, he said:

> All the great masterful races have been fighting races; and the minute that a race loses the hard fighting virtues, then . . . it has lost its proud right to stand as the equal of the best. . . . Better a thousand times to err on the side of over-readiness to fight, than to err on the side of tame submission to injury, or cold-blooded indifference to the misery of the oppressed. . . . No triumph of peace is quite so great as the supreme triumphs of war. . . . It may be that at some time in the dim future of the race the need for war will vanish; but that time is yet ages distant. As yet no nation can hold its place in the world, or can do any work really worth doing, unless it stands ready to guard its rights with an armed hand.

The audience knew what he meant by "the misery of the oppressed." As he spoke, the nation's newspapers were full of hair-raising accounts of Spanish oppression in Cuba. There, Roosevelt hoped, America would fight its next war.[4]

Located in the Caribbean Sea, the island of Cuba is ninety miles south of Florida; it is where Spain's overseas empire began four centuries earlier. Visited by Columbus during his first voyage in 1492, Cuba soon became a prize Spanish colony. There, as elsewhere in the New World, Spain was a harsh master. Seizing the land, settlers enslaved the native Tainos, who lived by farming and fishing. After most Tainos died of overwork and European diseases like smallpox, Spain replaced the Native Americans with enslaved Africans.

In the year of Roosevelt's birth, Cuba was the world's chief producer of cane sugar and a leading tobacco grower. Although Spain had abolished slavery by then, Cubans of all backgrounds resented living under a foreign government over which they had no control. When they protested, Spanish police arrested them, Spanish judges jailed them, and Spanish troops executed them by firing squad.

Resentment erupted into revolution. During the Ten Years' War (1868–78), Cuban rebels and Spanish rulers fought a bloody duel in which each side was too weak to win and too strong to lose. Finally, Spain ended the stalemate by a combination of force and reform. After slaughtering thousands, it promised reform if the rebels laid down their arms. Having restored order, however, Spain broke its promises and cracked down harder than ever.

In 1895, another revolution broke out. Crying *"Cuba Libre!"*—Free Cuba!— rebels swore to fight until their homeland gained its independence. Yet, outnumbered as they were by Spanish troops, the Cubans had no chance of winning in open battle. Instead, they began a guerrilla war. *Guerrilla* is Spanish for "little war"; that is, war made by small bands of fighters able to hide easily, move swiftly, and strike suddenly. Cuban guerrillas darted from the shadows, killed, then vanished into their island's mountains and jungles—until next time. Traveling lightly, they lived off gifts of food from friendly villagers and whatever they could take from the enemy. It was essential for them to stay on good terms with the *campesinos,* or peasant farmers, who also provided valuable information and hid wounded fighters until they could travel again. Most guerrillas were *campesinos* themselves.

In February 1896, General Valeriano Weyler took over as Spain's military governor in Cuba. A veteran of campaigns against the desert tribes of North Africa, Weyler believed that, in war, cruelty is kindness. Humane measures merely prolong the agony, he said. But harshness ends a war quickly, thus limiting the suffering.

Since guerrillas depended upon the *campesinos,* Weyler hit them first. Columns of Spanish troops forced peasants from their homes and drove them at gunpoint to encampments ringed by barbed wire. The general called these "reconcentration" camps; we know them as concentration camps. Hastily built, lacking proper shelter, sanitation, or medical care, they made the slums Roosevelt visited on Manhattan's East Side seem almost comfortable. Inmates fell ill and died in droves. Lack of food turned them into walking skeletons, forced to scrounge in the garbage outside Spanish-army field kitchens. To keep them inside, Weyler left no place to go if they escaped. His patrols turned the lush countryside into a desert, burning crops, poisoning wells, and destroying buildings. William J. Calhoun, an American special envoy to Cuba, described the scene during a tour in the spring of 1897:

> The island is one of the most unhappy and distressed places on the earth. I travelled by rail from Havana to Matanzas. The country outside of the military posts was practically depopulated. Every house had been burned, banana trees cut down, cane fields swept with fire, and everything in the shape of food destroyed. It was as fair a landscape as mortal eye ever looked upon; but I did not see a house, man, woman or child, horse, mule, or cow, nor even a dog. I did not see a sign of life, except an occasional vulture or buzzard sailing through the air. The country was wrapped in the stillness of death and the silence of desolation.

Historians estimate that Weyler's reconcentration scheme killed 400,000 men, women, and children; that is, one quarter of the Cuban population.[5]

Americans looked toward Cuba with growing anxiety and anger. The island had interested them for generations. Before the Civil War, Southerners saw it as ideal for growing cotton. Had President James Monroe allowed him, General Andrew Jackson would have taken it in the early 1820s. Seventy years later, American businessmen had invested millions in Cuban sugar plantations and other ventures. Countless other Americans, immigrants and the children of immigrants, automatically sympathized with its suffering people. To refugees from places like Russia, *freedom* and *independence* were not mere words, but precious things that any decent person would fight for.

American newspaper owners saw Cuba's suffering with dollar signs flashing before their eyes. The story of the Cuban people was dramatic and exciting—it would sell lots of newspapers. At one time, newspapers had aimed at the educated minority. Expensive and unattractive, they had small type and line drawings for illustrations, and cost up to twenty-five cents. By the 1880s, however, inventions like high-speed presses and photoengraving made it possible to produce enormous numbers of newspapers with pictures made instantly, as events unfolded.

Now priced as low as a penny, newspapers had to attract ever more readers to stay profitable. The *New York World* and the *New York Journal* solved the problem by creating the mass-circulation daily. Appealing to their readers' emotions, they printed grisly accounts of murders, sex crimes, and disasters written in simple words and short sentences. Articles like "Why Young Girls Kill Themselves" and "Strange Things Women Do for Love" were aimed at women readers. For children, they had color comic strips, a first anywhere. One, the *World's* "Yellow Kid," featured the pranks of a tiny terror of a boy in a bright yellow nightshirt. Other newspapers followed with similar comic strips. The flashy news featured in these newspapers became known as "yellow press" or "yellow journalism."

The atrocities of "Butcher Weyler" were natural circulation boosters. As terrible as General Weyler's actions were, the yellow press exaggerated them even further. This, in turn, inflamed public opinion, triggering demands for a "crusade" to liberate the island. But President McKinley had already suffered a bellyful of crusades. "The Major," as friends called him, had fought in the Union Army's bloodiest Civil War battles. "I have been through one war," he would say. "I have seen the dead piled up, and I do not want to see another." Still, as president, he could not ignore Cuba. So, in September 1897, he told the Spanish government that America could not tolerate Weyler's atrocities. Unless matters improved soon, public opinion would force him to take drastic action.[6]

Fearing bloodshed, McKinley sent the seven-thousand-ton battleship *Maine* to Havana Harbor. Although it was officially on a goodwill visit, the Spanish authorities understood its unspoken message. If they did not protect the lives and property of Americans living in Cuba, the *Maine's* guns would. The press, hot for war, cheered the president's action. Those cheers, however, soon turned to howls

The battleship U.S.S. Maine *explodes in the harbor of Havana, Cuba, on the night of February 15, 1898. The American artist who drew this picture had not actually seen the explosion but imagined what it must have looked like.*

of rage. For on the night of February 15, 1898, a month to the day after its arrival, an explosion sank the mighty warship. Of its 354-man crew, 266 died in the explosion, drowned, or later died of their wounds.

A committee of naval experts investigated the disaster. After studying the wreck, in March it reported that an underwater mine had caused the explosion, but could not say who had set it. In 1976, Admiral Hyman G. Rickover, "the father of the nuclear navy," issued another report, *How the Battleship "Maine" Was Destroyed.* In it, Admiral Rickover claimed that the explosion was an accident. Apparently, a fire in a coal storage room located next to an ammunition room heated the steel wall between them, igniting the fatal blast. Yet neither report solves the mystery beyond doubt. We simply do not know who or what destroyed the *Maine.* Nobody has ever proven beyond doubt that a mine, or a coal fire, caused the tragedy.

Even before the March report came out, the yellow press detonated its word mines. The *Journal* printed a slogan that swept the nation:

Remember the Maine!

To hell with Spain!

THE WARSHIP MAINE WAS SPLIT IN TWO BY AN ENEMY'S INFERNAL MACHINE the paper announced in bold headlines. The *World* declared DESTRUCTION OF THE MAINE BY FOUL PLAY. Newspapers explained how Spaniards did the dirty deed, with drawings by artists who had never been aboard a battleship. But the American public had little interest in such details. All it knew was that a proud warship had gone down with heavy loss of life. The nation wanted revenge.[7]

Meanwhile, an impatient Roosevelt waited for war. His boss, navy secretary John D. Long, sixty, a former governor of Massachusetts, despised war. A fussy little man with "delicate health" and a short attention span, Mr. Long was also bored by the details of running the navy. Since these were so technical, Long left them to his energetic assistant. Roosevelt liked discussing warship design, big guns, and armor plate with experts. During fleet exercises, he, not Long, stood on the deck of a battleship, hat in hand, saluting the vessels as they steamed by.

On February 25, Long left the office early to visit his dentist. Roosevelt, in charge of the navy for the rest of the day, lost no time in reeling off a string of commands. Buy extra ammunition! Increase coal stocks! Rent extra cargo ships! Station warships closer to Cuba! Finally, he cabled Commodore George Dewey, chief of the Asiatic Squadron. Dewey must gather his ships at Hong Kong, a British possession on the China coast:

KEEP FULL OF COAL. IN THE EVENT OF DECLARATION OF WAR SPAIN, YOUR DUTY WILL BE TO SEE THAT THE SPANISH SQUADRON DOES NOT LEAVE THE ASIATIC COAST AND THEN OFFENSIVE OPERATIONS IN PHILIPPINE ISLANDS.[8]

A busy afternoon! Although his country was still at peace, Roosevelt had issued the first orders of the Spanish-American War on his own authority. The next day, Long returned to the office. Shocked, he declared that his assistant "has come very near causing more of an explosion than happened to the *Maine*. . . . The very devil seemed to possess him yesterday afternoon." Devil or no devil, Long let Roosevelt's orders stand, because they made sense. A nation's military cannot go to war at the drop of a hat. Even if there is little chance of conflict, military planners must prepare for action—just in case.[9]

McKinley still refused to rush into war. Perhaps he should offer to buy Cuba, say for $300 million, a bargain compared to the cost of a war? Spain refused to sell. Nevertheless, he hoped for a diplomatic solution. Public opinion, however, wanted nothing of the kind. Whipped into a fury by the press, citizens turned on the president. Mobs burned him in effigy. Visitors to the Senate and House galleries sat wrapped in the Stars and Stripes, silently demanding war. Congressmen called the president "Wobbly Willie."

Roosevelt could hardly contain his rage. Always master of the stinging one-liner, he called McKinley "that white-faced cur," a man with "no more backbone than a chocolate éclair." Nor would he let Edith's operation to remove a dangerous growth on her hip cool his zeal for war. Years later, as president, he told an aide: "You know what my wife and children mean to me; and yet I made up my mind that I would not allow even a death to stand in my way. . . . I know now that I would have turned from my wife's deathbed to have answered the call."[10]

Finally convinced there was no other way to end the Cuban horror, on April 11, McKinley asked Congress for authority to use force to avenge the *Maine* and end Spanish oppression. Two weeks later, Congress formally declared war on Spain. Crowds celebrated the war as if it were a national holiday.

On the day Congress declared war, the United States Army numbered exactly 28,183 officers and men. Nicknamed "doughboys," from "adobe," the white clay dust that covered marching troops in desert country, for the past thirty years most soldiers had served on outposts scattered across the West. There they had defeated Native American tribes such as the

Lieutenant Colonel Theodore Roosevelt in his cavalryman's uniform. Unlike most officers, the wealthy New Yorker had his uniform custom made by Brooks Brothers, the exclusive New York men's tailors.

Sioux, Cheyenne, Comanche, and Apache, herding them onto reservations. The army's last campaign ended in 1890 with the slaughter of a Sioux band at Wounded Knee, South Dakota.

Since a larger force was needed to fight Spain, the president called for 125,000 volunteers, including three cavalry regiments of a thousand men each. Roosevelt was so eager to fight that friends feared he was "going mad." Edith knew better. Although still weak and in pain from her operation, she supported his decision, knowing he had to go for his own self-respect.[11]

Roosevelt resigned his post as Assistant Secretary of the Navy and enlisted in the First U.S. Volunteer Cavalry. A few days earlier, he had ordered an officer's uniform from Brooks Brothers, an exclusive New York men's tailor. No army-issue duds for him! Knowing his reputation as an organizer, the War Department asked Roosevelt to become the regiment's colonel. He refused, claiming lack of battlefield experience. However, he accepted the rank of lieutenant colonel when it offered to name a friend, Dr. Leonard Wood, colonel. Two years younger than Roosevelt, Wood was a talented surgeon. A brilliant officer, too, Wood was awarded by Congress the Medal of Honor for fighting Geronimo, the famous Apache chief.

Before leaving for the regiment's training camp at San Antonio, Texas, Roosevelt practiced shooting on the lawn of Sagamore Hill. There he would lie on his belly, squinting along the barrel of a rifle. Should the children dare speak, he silenced them. "Bunnies mustn't talk," he would say, because Father must be ready to kill enough Spaniards to win the war. When the big day came, and he left for the Oyster Bay railroad station, the children grew fearful. Ted and Kermit cried and buried their heads in their mother's lap. The girls, Alice and Ethel, trembled at the thought that Father might not return. Afterward, when little Archie played with his toy train, he did not say "choo-choo," but "Father come home."[12]

Dr. Leonard Wood was the first commander of the Rough Riders. Theodore Roosevelt, who later led the regiment, served as his second in command. A surgeon as well as a professional soldier, Wood later rose to the rank of general.

Roosevelt and Wood made a fine team. While Wood used his contacts in Washington to have supplies rushed to San Antonio ahead of other outfits, Roosevelt handled recruiting. He wanted the regiment to represent the "best" America had to offer. In Roosevelt's mind, these were old-line Knickerbockers, like the lieutenant colonel himself, graduates of Harvard and other Ivy League colleges, members of exclusive clubs, tennis and polo champions.

However, men of the sort Roosevelt had known in the Dakota Bad Lands formed the regiment's backbone. Tough, resourceful Westerners, they were at home in the saddle and could fire a gun at full gallop. A colorful lot, they had nicknames like "Pork Chop," "Metropolitan Bill," "Rattlesnake Pete," and "Prayerful James." Eight sheriffs, a Pawnee warrior, and an unreported number of outlaws served in the regiment. William "Bucky" O'Neill, sheriff of Prescott, Arizona, had killed several men "in the line of duty." Charlie Younger's father, Bob, had ridden with the Jesse James gang. Since they were used to "riding rough"—over rough country—they called themselves the Rough Riders.[13]

From the moment he reached camp, Roosevelt showed natural leadership ability. He began by learning the Rough Riders' names; within a week, he could match every name to a face. While Colonel Wood saw that things ran smoothly, Roosevelt put the troopers through their paces. That was not easy, since he had to learn by trial and error. It was mostly error at first. Mounted on his favorite horse, Little Texas, he would try to form an attack line. When he finally succeeded, the happy men blazed away with their six-shooters, making onlookers dive for cover. The Rough Riders came to love Roosevelt, regarding him as their real leader. Wood realized this, but did not take offense. If the war lasted more than a few months, he expected a promotion, leaving Roosevelt to command the outfit.

Meanwhile, the navy took all the glory. On May 1, Commodore Dewey carried out Roosevelt's orders without a hitch. Sailing from Hong Kong, bound for the Philippines, he caught the Spanish fleet in Manila Bay. The enemy vessels were old and rusty, no match for his six modern warships. The sleek vessels fired often and well. At the end of the battle, all ten Spanish ships were smashed to fiery junk, with heavy loss of life among their crews. American losses were one dead and eight wounded.

Manila Bay cheered most of America, but put the Rough Riders in the dumps. Itching for action, they went about camp chanting:

Rough, rough, we're the stuff.
We want to fight, and can't get enough,
Whoo-pee![14]

At this rate, they feared, the war would end before they could show the enemy their stuff. But they had no need to worry. For on May 28, orders came to join the army massing at Tampa, Florida, for the invasion of Cuba.

America's warships had trapped the six vessels of Spain's Caribbean squadron in Santiago Bay, near the southeastern tip of Cuba. To win the war, the navy had to destroy Spain's ships or make them surrender. However, Spain had given the bay strong land defenses. Because of the Spanish troops, it would be suicide for the U.S. ships to go after Spain's ships inside the bay. Here is where the American army came in. Planners wanted it to land on the coast nearby the bay and take the city of Santiago de Cuba from the land side.

On June 14, the largest military force ever to leave American shores put to sea. It consisted of 16,000 fighting men, including four regiments of "Buffalo Soldiers," some 2,500 black veterans of the Indian wars. Given the limited space aboard the thirty troop transports, only officers could take their horses. All cavalrymen would have to fight on foot. No matter. When the sailing order came, Roosevelt grinned from ear to ear and did his war dance.[15]

On June 22, the troops landed without opposition at Daiquirí, a village sixteen miles east of Santiago de Cuba. Marching inland, two days later the Americans met a Spanish force at a vital pass in the hills to the north of the landing site. The First and Tenth Cavalry, both Regular Army units, attacked from the right, the Rough Riders from the left. This was Roosevelt's baptism by fire, and he relished every moment of it, literally jumping up and down with glee. Seeing a dying man, he shook his hand and said, "Well, old man, isn't this splendid!" We do not know what, if anything, the poor fellow said in return. Anyhow, Roosevelt grabbed a rifle from a wounded soldier and led a charge. The Spaniards, pressed from both sides, retreated.[16]

Roosevelt wrote home about his first battle. He spared the family no detail of the event. Although his letters told of missing his family very much, they also told of vultures plucking out the eyes of dead Spaniards, of flesh-eating land crabs feasting on bodies, of swarms of buzzing, biting, blue-bellied flies. Edith cherished his letters. "Last night," she wrote, "I slept better because I held your dear letters to my heart instead of just having them under my pillow. I felt I was touching you when I pressed against me what your hand had touched." The children were terrified. Although Kermit was eight years old, he was so worried about Father that he asked Mama to cuddle him in her arms like his baby brother, Quentin.[17]

The Spaniards retreated to their main defense line on San Juan Heights, a chain of hills overlooking Santiago de Cuba. Their key positions were trenches and barbed-wire entanglements on San Juan Hill and Kettle Hill, named for a huge iron kettle used in sugar refining at the top. The American commanders planned to storm these positions. With the army controlling the two hills, and navy warships waiting at the mouth of the bay, the city must surrender or face destruction.

The attack began on July 1, but stalled almost immediately. To reach their forward assault positions, doughboys had to follow narrow jungle trails that opened onto meadows at the foot of each hill. When they tried crossing the meadows, Spanish riflemen on the heights picked them off. Forced to take cover in patches of tall grass, the Americans waited for orders.

Colonel Wood's assignment to a new post had come through, so Roosevelt commanded the Rough Riders at Kettle Hill. Sitting atop Little Texas, he was an easy target as he rode from one group of crouching men to another. Theodore's only fear, he recalled, was losing his spectacles; to avoid this calamity, he had four extra pairs clipped to his uniform and one pair sewn inside his hat. Eventually, with bullets whining near his head, even Theodore dismounted and took cover. Captain Bucky O'Neill did not. He stood up, all six feet of him, calmly smoking a cigarette. "Captain, a bullet is sure to hit you, sir," cried a sergeant, begging him to get down. "Sergeant," O'Neill replied, laughing, "the Spanish bullet isn't made that can kill me!" Instantly, one flew into his open mouth, killing the confident captain.[18]

Finally, orders came for an all-out assault. At a signal from a bugle, doughboys broke from cover and ran toward San Juan Hill. Roosevelt had his bugler sound the charge, too. Every man but one rose and went forward. That man, paralyzed with fear, would not move. Roosevelt had no mercy. "Are you afraid to stand up when I am on horseback?" he shouted. Just then the poor fellow stiffened and pitched forward. A bullet, probably aimed at Roosevelt, had drilled through him lengthwise from the top of his head.[19]

The Rough Riders raced toward Kettle Hill on foot, joined by Buffalo Soldiers of the Ninth and Tenth Cavalry. Now began what Roosevelt would always remember as his "crowded hour," his hour of glory. The charge ignited something deep within him, something wild, primitive—beastly. "All men who feel any power of joy in battle," he would write, "know what is it like when the wolf rises in the heart."[20]

With the wolf rising in his heart, Roosevelt led his men up Kettle Hill. He was armed only with a pistol salvaged from the wreckage of the *Maine*. Reaching a barbed-wire fence, Theodore dismounted just as a Spanish officer appeared. A single shot dropped the officer "neatly as a jackrabbit." Moments later, troopers cut through the fence and rushed the Spanish trenches. Overwhelmed, the enemy fled down the other side of Kettle Hill. Then, after a brief pause, Roosevelt joined his force with the units charging up San Juan Hill. As it became clear that both hills would be taken by the Americans, every living Spaniard fled toward Santiago de Cuba. The victors, panting and sweating, sat on the ground and looked back at the way they had come, thankful to be alive.[21]

Colonel Roosevelt poses with a group of Rough Riders soon after his "crowded hour," the victorious charge up Kettle Hill.

The only Spaniards remaining on the hills lay sprawled in pools of blood. Another person might have been sickened at the scene. Not Roosevelt. Jubilant, perhaps because he had made up for his father's lack of service in the Civil War, Theodore strode around, urging his men to look at those "damned Spanish dead." A family friend, Lieutenant Bob Ferguson, wrote Edith about the battle: "No hunting trip so far has ever equaled it in Theodore's eyes. . . . T. was reveling in victory and gore." No fewer than 215 Spaniards died that day. The American forces suffered 205 killed. The dead included 88 Rough Riders, the highest loss suffered by any of the attacking units.[22]

After the Battle of San Juan Heights, the end came quickly for Spain. On July 3, American naval guns sank the entire Spanish Caribbean squadron during a desperate escape attempt from Santiago Bay. Spanish forces in the city of Santiago de Cuba surrendered two weeks later. The next day, July 18, Spain asked for peace talks. President McKinley immediately named Leonard Wood, recently promoted to general, military governor of Cuba. (As we will see later, a treaty signed in December formally ended the war with Spain.)

Meanwhile, Roosevelt came to know firsthand how horrible war really is, even in a just cause. While his own health had never been better, all around him sick and wounded American troops suffered in the tropical heat. Yellow fever ravaged the victorious army, the disease proving deadlier than Spanish bullets. When rations ran low, Roosevelt spent his own money to buy his men food in the captured city. Then there were the Cuban children, "some like Archie and Quentin," homeless and hungry. At this point, perhaps his ideas about war began to change. Although Roosevelt would always support war in a "just" cause, as president he would try to minimize the chances of an outbreak of violence through diplomacy. But he had no regrets about his war service in Cuba. Well, just one regret. As he would tell a reporter, "I have always been unhappy, most unhappy, that I was not severely wounded in Cuba . . . in some striking and disfiguring way." For Theodore, a hideous wound was a kind of medal, visible proof that he had served his country as faithfully as the Civil War heroes he idolized.[23]

On August 15, 1898, Rough Riders returned to a camp at Montauk Point, New York, a short train ride from Theodore and Edith's home at Oyster Bay. After receiving their discharge papers, on September 13 Roosevelt said farewell to his men. His face streaked with tears, he praised the veterans as a band of brothers. "Between you and the other cavalry regiments there is a tie which we trust will never be broken," said the colonel. Then, as the troopers filed by, he shook the hand of every man. When he finished, Theodore left camp, bound for a new adventure.[24]

If San Juan Heights gave Roosevelt his crowded hour, it also made him a celebrity. This was no accident. Although there were other officers who had fought as bravely as he, none had Roosevelt's savvy about the need for "good press." Since his days as police commissioner, Roosevelt had courted newspaper reporters so that they would write about him favorably. In Cuba, he arranged for reporters and photographers to live with the Rough Riders. These included two men with that newfangled device, a movie camera. After the charge up San Juan Hill, for example, reporter Edward Marshall told readers of the *New York Journal* that Roosevelt was "the most magnificent soldier I have ever seen," a marvel of "coolness and calm judgment and towering heroism."[25] Thanks to the coverage of men like Marshall, the American public saw Roosevelt's actions at San Juan Hill as the high point of the Cuban campaign. Roosevelt's own account of the campaign, *The Rough Riders,* made it seem as if he defeated the enemy single-handedly. The word *I* appears so often in the text that, supposedly, the printer had to order an extra supply of that letter.

The head of the New York Republican Party, U.S. Senator Thomas Platt, was an avid newspaper reader. Described by critics as "a little old mangy rat," he had watery eyes, a face blotched with brown spots, and a hunger for money. An ally of big business, he had his cronies defend the interests of corporations (for a price) in the state legislature. In 1898, Platt had a problem. A financial scandal made it impossible for Governor Frank S. Black to win reelection to another two-year term. To keep the governorship in Republican hands, Platt needed a candidate to replace Black. How about war-hero Roosevelt?[26]

Platt had his doubts. He remembered Roosevelt as a troublemaker in the state assembly. Before supporting Roosevelt for governor, Platt had to make sure of his party loyalty; that is, his loyalty to Platt. For his part, Roosevelt despised the corrupt senator. Yet Theodore was also a practical man—a practical politician. If he hoped to get anything done, he knew he had to go along with powerful men like Platt as far as his conscience would permit. So, in return for Platt's support, Roosevelt promised that, should he win the election, he would consult Platt about appointments to state jobs and ideas for new laws. On September 27, at Platt's urging, the Republican Party nominated the Rough Rider for governor.

Roosevelt's campaign train crisscrossed New York State, stopping for speeches in small towns and large cities. Uniformed Rough Riders rode aboard the train. Before each speech, a bugler blew a cavalry charge to announce the hero's arrival. Sometimes Rough Riders warmed up the crowd with war stories. "My friends and fellow citizens," said ex-sergeant Buck Taylor, "my colonel was a great soldier. He will make a great governor. He always put us boys in battle where we would be killed if there was a chance, and that is what he will do with you." With that friendly slip of the tongue, the crowd roared with laughter and warmed to Roosevelt.[27]

The candidate gave as many as twenty speeches a day. This was hard work, since microphones did not exist yet. In those days, it took a powerful voice to reach an audience. Roosevelt stood on the train's rear platform, practically shouting at the crowd. Nearby, stenographers, or secretaries, all men in those days, took down the speech in shorthand. Now and then, for emphasis, Roosevelt waved his arms around and slammed a fist into his other hand.

Without any program except "honest government," Roosevelt stressed his good intentions and patriotism. "The speech was nothing," an onlooker noted, "but the man's presence was everything. It was electrical, magnetic. . . ." The candidate, people said, projected "sincerity six feet high." Even so, out of more than 1.3 million votes cast, Theodore beat his Democratic opponent, Judge

A formal portrait of Governor Roosevelt's children, 1900. Left to right: Ted Jr., Ethel, Alice, Quentin, Kermit, and Archie.

Augustus Van Wyck, by just 17,794 votes. Still, as he had learned in battle, a miss is as good as a mile. On December 31, 1898, Theodore Roosevelt was sworn in as the governor of New York State.[28]

As promised, Roosevelt asked Platt's approval on job appointments. In return, the senator had Republican legislators support Theodore's reforms, such as a law to regulate working conditions in sweatshops. The governor also won an eight-hour workday for state employees and raised teachers' salaries. Inspired by his father's ideals of morality and fairness, he banned racial segregation in public schools. At Oyster Bay, he explained, "My children sit in the same school with colored children." However, Platt became furious when the governor called for higher corporation taxes and attacked fraud in the management of the Erie Canal. "I don't want him raising hell in my state any longer," the senator barked. "I want to bury him."[29]

In November 1899, Vice President Garret A. Hobart died. Since President McKinley would need another running mate in the upcoming election, Platt decided to "bury" the governor in the vice presidency. Roosevelt objected; he thought the office a dead end, since vice presidents (even today) usually do very little and have no real power. However, Platt used his influence to get delegates to the 1900 Republican convention in Philadelphia to pledge themselves to Roosevelt, whether Theodore liked it or not. No second term as governor, Platt told Roosevelt. If he refused the nomination, Republicans would never again support him for anything. Only McKinley, who thought Roosevelt reckless, stood in the way, but he soon buckled under pressure from Senator Platt and his allies.

To cheers of "We want you, Teddy! Yes we do!" the convention nominated the New Yorker. Yet Senator Mark Hanna, a wily political veteran, did not cheer.

ABOVE: *The reluctant candidate. Held by William McKinley, a pistol-shooting Roosevelt shouts "I Don't Want to be Vice President," while his enemy Mark Hanna looks on. TR felt that the vice presidency was a dead end and would destroy his political career. He was wrong.*

LEFT: *A poster for the 1900 presidential campaign shows the Republican candidates, McKinley and Roosevelt. This poster is a lithograph by George Prince. It is an early example of mass-production color printing for political purposes.*

As McKinley's closest friend and strongest political backer, Hanna was deeply troubled by Roosevelt's nomination. Senator Hanna distrusted the New Yorker, thought Roosevelt too eager for war, too excitable, to be the man a heartbeat away from the presidency. "Don't any of you realize that there's only one life between that madman and the Presidency?" he asked friends.[30]

The Democrats nominated William Jennings Bryan as their candidate in the presidential campaign and the Socialists chose Eugene Debs. Speaking only rarely, President McKinley campaigned from the front porch of his home in Canton, Ohio. Meanwhile, Roosevelt acted as McKinley's mouthpiece—literally. In eight weeks of campaigning, he covered twenty-one thousand miles in twenty-four states and gave several hundred speeches, all denouncing the opposition as enemies of prosperity and private property. In November 1900, the Republicans won in a landslide. Not only did they keep the White House, they captured both houses of Congress.

Roosevelt hated being vice president. The post "ought to be abolished," he fumed. The job demanded very little of his time or energy, and for a workhorse like Theodore, that was a problem. He was bored and frustrated. McKinley all but ignored Roosevelt, not giving the vice president a role in shaping administration policies. The only active part of his job, presiding over the Senate, lasted four days, from March 4 to March 8, 1901. After that, Congress adjourned for a long recess.[31]

Roosevelt spent the summer at Sagamore Hill, reading, writing, and sailing on Long Island Sound. In September, he took the family on vacation to the Adirondack Mountains. He was there when, on September 6, Leon Czolgosz shot the president. Upon receiving the news, Theodore rushed to Buffalo to be at McKinley's side. After a few days, since McKinley seemed to be recovering, Roosevelt returned to the Adirondacks. Eight days later, President McKinley died.

News of the president's death left Mark Hanna sad and angry. He was sad that his friend had died, but at the same time angry at McKinley for choosing that "madman" Roosevelt as his running mate. "Now look, that damned cowboy is President of the United States," he cried.[32]

5

AT **HOME** IN THE
WHITE HOUSE

I do not think any two people ever got more enjoyment out of the White House than Mother and I. We love the house itself, without and within, for its associations, for its stillness and its simplicity.

—THEODORE ROOSEVELT TO TED JR., MAY 28, 1904

Roosevelt thought it "a dreadful thing" to become president in the way he did. McKinley's assassin, he believed, had aimed his shots not just at a person, but at democracy itself. By shooting an elected president, one man—Leon Czolgosz—had shown that his wishes meant everything, while those of the American people, who had elected McKinley as their president, meant nothing. No republic, no free government, Theodore believed, could exist if the gun of an assassin replaced the people's will.[1]

Yet we cannot undo the past. No matter how it happened, Roosevelt was president, and *very* glad of it, too. Lincoln Steffens, editor of the New York *Commercial Advertiser,* visited him a few days after taking the oath of office. "He strode triumphant around among us, talking and shaking hands, dictating and signing letters, and laughing. Washington, the whole country, was in mourning, and no doubt the president felt that he should hold himself down; he didn't; he tried to, but his joy showed in every word and movement," the journalist recalled. "With his feet, his fists, his face and with free words he laughed . . . with glee at the power and place that had come to him."[2]

Ever since John Adams and his wife, Abigail, unpacked their bags in 1800, the nation's First Family has lived in the White House. When the Roosevelts moved in a century later, they found it not nearly as comfortable as their own home, Sagamore Hill. The president's eldest daughter, Alice, seventeen, described it as "both ugly and uncomfortable."[3]

She was right. Over the years, workers had installed electric lighting, a steam-heating system, bathtubs with running water, and an elevator. By 1901, however, the mansion had become seedy. Its furniture and carpets, dating to the time of Abraham Lincoln, had grown musty with age; slapping a cushion sent dust clouds into the air. Offices for the president and his staff were on the second floor, above the East Room, a grand reception area. People on the second floor walked lightly, fearing rotten beams would give way, plunging an unlucky staffer through the ceiling of the East Room. Only a glass screen separated the offices of the president's staff from the family living quarters, also on the second floor. There were five bedrooms, two bathrooms, a library, and a maid's room. Rats were everywhere, rummaging in the walls and scurrying down the hallways in broad daylight. When exterminators spread poison, rats died in the walls, their bodies stinking to high heaven. Sometimes the president led his sons on rat hunts in the dining room.[4]

At Roosevelt's request, in 1902 Congress approved $540,000 to modernize the White House. This renovation created the landmark we know today. Workmen turned the second-floor offices into bedrooms and a private study for the president. A separate new building, called the West Wing, held the president's office and the offices of his thirty-eight assistants. It also contained the cabinet room, where he met with the heads of the various government departments. A

The People's House, 1908. Normally, in peacetime and before the rise of terrorism, the White House was open to visitors. Guides escorted visitors through the public rooms but not the private offices or the First Family's living quarters.

The twenty-sixth President of the United States at his desk. This picture was taken about 1908, when TR was fifty years old.

colonnade, or covered walkway formed by a double row of columns placed at regular intervals, connected the West Wing to the mansion itself.

The typical White House day began at 7:30 A.M. Upon rising, the president bathed, dressed, and ate breakfast. When it came to food, Roosevelt had no self-control. Unless Edith stepped in, he ate whatever he pleased. Breakfast, for example, consisted of heaping plates of fried liver, bacon and eggs, and thickly buttered bread. Young Ted reported that Father would down a dozen fried eggs, followed by two glasses of milk and four oranges. He also ate soup bowls heaped with peaches and cream. Addicted to coffee, each day the president drank about a gallon of it, thick with sugar, from a special cup the size of "a bathtub." Lincoln Steffens described his friend as "a fast and enormous eater," and it showed. When he became president, Roosevelt weighed 195 pounds. By the time he left office, his weight had shot up to 240 pounds.[5]

After breakfast, Roosevelt went to work. He used the old second-floor study as an office; the famous Oval Office was added in 1909, during the term of Roosevelt's successor, William Howard Taft. A plain room, Roosevelt's office had a portrait of Abraham Lincoln as its only decoration. Piles of papers lay on the desk, but there was no telephone. Its ring jarred the president's nerves; long phone conversations, he found, only wasted time. Always keen to learn about public opinion, his day began with reading newspaper articles and the mail. Edith helped with both tasks. She read four newspapers every day, marking articles for her husband's attention; so did an aide, only his task was to sift through 350 news-papers. Edith saw the mail before anyone else, selecting letters for his personal attention. Educated by tutors—most women did not attend college during her growing-up years—Edith, like her husband, had a fierce desire to do the "right" thing. And, like Theodore, she loved literature, especially the plays of William Shakespeare; she was also fluent in French. During secret cabinet and political meetings, Edith would sit in a corner, quietly knitting but taking in every word. Afterward, she gave the president her opinion.[6]

Unlike nowadays, when nearly every minute of the president's schedule is programmed far in advance, Roosevelt kept to a relatively leisurely pace. Members of Congress would see him from 10 A.M. until noon; all others needed an appointment. Visitors usually found him outgoing and friendly, even playful. Once, when a senator came in, the president leaped from behind his desk, threw his arms around the man, and danced about the room with him. As they danced, they sang:

> Oh, the Irish and the Dutch
> They don't amount to much,
> But huroo for the Scandinoo-vian![7]

Perhaps nothing impressed visitors more than Roosevelt's laughter. The man loved his job and let everyone know it. "A hundred times a day the President will laugh, and, when he laughs he does it with the same energy with which he talks," a reporter noted. "It is usually a roar of laughter, and it comes nearly every five minutes. His face grows red with merriment, his eyes nearly close, his utterance becomes choked and sputtery and falsetto, and sometimes he doubles up [laugh-ing]. You don't smile with Mr. Roosevelt; you shout with laughter with him, and then you shout again while he tries to cork more laugh[ter] and sputters: 'Come gentlemen, let us be serious. . . .'"[8]

Security was no laughing matter, not when America had suffered three presi-dential assassinations in thirty-five years. Created in 1864, the Secret Service was a government organization originally formed in order to catch counterfeiters, smugglers, and illegal liquor makers. Following Abraham Lincoln's death in 1865, its chief responsibility became presidential security. After the assassination of James Garfield (1881) and William McKinley (1901), the Secret Service set out to improve its methods. In the Roosevelt White House, Secret Service men stood at key places throughout the mansion and the West Wing. Agents seized visitors' bundles, inspected their hats, and made sure their hands were always visible. Whenever Roosevelt traveled, agents ran a decoy train ahead of his so that any assassins would have trouble figuring out which train the president was on. Sometimes the service even ignored the law for the sake of presidential security. For example, during a visit to San Francisco, agents arrested John Czolgosz, the brother of McKinley's assassin. No charges were pressed because he had done no wrong. Instead, he stayed under lock and key until Roosevelt left town. Even today, the Secret Service may ignore the legal principle that a person may not be arrested without evidence if it is felt that the president's life might be in danger.

Still, Roosevelt's security was far from being perfect. Out west, cowboys packing loaded six-shooters greeted the president. Once, a tailor appeared at the White House, asking to see the president. Admitted to Roosevelt's office, he whipped a long scissor blade from the sleeve of his coat. It is not known why he did so, but he proved to be harmless. Another time, a lady arrived with a pistol in her handbag. Although she proved harmless, too, another lady, Mrs. Laura Morris, was not. Accusing the president of persecuting her husband, she went for him as if to scratch out his eyes. Two Secret Service agents carried her out of the White House kicking and screaming.[9]

Roosevelt did not worry about his personal safety. Like his hero, Lincoln, Theodore was a fatalist. This meant he believed that what will be, will be. Anything destined to happen cannot be prevented. Yet he had no intention of giving a would-be assassin a free shot. Although always escorted by an armed Secret Service agent, Roosevelt carried a pistol whenever he went out, even in states that banned concealed weapons. If he slept away from the White House or Sagamore Hill, he kept the weapon on the night table, within easy reach. A friend once brought up the subject of assassination. "Oh," Roosevelt replied, patting his right hip pocket, "I go armed, and they would have to be mighty quick to get the drop on me."[10]

Friends always found a warm welcome at the White House. Roosevelt left orders that "the cowboy bunch" could drop in to the mansion anytime, although a newspaper grumbled about the "thugs and assassins" who darkened the president's door. Occasionally, however, the police guards gave Roosevelt's friends a hard time. It took Sylvane Ferris, the president's former ranching partner, two days to talk his way past them. "The next time they don't let you in, Sylvane," said an irate Roosevelt, "you just shoot through the windows." This was bad advice, since anyone shooting at the White House would have drawn a hailstorm of lead from Secret Service pistols in return.[11]

Similarly, ex–Rough Riders were always visiting or writing to ask advice or to borrow money. Letters often told of babies named for the president or informing him of the men's activities. "I have the honor to report," a former major wrote, "that Comrade Webb, late of Troop D, has just killed two men at Bisbee, Arizona." Another fellow just wanted to tell his tale of woe. "Dear Colonel, I write you because I am in trouble. I have shot a lady in the eye. But Colonel, I did not mean to shoot that lady. It was all an accident, *for I was shooting at my wife.*" No wonder Edith felt that she and her husband were "the parents of a thousand very large and very bad children."[12]

Roosevelt's salary was $50,000 a year (what cost $50,000 in 1900 would cost $1,107,780 in 2005). Since Congress gave no allowance for entertaining the president's visitors and guests, Roosevelt usually spent most, and in some years all, of his earnings on hospitality. He and Edith liked having company. At least once a week, up to twenty guests joined them in the Red Room for a big meal and lots of talk. Guests came from all walks of life: politicians, cowboys, musicians, novelists, scientists, historians, big-game hunters. Bat Masterson, the famous "shootist"— or gunfighter—was a favorite of the president's, as was heavyweight boxing champion John L. Sullivan, who could "lick any bum in the house."[13]

As usual, Roosevelt cultivated the press. No president has ever had friendlier relations with reporters than he. Nowadays the president has formal press conferences, where scores of newspaper and television reporters bombard him with questions. Roosevelt never held a press conference. Instead, he met with five or six reporters in his office or in the pressroom, which he set up in the West Wing. There he answered their questions freely, but expected anything said in confidence to stay secret. If that trust was violated, the reporter and all others from his newspaper were never allowed to enter the Roosevelt White House again.[14]

In using the press to explain his ideas to the public, Roosevelt pioneered methods still used by today's elected officials. He invented the *leak;* that is, he gave reporters information "off the record," with the understanding that they would not reveal their source. "If you even hint where you got it," he told one, "I'll say you are a damned liar." Leaks, for example, might embarrass opponents

A close-up of TR soon after his election to his first full term as president.

or lessen the impact of bad news later. Roosevelt also invented the *trial balloon.* This tested public opinion by suggesting a plan or idea through an unnamed person. For example, an "informed source" or "high administration official" might suggest raising the duty on imported clocks. If the public raised an outcry, the president could easily back down, saying there was nothing to the story.[15]

It could be argued that few presidents have been as qualified as Roosevelt to hold office. No president had ever traveled as widely as he, both in the United States and overseas. Moreover, he had an uncanny ability to absorb information, mostly from reading. "Reading with me is a disease," he said, a lifelong addiction formed in childhood. Roosevelt used every spare minute for reading, and even kept a book near the White House entrance to read while waiting to welcome foreign dignitaries. Once, during a long train ride, the president disappeared. A friend searched the train, and finally found him in a tiny toilet with its door half-open. There Roosevelt stood under an electric light, "busily engaged in reading, while he braced himself in the angle of the two walls against the swaying motion of the train."[16]

Most people can read a sentence or a paragraph at a time. Roosevelt read by pages, two to three a minute. Normally, he read a book a day; on quiet evenings, he read three books. Blessed with a photographic memory, he could recite long passages from books read years earlier. His reading tastes ranged from the Greek classics in English translation to modern novels, as well as nonfiction texts from biology to history. "This man is ignorant about nothing," a reporter noted. "There is nothing about which he does not know something; in most cases it is a good deal." The president constantly amazed experts with his knowledge of their fields. Guglielmo Marconi, inventor of wireless telegraphy, said Roosevelt knew as much Italian history as a university professor. The greatest ornithologist of the day, Frank M. Chapman of the American Museum of Natural History, said he "knows more about birds than I do."[17]

Roosevelt was our most athletic president, bar none. His indoor sports included singlestick, a bruising "game" he played with General Leonard Wood. "We put on heavily padded helmets, breastplates and gauntlets and wrap bath towels around our necks," he wrote Kermit, "and then we turn and beat one another like carpets with the sticks." They went at it until Wood broke the commander in chief's right arm.[18]

Recovering from the broken arm, the president hired a Japanese champion, Professor Yamashita, to teach him "Jiudo"—jujitsu, a Japanese martial art. After mastering the basics, he worked out with two Japanese trainers three times a week in his office. All wanted to win. An opponent once got Roosevelt in a choke hold. So "I also got hold of his windpipe and thought I could perhaps choke him off before he could choke me. However, he got ahead." The trainer's choke hold resulted in a severe presidential sore throat. Roosevelt also boxed with young army officers. During one bout, an uppercut broke a blood vessel in his left eye, eventually costing him the sight in that eye. Yet, the president explained, he never said a word about it to the officer, because it "would only have caused him to feel badly."[19]

Outdoors, Roosevelt went for a wide range of activities. At night, under the watchful eyes of a Secret Service agent, he ran around the base of the Washington Monument. The president never tired of horses; he rode, jumped, and galloped them whenever possible. Although he hated golf, calling it a sport for "sissies," he was an avid tennis player. Roosevelt once played ninety-one tennis games in a day, followed by a vigorous three-mile walk. He climbed trees, too, at least until Edith put her foot down. "Theodore!" she cried. "If you knew how ridiculous you look up that tree you'd come down at once!" The president obeyed.[20]

Nothing compared to his outings in Rock Creek Park in Washington, D.C. Rock Creek Park was a wild place. It had a swift stream that rushed through steep hills, strewn with huge boulders and cut by deep ravines. Roosevelt used his outings there, called "point-to-point hikes," for exercise and as character tests for selected guests. The idea was to always go in a straight line, no matter what stood in the way. With Roosevelt in the lead, the party went over, under and through obstacles, but never around them.

The French ambassador, Jules Jusserand, passed the test with flying colors. Expecting a pleasant stroll in a manicured local garden, this elegant gentleman was invited on one of Roosevelt's Rock Creek walks and arrived at the White House wearing a dress suit and a tall silk hat. To his surprise, Jusserand found the president and a few others wearing grungy clothes. He recalled:

> We started off at what seemed to me a breakneck pace, which soon brought us out of the city. On reaching the country, the President went pell-mell over the fields, following neither road nor path, always on, on straight ahead! . . . At last we came to the bank of a stream, rather wide and too deep to be forded. . . . I thought that now we had reached our goal and would rest a moment and catch our breath before turning homeward. But judge my horror when I saw the President unbutton his clothes and heard him say, "We had better strip, so as not to wet our things in the Creek." Then I, too, for the honor of France, removed my apparel, everything except my lavender kid gloves. The President cast an inquiring look at these as if they, too, must come off, but I [said], "With your permission, Mr. President, I will keep these on; otherwise it would be embarrassing if we should meet ladies."

As Roosevelt roared with laughter, they slid into the water and swam to the other side. Jusserand had made a friend, and a friend of France's, too. Another time, a less-athletic diplomat lagged behind. "Very soft! Very soft!" the president snorted. He could not trust such a fellow.[21]

Never before, or since, has the White House been home to such an energetic family as the Roosevelts. Always poised and dignified, Edith shaped the position of first lady, a term first applied to Mary Lincoln. It was Edith who gave the president's wife a public role. Taking charge of the social side of her husband's work, Edith planned official dinners and receptions. She also formed the White House china collection and created the gallery of portraits of first ladies. Even gruff, bad-tempered Mark Hanna fell under her spell. Once he saw a little boy standing beside a carriage and talking to its passengers, Edith and her youngest son, Quentin. As the carriage drove away, Hanna poked the boy in the back with his cane. "You!" he growled. "You ought to take your hat off when a woman speaks to you. When Mrs. Roosevelt speaks to you, keep it off a week!"[22]

Not all the children lived in the White House. Alice lived with Aunt Bamie in Connecticut, visiting only occasionally. Her brothers—Ted, fourteen, and Kermit, twelve—attended Groton, a boarding school in Massachusetts; sister Ethel, ten, stayed at a private Washington girls' academy during the week. The younger boys lived in the White House. Archie, seven, went to a public school nearby. When Quentin, four, came of age, he also attended public school.

Roosevelt family portrait, Sagamore Hill, 1903. Left to right: Quentin, TR, TR Jr., Archie, Alice, Kermit, Edith, and Ethel.

Although they walked to school by themselves, and even rode public omnibuses, Secret Service men always kept them in sight, for fear they might be kidnapped or otherwise harmed. When the boys played on the White House lawn, agents watched them from behind bushes.

The White House staff soon got used to the president's "romps," as he called wrestling matches and pillow fights with Archie and Quentin. One night, before a diplomatic reception, Father, grand in "white tie and tails," went upstairs to tuck them in; the Roosevelt boys always kissed their father good night. "The two small persons in pink tommies," he wrote, "instantly raced for the bed and threw themselves on it with ecstatic conviction that a romp was going to begin. I did not have the heart to disappoint them, and the result was that my shirt got so mussed that I had to change it." At other times, the boys waited in ambush. When the President of the United States came along, thinking great thoughts, they pounded him with pillows.[23]

Roosevelt never lost the fascination with animals that he developed as a boy. During his presidency, the White House often seemed like a zoo. Pets were everywhere. Tom Quarts, usually a mild-mannered cat, took a hissing, scratching dislike to House Speaker "Uncle Joe" Cannon of North Carolina. There were dogs like Jack, the terrier, and Sailor Boy, the retriever, and an assortment of rabbits, flying squirrels, kangaroo rats, and the hens Baron Speckle and Fierce. The president thought Jonathan, the piebald rat, a cuddly darling; he "always crawls over everybody." Eli, a gorgeous parrot with "a bill that I think could cut through boiler plate, but crawls all over Ted," endeared himself by screeching "Hurrah for Roosevelt!" The boys had several horses, too. Quentin once took his favorite, Algonquin, a Shetland pony, upstairs in the elevator to visit Archie when his brother lay sick in bed.[24]

Like their father when he was a boy, the children adored snakes. Whenever Alice stayed at the White House, she went about with Emily Spinach, a long, lean garter snake named after her aunt Emily Carow, a long, lean lady. Quentin's favorite was a four-foot king snake. One day, he burst into Father's office, proudly plunking it down on the desk. Yes, the president agreed, such a creature was truly worthy of such a boy as Quentin. But since he was in conference with the attorney general, he asked his son to show it to four congressmen waiting impatiently in the next room. The whiskered gentlemen mistook the creature for a stick, until it began to move. "Then the king snake went up Quentin's sleeve," Roosevelt gleefully recalled. "The last I saw of Quentin that afternoon, one Congressman was gingerly helping him off with his jacket, so as to let the snake crawl out the upper end of the sleeve."[25]

Left to themselves, Archie and Quentin always managed to find something to keep them busy. The White House became their playground. The boys slid down flights of stairs on silver trays, shouting all the way. As Quentin grew older, he and his "gang" of schoolmates tore down the hallways on bicycles, clumped about on stilts, and roller-skated on the polished floors. Armed with water pistols, they battled in the East Room. Visitors saw little boys pop their heads out of tall vases. Bold explorers, they crawled in the spaces between the floors and ceilings, no doubt meeting rats now and then. They found the attic heaven for hide-and-seek. The president was not shy; he could not resist joining in the fun. "Do you recollect," he wrote Archie later, "how we all of us used to play hide-and-go-seek in the White House and have obstacle races down the hall when you brought your friends?"[26]

Sometimes the boys went too far. One night, ugly growths—spitballs— appeared on a portrait of President Andrew Jackson. Quentin and three of his gang had chewed bits of newspaper into wet, mushy globs and stuck them on the end of Old Hickory's nose. Roosevelt hauled his son out of bed and made him remove the mess. Next morning, the culprits got a tongue-lashing. "Just imagine how I would feel if you rowdies, gangsters, villains, threw spitballs at my portrait!" he said. He wrote Kermit that he forbade the chief villain, Quentin, from having visitors "until I felt that a sufficient time had elapsed to serve as punishment. They were four very sheepish small boys when I got through with them."[27]

This punishment did not break Quentin of his spitball habit. In school, he threw one at a classmate. It went astray, hitting their teacher squarely in the face. Next day, a heavyset man strode into the classroom, followed by a nervous principal. The visitor looked exactly like the photograph hanging over the chalkboard. Somehow, Quentin had let the cat out of the bag, admitting what he had done. "I really had to come to offer my apology for Quentin's rude and thoughtless behavior of yesterday," Roosevelt said, handing the teacher a large bouquet of flowers. Another time, he wrote her that, should Quentin misbehave again, "let

me know and I will whip him." If she wanted to, the teacher had the president's permission to do the same.[28]

The president could not whip his eldest child. Alice had always been a rebel. At age nine, she said she no longer wanted to be a girl and took to wearing pants. By her late teens, she had grown into a beautiful young woman nicknamed "Princess Alice." Yet she was an angry princess, feeling that Father did not love her as much as the other children. Unlike her solemn cousin Eleanor, Alice smoked cigarettes in public, an unheard-of thing for "decent" girls at the turn of the century. She fired cap pistols at garden parties, gambled at racetracks, and drank whiskey. She socialized with gaudy multimillionaires, people, as we will see, her father loathed. Forced to attend church, she would read a book or practice her special "one-sided nose wrinkle" to show her disdain for religion and her father's authority. Alice even became a fan of the hootchie-kootchie, a risqué dance favored by "fast" women.[29]

Father found her a handful. When a friend asked why he did not discipline Alice, Roosevelt replied, "I can be president of the United States, or I can attend to Alice. I can't do both." But he knew that was a false choice, for Theodore did not feel he could choose to neglect his presidential duty for any reason. The president had a job to do for his country, and he dared not let anything stand in the way of *that*.[30]

6

"I BELIEVE IN POWER"

There inheres in the Presidency more power than in any other office in any great republic or constitutional monarchy in modern times. . . . I believe in a strong executive. I believe in power.

—THEODORE ROOSEVELT

Sitting presidents are often fans of past presidents, whose example and ideals they admire. Theodore Roosevelt's favorites were Andrew Jackson and Abraham Lincoln. Although they had different governing styles, Jackson and Lincoln were strong leaders who believed the president was the people's chief servant. In their day, both aimed at preserving the Union, if necessary by armed force. Similarly, Roosevelt strove to do what was best for the nation as he wrestled with the leading challenges of his day: the effects of the Industrial Revolution, safeguarding the environment, America's role in world affairs, and racial justice.

Concerning African-Americans, he told a friend, "as a race and in the mass they are altogether inferior to whites." Sadly, at least in terms of economic standing, that was all too true. Most African-Americans had few opportunities compared to whites. Racists thought this was as it should be, for in their eyes nothing—not even equal opportunities—could improve the condition of "backward" blacks. The president, however, saw the problem as one of social conditions, not biological laws. Human nature, he believed, is flexible, able to change as society changes. History proved that a talented minority of blacks had always overcome obstacles with their intelligence and energy. Where a minority had gone, he saw no reason why the majority should not follow, given enough time.[1]

Roosevelt believed in judging people on their merits, not on their color. It was a question of morality. We must "treat the individual Negro just as we treat the individual white man," he wrote a friend. We must "give him a fair chance. . . . Punish or penalize him as we would a white man if he falls short or goes wrong . . . encourage him if he goes right." Yet there was a difficulty. While wishing blacks well, the president never used his power on their behalf, never proposed government help, never forcefully defended their right to vote. Denouncing lynching as lawlessness, he left it to the Southern states to deal with the problem—which was like having wolves guard sheep. Sadly, despite Roosevelt's fine words, protecting black rights was not a major concern during his years in office. Apparently, the reason was political. Roosevelt believed that fighting for racial justice would harm his ability to bring about reform in areas that he judged needed change even more urgently.[2]

We see this in an incident involving a man named Booker T. Washington. Here was a person after the president's own heart, a leader of those Roosevelt called the "better element" of blacks. Tall and straight as an iron rail, Washington was two years older than the president and of mixed heritage: his mother was a slave and his father was a white man, perhaps her owner. Through sheer grit, Washington overcame enormous obstacles in order to obtain "book learning" and began a career as an educator. In 1881, as Roosevelt entered the New York State Assembly, Washington established an all-black school, the Tuskegee Institute, in Tuskegee, Alabama. As the institute's reputation for excellence grew, Booker T. Washington became the most prominent African-American of the day.[3]

Booker T. Washington in 1903. Born into slavery, after the Civil War he became the nation's leading African-American educator.

On October 16, 1901, a month after taking office, Roosevelt asked the famous educator to dinner at the White House. African-Americans had visited the mansion before, but Washington was the first to get a dinner invitation. Afterward, the two men discussed appointing certain highly qualified "colored persons" to government posts in the South.[4]

Southerners became enraged. For in treating a black as a social equal, the president had done the unforgivable, they thought. The Memphis, Tennessee, *Scimitar* called the dinner "the most damnable outrage ever perpetrated by any citizen of the United States." Fire-eaters in the Senate spewed their hatred in vile, murderous tones. South Carolinian "Pitchfork" Ben Tillman warned: "The action of President Roosevelt in entertaining that nigger will necessitate our killing a thousand niggers in the South before they will learn their place again." Mississippi rabble-rouser James K. Vardaman said the White House had become "so saturated with the odor of the nigger that the rats have taken refuge in the stable."[5]

Before issuing the invitation, Roosevelt admitted to worrying about bad publicity. But that "made me ashamed of myself, and made me hasten to send the invitation." Now he lashed out at his critics. I will choose my company, he insisted, whatever an "unspeakable creature" like Vardaman might say! However, the incident taught the president a lesson he dared not ignore. As a private citizen, Roosevelt might feel shame at discriminating against anyone. Yet, as a politician, he knew he would need Southern support in Congress and Southern votes when he ran for president in his own right in 1904. So, for the rest of his presidency, he never had another black person to dinner. Although not courageous, it seemed like good politics. In this case, at least, Roosevelt thought the end justified the means, that the moral issue of racial justice had to take a backseat to a "greater" moral issue, the well-being of the nation as a whole. We will never know whether he was right, for the president could not use the "bully pulpit" to take the issue forcefully to the American people.[6]

Among friends, the president wondered whether the American experiment in self-government could last, and for how long. His gloomy prediction: "The republic cannot live ten years longer if things go on this way."[7]

What way? The danger did not come from overseas; no foreign country could conquer America. Roosevelt saw the danger lurking within. It grew out of "the great dumb forces," his term for the powers unleashed in America by the Industrial Revolution. These forces were operating on society in two ways at once, by producing great fortunes for a few wealthy families and great misery for millions of poor people. Left to themselves, the president thought, the fighting between rich and poor would tear the country apart.[8]

Roosevelt believed this partly because of his upbringing. Knickerbocker families like his had become wealthy before the Industrial Revolution arrived in full force. During the seventeenth and eighteenth centuries, we recall, Knickerbockers had prospered in foreign trade, banking, and real estate. Although wealthy, these "old-money" families were poor compared to the new tycoons of industry and finance. Even so, the Knickerbockers saw themselves as society's rightful leaders. Robert Roosevelt, the president's uncle, praised America's old-money society as "the best people in the world, the most generous, the most intelligent, the most public-spirited, most upright, most philanthropic." For generations, they had set the fashion in style and manners. Prizing education, interested in life's "finer" things, they founded museums, built concert halls, and supported charities. In the tycoons, the "suddenly rich," the Knickerbockers saw people with different values.[9]

None loathed the newly rich more than Theodore Roosevelt. These "selfish barbarians," these "Vikings," led "lives of rotten frivolity [and] rotten vice." While poor Americans might suffer in bad economic times, the tycoons lavished fortunes on extravagant dinners and gaudy possessions. Having to be in their company made him yawn with boredom. Such dull, silly people! "It tires me to talk to rich men," he moaned. "You expect a man of millions, the head of a great industry, to be a man worth hearing; but as a rule they don't know anything outside their own business."[10]

Roosevelt liked their growing power even less. Not only on the state level, but on the national as well, "big moneyed men" corrupted politics. Roosevelt feared that their influence was a tyranny in the making, one that would conquer democracy. "Of all forms of tyranny," he wrote, "the least attractive and the most vulgar is the tyranny of mere wealth, the tyranny of a plutocracy." In stinging one-liners, he denounced "the criminal rich and the fool rich," "the wealthy criminal class," and the "malefactors of great wealth." Blinded by greed, lacking all sense of social responsibility, the "colossal lawless corporations" did as they pleased. And it pleased them to bribe lawmakers, buy judges, and hire thugs to break strikes. A reckoning was coming, Roosevelt thought, a destructive workers' revolution provoked by the stupidity and selfishness of irresponsible wealth.[11]

Roosevelt realized that the impoverished people's struggle for work and bread might kindle violence. Yet, while he despised the suddenly rich, he had what historian John Morton Blum called a "jagged dread of violent revolution." Nothing infuriated him more than events like the Haymarket bombing. Lawless violence, he believed, threatened the very existence of civilization. In 1886, Roosevelt wrote from the Badlands regretting that he could not lead his cowboys in shooting anarchists. As New York police commissioner, he warned: "The mob takes its own chance. Order will be kept at whatever cost. If it comes to shooting, we shall shoot to hit." During the Pullman strike, he demanded the arrest of strike leaders "and shooting them dead." If that meant killing the likes of Eugene Debs, then so be it.[12] Though Roosevelt sympathized with the workers' plight, he would not tolerate their violence. While a foreign war might be necessary to protect the nation, social violence, Roosevelt insisted, was never justified.

How to save America from the twin demons of corruption and revolution? Roosevelt answered with the "Square Deal," his policy of dealing fairly (squarely) with everyone. Writing to a friend, he described his method with a favorite West African proverb: "Speak softly and carry a big stick; you will go far." The president would have the United States government speak softly; that is, interfere in the nation's life—and the mighty influence of the wealthy—as little as possible. But if need be, it must use its full power, its big stick, to defend the public. Much of the rest of this chapter will deal with his "Square Deal" domestic policies.[13]

J. P. Morgan was the first to feel the stick's force. Shortly before Roosevelt took office, the financier combined three railroads to form the Northern Securities Company. With Morgan controlling nearly all rail traffic between Chicago and the Pacific coast, competition among the railroads in the northern part of the country vanished overnight. As freight charges rose, Morgan's profits soared.[14]

Roosevelt saw nothing wrong with soaring profits; after all, nobody goes into business to lose money. He also knew that well-run trusts like Carnegie Steel and Standard Oil increased productivity. In turn, high productivity meant cheaper consumer goods, more jobs, and a higher standard of living for everyone. Big business, then, was not necessarily evil. There were, the president said, good trusts and bad trusts. There was no reason, according to Theodore, to break up trusts, leaving a host of small, inefficient companies. Instead, Roosevelt wanted to prevent trusts from doing harm while allowing the nation to enjoy the

Some critics thought President Roosevelt's "trust-busting" went too far. Here, a cartoonist depicts him wielding his big stick against the trusts and "everything in general."

benefits of mass production. "Big business has come to stay," he said. "The proper thing to do is to socialize it, to moralize it, to make it an agent for social good. . . ." In short, the president wanted big business to be a good citizen.[15]

J. P. Morgan was behaving like a bad citizen. "I owe the public nothing," he said about the stranglehold Northern Securities had on the railroads, his eyes bright as the lights on an oncoming locomotive. Now, for the first time in American history, a president stood up to a giant corporation. In February 1902, Roosevelt grasped the big stick. Turning to the Justice Department, he ordered it to sue to break up Morgan's company as an illegal monopoly under the Sherman Antitrust Act of 1890.[16]

"Jack and the Wall Street Giants" appeared in the January 13, 1904, issue of Puck *magazine. The cartoonist, a man named Keppler, depicts a tiny TR preparing to battle America's most powerful business leaders, all armed to the teeth and led by J. P. Morgan.*

The lawsuit shocked Wall Street. Roosevelt was not playing by the rules, said irate business leaders. Presidents were not supposed to interfere in business affairs! Outraged, Morgan grumbled that the president had not acted like a "gentleman." To set things straight, he visited the White House with his ally Senator Mark Hanna.[17]

"If we have done anything wrong, send your man to my man and they can fix it up," demanded Morgan. In other words, he wanted the attorney general, Philander Knox, to work out a deal with his representative.

"That can't be done," replied Roosevelt.

Wall Street's "Jupiter" had missed the point. Roosevelt was no business rival with whose "men"—aides, lawyers, managers—Morgan could make a deal. The president did not want to "fix" up anything; he wanted to stop bad behavior. Let Morgan do right by the country, and the government would leave him alone. Northern Securities was broken up by court order.

The next crisis came in the anthracite coalfields of Pennsylvania. Anthracite, or hard coal, was America's chief home-heating fuel. More important still, anthracite fueled the industrial system. Steam locomotives burned it in their boilers. Blast furnaces used it in making steel. Factories drove their steam engines with it.

Coal mining was not for weaklings. Miners worked a ten-hour day, six days a week, earning $250 to $450 a year. Mine owners, or "operators," based each man's pay on the amount of coal he dug. However, by using scales rigged to give false weights, three thousand pounds of coal might register as a standard two-thousand-pound ton. Thus miners were frequently cheated of wages. On payday, the miner often received not cash, but "scrip," printed IOUs good only in the company store. Because these stores charged more than any others, most miners were in debt to the operators of the company. In a song of the day, an ailing miner tells Saint Peter he cannot afford to die, "for I owe my soul to the company store." Coal mining was also dangerous: in 1901 alone, 513 men died in accidents. Countless others suffered a lingering death from "black lung," or "miner's asthma," a disease caused by inhaling coal dust. "By the age of fifty," an observer noted, "the miners were worn out and broken, good for little but the human slag heap."[18]

In 1908, boys like this young teenager still dug coal for twelve hours a day in deep, dark, dangerous coal mines. Every year, scores of child workers died in mine cave-ins and explosions.

Because men earned so little, their sons were usually forced to quit school by age ten to work in the mines. "Trapper boys" opened and closed doors that allowed air to reach work areas in deep shafts. "Mule boys" drove the mules that pulled coal cars along iron rails. "Greasers" kept car axles greased so they moved smoothly. Most, however, were "breaker boys." When a coal car came above ground, it went to a building called a "breaker," where machines broke the coal into pieces the right size for burning. The pieces then sped noisily through long chutes where the breaker boys waited. John Spargo, an eyewitness, described what he saw:

> Work in the coal breakers is exceedingly hard and dangerous. Crouched over the chutes, the boys sit hour after hour, picking out the pieces of slate and other refuse from the coal as it rushes past to the washers. From the cramped position they have to assume, most of them become more or less deformed and bent-backed like old men. . . . The coal is hard, and accidents to the hands, such as cut, broken, or crushed fingers, are common among the boys. Sometimes there is a worse accident: a terrible shriek is heard, and a boy is mangled and torn by the machinery, or disappears in the chute to be picked out later smothered and dead. . . . I once stood in a breaker for half an hour and tried to do the work a twelve-year-old boy was doing day after day, for ten hours at a stretch, for sixty cents a day. . . . My hands were bruised and

Breaker boys sorting coal by size in an unidentified mine. Many of these boys were under eleven and had seldom, if ever, attended school. Long exposure to coal dust gave them "black lung," a disease that made them gasp for breath, cough up blood, and shortened their lives.

cut in a few minutes; I was covered from head to foot with coal dust, and for many hours afterwards I was expectorating some of the small pieces of anthracite I had swallowed.[19]

The United Mine Workers (UMW) union wanted to improve working conditions. Its leader, John Mitchell, an ex–breaker boy, had risen through the miners' ranks through his intelligence and dedication. A thin, delicate-looking man, neatly dressed in black, Mitchell had a magnetic personality. Able to inspire members' love, he avoided strikes whenever possible. A strike, after all, meant even more hardship for UMW members, and bloodshed, too, if the operators hired scabs. Roosevelt paid Mitchell the highest compliment, calling him a "gentleman."

Early in 1902, Mitchell called for higher wages, honest weighing of coal, and recognition of the UMW as the miners' official representative. George F. Baer, president of the coal operators' association, refused to deal with any union. "Anthracite mining," he huffed, "is a business, and not a religious, sentimental or academic proposition." If miners wanted justice, let them not rely on unions, but on "the Christian men to whom God in His infinite wisdom has given the control of the property interests of the country." Translation: Operators had a license from the Lord to do as they pleased, no matter what the workers suffered. Faced with such arrogance, on May 10, Mitchell led 147,000 miners off the job.[20]

The effect was immediate and severe. As coal supplies dwindled, prices rose from five to thirty dollars a ton. Shortages first brought slowdowns, then layoffs, in every industry that used the black stuff. Unable to pay their bills, laid-off workers in many industries went hungry. Unable to pay their rent, the families of laid-off workers became homeless. As the strike dragged into the fall, mobs seized the coal cars of passing trains, even cut down telegraph poles for fuel. Schools closed because there was no coal to heat the buildings. Hospitals struggled to keep patients warm. Generally, Mitchell's men were peaceful, but sometimes they exchanged gunshots with guards at the mines. Operators welcomed any violence as an excuse to draw the government into the strike on their side. The newspapers that the wealthy controlled shrieked "Reign of Terror," demanding the president send troops to break the strike.[21]

With winter near and the shortage of coal more critical than ever, Roosevelt had trouble sleeping. Usually a sound sleeper, during this crisis he might doze off

During the coal strike of 1902, people stood in line for hours to get enough of the fuel to heat their homes and stoves. Many schools shut down for lack of coal, and hospitals were forced to send patients home.

for an hour or so, until jolted awake by nightmares. The president knew that desperate people do desperate things. The "untold misery" caused by the strike, he said, made riots inevitable. Riots, in turn, "might develop into social war"—violence without end. Jacob Riis agreed. Unless his friend acted, and soon, Riis warned, "the arrogance of the money power will bring a revolution."[22]

What could Roosevelt do? History was no guide. Presidents had no *legal* right to force a just settlement. "There is literally nothing," Roosevelt told Senator Henry Cabot Lodge, "the national government has any power to do in this matter." However, as president of all the people, he thought he had a *moral* right to interfere. He simply could not stand by while the nation tottered at the brink of disaster. It was also good politics. If he ended the strike, grateful voters would surely reward him in the 1904 election.[23]

Roosevelt called both sides to a meeting. Appealing to their patriotism, he asked them to agree to arbitration; that is, having an impartial third party settle the dispute. John Mitchell, the workers' representative, welcomed arbitration. George F. Baer, the company man, did not. Worse, Baer insulted the president for putting him in the same room with "a criminal," as he called the union leader. Had it not been for his high office, Roosevelt told friends later, he would have chucked Baer out a window. Such arrogance! Such "extraordinary stupidity"! Here he was trying to save the operators from the results of their folly, but they ignored the dangers facing them and the country.[24]

If driven to it, Roosevelt announced he would send the army to seize and run the mines. "What about the Constitution of the United States?" a congressman asked. Under it, not even the president has the right to seize private property without legal authority. Almost shouting, Roosevelt replied, "The Constitution was made for the people and not the people for the Constitution." It was not a question of the welfare of the people being more important than the Constitution, the supreme law of the land. The Preamble to the Constitution says that it was created to "promote the general welfare." So, while no specific law gave the president a role in labor disputes, Roosevelt felt he had the right to act for the good of the nation as a whole. I am President of the United States! I am commander in chief of the army! "I will seize the mines by military force, I will operate them by military force," he said. "I will give the people coal!" His intentions were good. Yet Roosevelt was on dangerous ground. Presidents are human beings, subject to all the failings of humanity. Even a well-meaning president may delude himself into believing that he has the public good in mind when he really has other, more selfish reasons for acting. In this case, Roosevelt acted to uphold what he thought the *spirit* of the laws—the public welfare. Yet, as a politician, he also knew that ending the coal strike would enhance his popularity with voters.[25]

On October 9, Roosevelt sent his "man" to New York for a secret meeting with J. P. Morgan. Elihu Root, secretary of war and a top Wall Street lawyer, persuaded Morgan to put pressure on the coal operators. It took little effort. Morgan disliked the president, but the Northern Securities case had taught him to respect Roosevelt. Besides, like Roosevelt, he cringed at the thought of whole-sale violence. To keep the city calm, Morgan set up a depot on the East Side to sell coal below cost. The operators, who depended on Morgan for loans, dared not cross him. When the operators agreed to an arbitration commission, John

Mitchell ordered the miners back to work. In March 1903, the commission awarded them a 10 percent pay raise, a workday reduced to nine hours, and honest weighing of coal. It did not recognize the UMW as their sole representative.

American Federation of Labor president Samuel Gompers called the settlement "the most important single incident in the labor movement in the United States." The credit went to responsible labor leaders like Mitchell and cautious businessmen like Morgan. Most of all, it went to the president. By showing leadership in the coal crisis, he made his own kind of revolution. The Square Deal had a very big stick! Thanks to Roosevelt, the federal government showed that it could act fairly in a labor dispute. Equally important, it proved that it could make big business behave like a good citizen. "The public be damned!" was no longer an acceptable attitude in America.[26]

Running on his own. TR addresses a crowd during the 1904 presidential campaign. People tried to get as close as they could to hear them. Notice the men perched on the power pole at the left.

Roosevelt's handling of Northern Securities and the coal strike brought a political payoff. In 1904, the Republicans chose him to head their ticket. The Democrats, stung by William Jennings Bryan's failures as a presidential candidate, nominated New York State Appeals Court judge Alton B. Parker. The Socialists went for Eugene Debs.

Judge Parker charged "trust-buster" Roosevelt with taking campaign contributions from big business. It was true, the president admitted, but he insisted those contributions did not influence his policies; he was not for sale. The public agreed. By a popular vote of 7.6 million to 5.1 million, Roosevelt

defeated Parker and won the election. Over 402,000 men voted for Debs. "I had no idea there would be such a sweep," said Roosevelt. Elated over his victory, he announced that he would follow custom and not run for a third term as president. He would regret this hasty decision for the rest of his life.[27]

March 4, 1905. Inauguration Day. A sparkling, clear day, with a cold wind whipping off the Potomac River. Cheering crowds greeted the president-elect as he rode in a carriage along Pennsylvania Avenue, the capital's main thoroughfare. On his right hand Roosevelt wore a special token that Secretary of State John Hay lent him for the day. Hay, once Abraham Lincoln's private secretary, had asked Roosevelt to wear the ring, which contained strands of their hero's hair. We can imagine that the ring gave Roosevelt the feeling that Lincoln looked down on him from heaven.

Other carriages bore the First Family and the president-elect's close relatives, his sisters and their husbands. His niece Eleanor sat beside her handsome fiancé, Franklin Delano Roosevelt, twenty-two, a distant cousin from Hyde Park, New York. Although raised a Democrat, in 1904 Franklin had cast his first presidential vote for "Uncle Ted." The older man, in turn, encouraged him to go into politics, even as a Democrat. Learning of the engagement, he wrote Franklin: "I am as fond of Eleanor as if she were my daughter; and I like you, and trust you, and believe in you." Franklin lived up to the older man's faith in him. When he became president in 1933, another time of crisis, he modeled his

Roosevelt campaigning in Ohio from the back of a railroad car in 1904. Before the coming of the airplane, the nationwide system of railroads enabled candidates to campaign across the country quickly and efficiently.

ABOVE: *TR's favorite niece and her fiancé, Franklin D. Roosevelt. The president liked Franklin and encouraged him to pursue a political career, even if that meant as a member of the rival Democratic party.*

RIGHT: *March 4, 1905, President Theodore Roosevelt delivers his Inaugural Address at the U.S. Capitol.*

New Deal reform program in part on his uncle's Square Deal.[28]

Reaching the Capitol, Roosevelt took the oath first taken by George Washington, to "preserve, protect, and defend the Constitution of the United States." Then the parade kicked off. For hours, he stood on the reviewing platform, watching cowboys and Indians, patriotic clubs and Harvard students, Civil War veterans and Rough Riders, stream past. Bands blared rousing tunes, such as "There'll Be a Hot Time in the Old Town Tonight." Marchers shouted "Hooray for Teddy!" A Rough Rider set off waves of laughter by lassoing an onlooker and pulling him into the street. Roosevelt was "dee-lighted." He laughed, waved, and swayed to the rhythms of the marching bands. That night, back at the White House, family and friends drank a champagne toast to his success and to the future. He drank, too, but suddenly said something that must have been preying on his mind all day: "How I wished Father could have been here too!"[29]

Roosevelt's sweep did not guarantee him an easy time in Congress. Many Republican members had doubts about the Square Deal. Nicknamed the "Old Guard," today they would be called ultraconservatives. Where the president wanted to check "the wealthy criminal class," the Old Guard praised "free enterprise" and opposed governmental interference. Powerful in both houses of Congress, the Old Guard meant to resist further reform. Yet, thanks to Roosevelt's political skills and strength of character, he achieved a great deal in his second term.

The struggle with the railroads continued. In 1903, Roosevelt had persuaded Congress to pass the Elkins Act banning rebates, the price cuts railroads gave big shippers such as Standard Oil. Three years later, he saw that a new measure, the Hepburn Act, controlled railroad operations further. This law allowed the Interstate Commerce Commission to inspect railroads' financial records and set their maximum freight and passenger rates. It also banned railroads from handing out free passes to politicians and others they sought to influence.

Despite opposition from the Old Guard, Roosevelt still found allies. Calling themselves "progressives," Republican and Democratic reformers demanded progress in all areas of American society; today we call them liberals. Other progressives were not politicians at all, but reporters who aimed at arousing public opinion in the cause of reform. Slowly, carefully, they interviewed people, researched public records, and held personal inspections. Usually, they published their findings in books and in dime magazines: *McClure's, Collier's, Everybody's.* For example, in his book *The Octopus* (1901), Frank Norris exposed the railroads' stranglehold on farmers. Lincoln Steffens detailed corruption in city governments in *The Shame of the Cities* (1904). Ida Tarbell detailed John D. Rockefeller's sleazy dealings in *The History of the Standard Oil Company* (1904).

While wanting the same things the president did, these reporters could make his job harder. Roosevelt feared that the reform movement might get out of hand, inflaming the public and furthering demands for violent solutions to problems. As the debates on the Hepburn Act raged, David Graham Phillips blasted Senate corruption in a series of articles titled "The Treason of the Senate." Although filled with factual errors, the articles still had enough truth in them to anger the very men Roosevelt needed to pass this critical law. During a speech, Theodore compared Phillips and writers like him to a character in John Bunyan's *Pilgrim's Progress,* who was so busy raking up muck that he saw nothing else. "Muckraker!" The name stuck, becoming a badge of honor for crusading reporters.[30]

Some muckrakers took a hard look at the medicines Americans took and the food they ate. Early in the twentieth century, many people had little, if any, access to decent medical care. Few doctors practiced in rural areas. In towns and cities, doctors charged as much as two dollars a visit, a lot for a family struggling to make ends meet. As a result, people turned to "patent medicines"; that is, medicines sold without a doctor's prescription.

Patent medicines had catchy names like:

Foley's Honey & Tar for Coughs and Colds
Dr. Miller's Vegetable Expectorate for All Lung Ailments
Munson's Paw-Paw Pills to Coax Your Liver into Action
Pierce's Pleasant Pellets to Cure Constipation

There were also hosts of "soothing syrups" for jangled nerves, "teething potions" for young children, and "tonics" to restore vigor. Still, whatever its name or its claims, buyers of a patent medicine were wise if they followed an ancient bit of advice: "Buyer Beware!"

Patent-medicine manufacturers did as they pleased. No law required them to list a medicine's ingredients on its label. As a result, medicines were often adulterated, made impure by the addition of useless, spoiled, or dangerous materials. Brightly colored bottles often contained large amounts of alcohol flavored with spices and sugar. Touted for its ability to relieve "female complaints," the popular Lydia Pinkham's Vegetable Compound was 18 percent alcohol. A bottle of Paine's Celery Compound, for heavy whiskey drinkers, contained enough alcohol to make a user drunk.

Patent medicines might contain all sorts of addictive (habit-forming) drugs. Historians have called Roosevelt's America a "dope fiend's paradise." More than six hundred patent medicines contained opium and its by-products, morphine and heroin. These were freely imported and openly sold in pharmacies, groceries, and by mail-order firms. Other patent medicines had cocaine, extracted from coca leaves and first used by South American Indians for its stimulating effects. In the United States, stores sold cocaine cigarettes, cocaine snuff, cocaine-injecting kits, and cocaine drinks called "cordials." Originally, Coca-Cola was made from a syrup of coca leaves and kola nuts, an African plant rich in caffeine, the same stimulant found in coffee. By 1900, at least 200,000 Americans were drug addicts. According to one estimate, in New York City alone 60 percent of children had tried opium or cocaine in one form or another.[31]

Food, particularly meat, could be deadlier than any patent medicine. For centuries, farmers had raised animals for sale to local slaughterhouses. These, in turn, sold the fresh meat to neighborhood butchers, who trimmed it to suit their customers' wishes. That changed after the Civil War, as ranchers began raising cattle on government lands in the West. After the roundup, cowboys drove cattle to railroad depots for sale to dealers. Railroad trains then brought the cattle to meatpacking centers like Chicago, Kansas City, and St. Louis. Plants "processed" the animals under one roof, as on a factory assembly line. Each day, by the thousands, live cattle entered the line and emerged as packages of meat labeled by weight and cut. Refrigerated railroad cars then sped the packages to markets throughout the country. Many plants were filthy and dangerous. But when progressives drafted bills to regulate meatpacking and drugs, opponents blocked them in the Senate.

A muckraker, Upton Sinclair, helped Roosevelt break the logjam. Sinclair went to Chicago to research a novel about immigrant workers in the stockyards. During his seven-week stay, the author admitted, he paid little attention to the packinghouses, "as I do not eat much meat myself." Instead, he relied on talks with workers and his imagination. When his book *The Jungle* appeared in January 1906, it became the most famous muckraking work ever. *The Jungle* had hair-raising descriptions of how packers prepared things like sausages:

> There was never the least attention paid to what was cut up for sausage; there would come all the way back from Europe old sausage that had been rejected, and that was mouldy and white—it would be dosed with borax and glycerine, and dumped into the hoppers, and made over again for home consumption. There would be meat that tumbled out on the floor, in the dirt and sawdust, where the workers had tramped and spit uncounted billions of consumption [tuberculosis] germs. There would be meat stored in great piles in rooms; and the water from leaky roofs would drip over it, and thousands of rats would race about on it. It was too dark in these storage places to see well, but a man could run his hand over these piles of meat and sweep off handfuls of the dried dung of rats. These rats were nuisances, and the packers would put poisoned bread out for them, they would die, and then rats, bread, and meat

would go into the hoppers together. . . . All of their sausage came out of the same bowl, but when they went to wrap it they would stamp some of it "special," and for this they would charge two cents more a pound.[32]

Shocked by such descriptions, the public demanded change—at once. Roosevelt read *The Jungle* at breakfast. He was so upset, it was said, that he flung his sausages, which he dearly loved, out the window. This is a fine story, a dramatic story, but untrue. The president had wanted to do something about dangerous drugs and food for some time. As for Upton Sinclair, Roosevelt had "utter contempt" for the fellow, calling him "hysterical, unbalanced, and untruthful." The author, Theodore believed, had written an exaggerated account of things he had not seen. Conditions in certain plants were surely bad, but not a reason to condemn an entire industry, Roosevelt said.[33]

But the novel had roused the public, and Roosevelt made "real use" (his

An anonymous 1905 cartoon depicting TR's reaction to the scandal in the meatpacking industry. Thanks to his leadership, Congress passed the first law providing for federal inspection of meat products.

words) of the opportunity it offered. The president sent two Department of Agriculture investigators to Chicago to learn more about conditions in the packinghouses. They confirmed many of Sinclair's charges, particularly in the smaller houses, where owners cut costs by cutting corners. Roosevelt used their findings to pressure key congressmen into passing the reforms he wanted. Faced with a loud public outcry, they dared not stand in the way.[34]

In June 1906, America's first consumer-protection laws went into effect. The Pure Food and Drug Act banned the manufacture, sale, and transportation across state borders of adulterated food and drugs. It required labels listing all habit-forming drugs in patent medicines. (In 1914, Congress banned the selling of such drugs without a doctor's prescription.) In addition, a new agency, the Food and Drug Administration (FDA), would test all foods and drugs meant for human use, banning those it found unfit. The Meat Inspection Act gave the Department of Agriculture the power to inspect all meat shipped across state borders. It would decide if the meat came from healthy animals and if it was packaged under sanitary conditions. Violators faced a $10,000 fine and a two-year jail term. Over the years, Congress strengthened both acts, creating the system of consumer protection we have today.

Roosevelt had reason to be proud. Despite attacks from big business, despite the Republican Old Guard, he had begun curbing the special interests. While fighting these battles, he made such important contributions in other areas—the environment and foreign affairs—that they will require separate chapters. Yet his presidency also had its dark side. Twice he violated his own principles of fair play. His reaction to the Industrial Workers of the World (IWW) and to murder charges against black soldiers in Texas showed a nasty side to his character—his actions showed him as a bully.

The IWW was founded in 1905, in Chicago. Its president, William Dudley Haywood, thirty-six, had left school before his tenth birthday. Setting out on his own, he worked as a cowboy, miner, and gold prospector. Somehow he lost an eye and the use of a hand. "Big Bill," as folks called him, was over six feet tall and had the "strength of an ox." A gentle man, he enjoyed babysitting for friends' children; his strongest swear term was "gee fuzz." Big Bill learned about life from experience, not books; he knew firsthand the hardships workers endured. He once saw a black man lynched, an injustice that burned itself into his soul. Like his friend Eugene Debs, he gave businessmen, politicians, and, yes, presidents, the jitters. For Big Bill was not only a socialist, but a revolutionary.[35]

Like all IWW members, Haywood called himself a "Wobbly," a nickname of unknown origin. The IWW differed from the nation's leading labor organization, Samuel Gompers's American Federation of Labor. The AFL pooled the strength of highly skilled, better-paid craftspeople. For example, in the railroad industry, each craft, like the engineers, had a separate union, which in turn belonged to the AFL. The Wobblies, however, wanted everyone. Their idea was to gather all workers, whatever their skills, into "one big union." One big workers' army.

The IWW championed the left-outs, America's lowest paid, most needy and desperate workers. Among others, these included female textile workers in New England, migrant harvesters in California orchards, and blacks oppressed by Jim Crow. Yet few of the left-out workers lived such bleak lives as the lumberjacks. In American mythology, the lumberjack is an ax-swinging giant like Paul Bunyan. In reality, he lived in remote forest camps, housed in dark, dank, tar-paper shacks crawling with vermin. Underpaid, in debt to the company store, the lumberjack was a slave in all but name. Some company stores even went so far as to get him addicted to heroin and cocaine, sold on credit, to keep him in line. The Wobblies wanted the lumberjack, too.[36]

Together with his red membership card, a new Wobbly got a little red song-book with a motto printed on the cover: "To Fan the Flames of Discontent." The book had the words to some fifty songs. Sung at rallies, on picket lines, and in jails, these songs called for workers' solidarity. "There is Power in a Union," by the IWW's troubadour, Joe Hill, was a favorite.

> There is pow'r, there is pow'r
> In a band of workingmen,
> When they stand, hand in hand,
> That's a pow'r, that's a pow'r
> That must rule in ev'ry land—
> One Industrial Union Grand.[37]

Although the IWW fought for better wages and working conditions, it eventually wanted a revolution. By revolution, Haywood and other leaders meant taking over the nation's factories, mills, mines, banks, and railroads. Since there would be so many Wobblies, when the right time came they would chase the bosses away, and that would be that. Planners in the IWW thought that upon seeing workers in control of the economy, the army and police would just go along. Until then, however, Wobblies expected opposition from everyone who had a stake in the existing system.

They were right. Police broke up Wobbly meetings, arresting the speakers. Bosses fired Wobbly organizers and blacklisted them so no one else would hire them. Wobbly organizers ended up in ditches riddled with bullets. Even AFL craft unions refused to let Wobblies speak in their halls. Faced with such strong opposition, some members of the IWW favored "direct action." Like the anarchists, they saw guns and dynamite as "equalizers." Scores of "class enemies"—policemen, scabs, bosses—fell to the Wobblies' vengeance. Such violence threw President Roosevelt into a panic.

His reaction to one act of violence earned the scorn of millions who otherwise had no use for Wobblies. On December 30, 1905, as former Idaho governor Frank Steutenberg pulled the wooden slide that opened his front gate, a bomb exploded. The police quickly figured out the motive for the murder, or at least thought they did. Six years earlier, Steutenberg had broken a strike by the Western Federation of Miners, Haywood's union, with federal troops President McKinley sent at his request. Acting on a tip, detectives arrested Harry Orchard, a professional hit man. Under questioning, Orchard claimed Haywood and two aides, Charles Moyer and George Pettibone, had hired him to do the killing. After their arrest, prosecutors decided to try Haywood and his aides separately. Conviction meant the hangman's rope. The big fellow would go to trial first.

Normally, with pending trials, presidents keep their opinions to themselves. Roosevelt did not. He had already decided that the accused were guilty. Repeatedly, in letters to friends, he called them "thugs and murderers," "infamous creatures," and "scoundrels." Yet personal belief could never excuse what came next. In a letter to New York congressman James S. Sherman, he branded the three "undesirable citizens." Although it was supposedly a private letter, he made no effort to keep his opinion secret. A copy of the letter soon found its way into the newspapers.[38]

In effect, the president was using the prestige of his office, and the public's respect for him, to sway opinion on a life-and-death trial. Like most Wobbly haters, Roosevelt wanted a swift conviction, followed by a swift hanging. Big Bill understood this perfectly: "The President says that I am an undesirable citizen, the inference being that as such I should be put out of the way. His influence is all-powerful and his statement . . . will do more to prevent a fair trial than everything that has been said and done against me."[39]

Roosevelt had stirred up a hornet's nest. Nearly the entire socialist and trade-union movements accused him of playing dirty. Even Samuel Gompers questioned his old friend's fairness. But none was more critical than Eugene Debs. Denouncing the president as a "cruel and cowardly hypocrite," he noted that the Constitution protected every American, even a Wobbly. "Is this fair? Is it just? A square deal?" Debs asked in an open letter. "Is it not, in fact, Mr. President, cowardly to take such advantage of your high office to pronounce the guilt of three of your fellow citizens, who have not been tried and against whom nothing has been proved? . . . All we are asking and insisting upon is that our accused brothers shall have the protection of the law, a fair hearing and just verdict. . . ."[40]

Debs's attack was just the beginning. Every major city saw protest marches directed at Roosevelt personally. Over 50,000 marched through downtown Boston, denouncing the "legal lynching" in Idaho and chanting: "If Moyer and Haywood die; if Moyer and Haywood die,/Twenty million workingmen will know the reason why." In the largest demonstration, in New York City, some 100,000 marched up Fifth Avenue, the workers' "avenue of the enemies," carrying banners with inscriptions such as:

ROOSEVELT CAN SHOW HIS TEETH—
WE ARE NOT AFRAID.
WE STAND BY OUR BROTHERS IN IDAHO

In solidarity with them, many, including Harvard students, wore badges announcing I AM AN UNDESIRABLE CITIZEN. Stung by this explosion of outrage, Roosevelt became so cranky that Edith left him to eat his meals alone.[41]

He was just as cranky at the outcome of Haywood's trial. The chief of the defense team, Clarence Darrow, was a slouching, messy man with a gravelly voice. You would never know it by his appearance, but Darrow was a courtroom genius, the most famous defense attorney of the day. Yet he did not come cheap.

Hundreds of small donations from union members across the country, and not just the IWW, paid his $35,000 fee.[42]

Darrow trashed the prosecution's case. Proof? The only "proof" of Haywood's guilt, he said, was the word of Harry Orchard, an admitted liar, thief, and assassin who had been promised his life for turning state's evidence. In July 1907, the jury voted "not guilty," forcing the state to drop charges against Haywood's aides. "I suppose the jury was terrorized," Roosevelt fumed, refusing to admit that he might have been wrong. Orchard received life imprisonment, dying in 1954. To the end, he insisted that Haywood and his aides had put him up to the murder.[43]

In August 1906, as the IWW leaders awaited trial in Idaho, three companies of the all-black Twenty-fifth Infantry Regiment arrived at Fort Brown near Brownsville, Texas. Their mission was to replace a white unit and prevent Mexican smugglers from crossing the Rio Grande. These companies, totaling 167 men, were among the best units in the army. They included six winners of the Congressional Medal of Honor; another thirteen held certificates of merit for bravery. Many had served five to ten years in the ranks; one was a twenty-seven-year veteran. Several had fought beside the Rough Riders in Cuba.

Jim Crow stood tall in Brownsville. The presence of uniformed black men offended the town's white majority. Overnight, shops, saloons, and the town park sprouted signs reading NO NIGGERS AND NO DOGS ALLOWED. Local people scared themselves with imaginary images, expressed in a poem printed in the town newspaper:

> Our daughters murdered and defiled,
> Black fingers crooked around fair throat,
> The leering fiend—the tortured breath—
> Where's time for laggard red tape now,
> When moments may mean life or death?

With one voice, white Brownsville demanded that the army send the blacks away before they made trouble.[44]

Just after midnight on August 14, Brownsville awoke to the sound of gunfire. For ten minutes, a group of men, some in uniform, ran through the streets, shooting at streetlights and into windows. By the time the shooting stopped, a policeman lay wounded and a bartender lay dead. Empty cartridge cases from army-issue Springfield rifles littered the ground. At daybreak, Mayor Frederick J. Combe named a committee to look into the crimes. Witnesses said they heard black voices during the rampage, and saw unidentified black soldiers firing rifles. Immediately, the mayor sent a telegram to Roosevelt demanding action against the supposed killers.

Officers at Fort Brown had already taken action. Fearing trouble, company commanders had ordered an 8 P.M. curfew on the night of August 13. As shots rang out in a street near the fort, buglers blew the call to arms. Men sprang from their cots and assembled on the parade ground within five minutes, ready for action; a roll call showed everyone present. Meanwhile, officers unlocked the gun racks and inspected the rifles before giving them to the soldiers. None had been fired recently.[45]

Roosevelt ordered separate investigations by two high-ranking officers. Upon questioning, the men of the regiment denied any knowledge of the shooting. While accepting the statements of the white community as truthful, the officers took the soldiers' denials as a deliberate "conspiracy of silence." Even if innocent themselves, they were sticking together to protect guilty comrades, the investigators said.

What about the shooters wearing uniforms and the empty cartridge cases? Surely these proved that some soldiers had done the shooting and raced back to their barracks before the bugle sounded? Surely not!

The white unit the Twenty-fifth replaced had discarded piles of old clothes before leaving for its next posting. As for the cartridge cases, the Twenty-fifth had brought them from its last post, Fort Niobrara, Nebraska, where they had fired the bullets in target practice. Army units usually kept empty cartridges for reloading later. At Fort Brown, these lay in an open footlocker stored on a porch. Local boys made off with handfuls of them, selling them around town as souvenirs. Nobody has ever identified the shooters. Most likely, however, they were townsmen who planted the cartridges as "evidence" against the soldiers of the Twenty-fifth.[46]

Roosevelt could not believe the soldiers knew nothing about the shootings. Their claims of ignorance, he imagined, "proved" that they had planned the outrage, then carried it out with military precision. He warned that, unless someone confessed or revealed the culprits, all would pay the price. As commander in chief of the armed forces, he had the right to discharge any soldier at any time.

The soldiers could add nothing to their statements. So, on November 5, 1905, the day following congressional elections, Roosevelt discharged them "without honor." His order did more than leave 167 men jobless. It barred them from ever holding a government position, took away their pensions, and made them ineligible for old soldiers' homes. Dismissal meant almost certain poverty for the older men, who had devoted their lives to the army.

Roosevelt's action violated basic legal principles. The Fifth Amendment to the U.S. Constitution says "no person . . . may be deprived of life, liberty, or property without due process of law." Due process means that anyone accused of a crime is innocent until proven guilty in a fair trial. Moreover, American law holds individuals accountable for their actions alone, or for allowing others to commit a crime they know about in advance. By ignoring these principles, the president acted as judge, jury, and executioner. Without a trial, without defense lawyers examining witnesses under oath, he dismissed the soldiers without a shred of evidence. This is the only case of mass punishment, without trial, in the history of our military.

African-Americans reacted with shock and hurt. In a society that afforded them few opportunities, blacks took special pride in their military men. Deservedly so, for they had fought bravely in every war since the Revolution. The dismissals, then, came as a slap in the face by one they regarded as a friend. Although Booker T. Washington did not criticize Roosevelt publicly, he protested in private, asking him to reconsider the dismissals, but without success. Others spoke openly, at mass meetings in Washington and in the black press. Dr. W.E.B. Du Bois, a founder of the National Association for the Advancement of Colored People (NAACP), said of Roosevelt: "Without doubt he thought he was doing justice. The trouble is, and the crime lay, in the impulsive . . . judgment. Yet in this respect, he is not different from his fellows. He is an American. The pity of it is, we expected more."[47]

Justice won in the end. In 1970, historian John D. Weaver published *The Brownsville Raid.* Based on exacting research, his book convinced congressmen of the injustice. Two years later, the government gave all 167 dismissed men honorable discharges. President Richard Nixon signed a bill awarding Dorsie Willis, eighty-six, the group's last survivor, a payment of $25,000.

As for Theodore Roosevelt, he had no regrets, or at least said he had none. "Some of those men were bloody butchers; they ought to be hung. . . . It is my business and the business of nobody else," he told an audience. This outburst, however, may have been a cover for something else. As with other things that upset or embarrassed him, he did not mention the Brownsville affair in his *Auto-biography*. Roosevelt, apparently, could not admit, perhaps even to himself, that he might have done wrong. In time, as we will see, he would make amends and earn forgiveness from the African-American community. Even so, the dismissals of the Twenty-fifth Infantry Regiment were a terrible injustice.[48]

7

"CONSERVATION IS A GREAT MORAL ISSUE"

Of all the questions which can come before this nation, short of the actual preservation of its existence in a great war, there is none which compares in importance with the great central task of leaving this land even a better land for our descendants than it is for us, and training them . . . to inhabit the land and pass it on. Conservation is a great moral issue, for it involves the patriotic duty of insuring the safety and continuation of the nation.

—THEODORE ROOSEVELT

If we remember Theodore Roosevelt for nothing else, his efforts in safeguarding our natural heritage would guarantee his place in the front rank of our country's heroes. To understand what he did and why, we must see America as Europeans first saw it.

Our America barely resembles the land they found. To begin with, it was a land blessed with trees. On days when the wind was just right, sailors in the 1600s smelled the northern pine forests while far out at sea, hours before sighting land. Vast forests of pine, hickory, oak, chestnut, walnut, and evergreen stretched from the Atlantic coast westward to the horizon and beyond. The treetops, a traveler wrote in 1751, were "so close to one another for many miles together . . . it seemed almost as if the sun had never shone on the ground since the creation." Those trees were also larger than most of ours today, for they grew undisturbed, reaching their full natural size over the centuries. Travelers reported white pines two hundred feet tall and sycamore trunks fifteen feet in diameter. Grapevines thick as a man's thighs entwined the trunks, growing to the very treetops.[1]

Wildlife abounded. In colonial times, coastal waters had oysters the size of dinner plates and crabs big enough to feed four men. Lobsters were so plentiful that slaves on Southern plantations complained of having them at every meal. Inland, streams of clear, cold water churned with "fishes as bigg as children of 2 years old." The land teemed with big, and sometimes dangerous, animals: grizzly bear, wolf, moose, elk. During their exploration of the Louisiana Territory, from

1804 to 1806, Meriwether Lewis and William Clark reported uncountable herds of deer and antelope.[2]

The buffalo, or American bison, ruled the Great Plains west of the Mississippi River. Buffalo moved in vast herds, feasting on the succulent grasses. In May 1871 Major Richard Irving Dodge set out in a wagon across southwestern Kansas. In one place, he reported, the country "appeared one mass of buffaloes, moving slowly northward." The herd "was about five days passing a given point, or no less than fifty miles deep. From the top of Pawnee Rock I could see from six to ten miles in almost every direction. The whole space was covered with buffaloes, looking at a distance like one compact mass. . . ." Dodge did not try to calculate the herd's size. Other travelers, however, thought some herds had upward of two million animals, and these were nothing special. A really large herd might form a tightly packed mass larger than the state of Rhode Island.[3]

Birds lived in numbers that seem incredible today. Travelers described flocks of wild turkeys, many standing three feet tall and weighing up to fifty pounds. In Pennsylvania, "clouds of owls rose out of the valleys" on their evening hunts. Yet nothing compared to the passenger pigeon, the most numerous bird in recorded history, perhaps of all time. New Englanders reported flocks of "millions of millions" of these graceful, long-tailed birds. Some flocks took fourteen hours to pass a given point and "shaddowed the skie from us." Travelers noted "pigeon cities," or nesting sites, forty miles long by two miles wide, containing countless adults and hatchlings. Ornithologist John James Audubon saw such a city in Kentucky in the year 1813:

> The dung lay several inches deep, covering the whole extent of the roosing-place, like a bed of snow. Many trees two feet in diameter, I observed, were broken off at no great distance from the ground; and the branches of many of the largest and tallest had given way, as if the forest had been swept by a tornado. . . . As [more] birds arrived and passed over me, I felt a current of air that surprised me. . . . Here and there perches gave way under the weight with a crash, and, falling to the ground, destroyed hundreds of the birds beneath. . . . It was a scene of uproar and confusion. I found it quite useless to speak, or even to shout to those who were nearest to me.[4]

Native Americans treated the land with a care and understanding gained through centuries of experience. The forest tribes east of the Mississippi River used little timber, except for dugout canoes, lodge poles, cooking fires, and arrows. Their trails crisscrossed the forests, but were narrow, only inches wide. Although they made fires in the forest, they carefully avoided causing forest fires. Native Americans set surface fires to clear leaves, seedlings, and fallen branches. Yet their fires were not large enough, or hot enough, to harm the large, healthy trees. Controlled burning during what whites called "Indian summer" cleared the ground, fertilizing the soil with nutrient-rich ashes. This, in turn, allowed Indians to grow larger crops and produced more grass for the deer they hunted.[5]

Yet hunting was more than getting a meal; it was a religious experience. Native Americans believed that all life is sacred, a gift from the Master of Life, or Great Spirit, called God by whites. When they hunted, it was done sorrowfully, prayerfully, and with respect for their prey. About the year 1760, for example, an English trader met some Ojibways on a bear hunt. After the kill, he reported, the hunters took the animal's head "in their hands, stroking and kissing it several times, begging a thousand pardons for taking away her life," because they were hungry. To make sure they had not offended an animal's spirit, hunters would put a tobacco pipe in its mouth, then blow smoke down its throat in gratitude to its spirit. Indians considered tobacco sacred, since its smoke gladdened the Master of Life. They also apologized to plants before the harvest, explaining that they must eat them to live, and sprinkled powdered tobacco on the fields afterward.[6]

Whites thought differently. Europeans came from a continent where kings, nobles, and churches owned much of the land. Cutting timber and hunting were usually privileges of the few; offenders faced fines, jail, and even death. In some countries, those who gathered fallen branches illegally might have a hand cut off or an eye put out by the public executioner. America, however, had more wood and wildlife than the old world. Whites arriving in the New World saw its natural resources as limitless. In other words, they saw nothing sacred about nature, believing it existed for the benefit of people. Nature was so bountiful, it seemed, that no matter what men did, there would always be more.

The forest, to whites, was both an enemy and a resource. A place of constant danger, it held fierce animals with teeth and claws, and warlike people with tomahawks and bows and arrows. Before a seed went into the ground, at least part of "the ocean of trees" had to go. According to Benjamin Franklin, "By clearing America of Woods," settlers were "Scouring our Planet," cleansing it in the cause of progress. However, the nation also needed vast quantities of wood for building, warmth, light, and cooking. From potash, made by burning hardwood trees, it produced soap, glass, gunpowder, and textile bleach.[7]

Working with his family, an experienced man could fell an acre of trees a week. Sometimes he chopped down tall trees just to get at the fruit growing on their branches. He might also kill trees by "girdling," stripping a wide ring of bark from the trunk to prevent the sap from rising. Amazingly, farmers would clear large areas by deliberately setting forest fires, which burned until they ran out of fuel or reached a natural barrier such as a river. In the summer of 1781, for example, the French army set out across New York to join George Washington's forces. As they marched, the French often saw smoke clouds from raging forest fires. An officer wrote that the fires "caused no excitement at all among the nearby Americans, whose country is full of forests. Sometimes they even congratulate themselves on having a big conflagration, as it saves them the trouble of cutting down the trees to clear the land."[8]

The Industrial Revolution increased the demand for wood. Laying railroad tracks required millions of ties to hold the rails in place. Even after coal burners appeared, locomotives and steamboats used vast quantities of wood. In the 1850s, American locomotives burned three million cords of wood and steamboats another four million cords a year. (A cord is a pile of wood eight feet long, four feet high, and four feet wide.) Each day, a mass-circulation newspaper used paper made from thousands of trees.

Lumber barons became the Carnegies and Rockefellers of the forests. Men like Frederick Weyerhaeuser controlled millions of acres of timberlands. Instead of selecting individual trees, as the Indians had done, they "clear-cut" the forest, felling every tree, whatever its size. As the Eastern forests fell, they moved their operations to the forests bordering the Great Lakes, then to the South, and finally to the Pacific Coast. In Oregon, Washington, and California, the lumber barons found redwoods, the oldest, largest living things on the planet. By the time Roosevelt became president, America's original forest cover had shrunk from an estimated 850 million acres to 500 million acres. Speaking of the forest, a lumberman confessed: "It was almost a crime against Nature to cut it, but we lumbermen were never concerned with crimes against Nature. We heard only the demand for lumber, more lumber and better lumber."[9]

Deforestation had devastating effects. Tree roots absorb water, slowly

releasing it into the atmosphere throughout the year. Without tree cover, melting snow and spring rains made rivers go haywire. Floods washed away farms, wrecked towns, and carried millions of tons of fertile topsoil to the sea. In summer, the topsoil, exposed to the sun's heat, dried to powder and blew away. This resulted in "dust bowls," wide areas subject to ferocious dust storms. Fires unlike any ever seen broke out, too. For clear-cutting did not clear away every bit of wood, just the valuable timber. When the lumberjacks finished, they left behind vast amounts of "slash"—unusable tree trunks, stumps, branches, leaves, brush. In healthy forests, Indians had gotten rid of these each year with controlled fires. When lightning struck, the fires it started usually spared large, mature trees. Clear-cut areas, however, became tinderboxes.

These tinderboxes bred firestorms. A firestorm happens when hot air from a big fire rises fast, creating a vacuum at ground level. The vacuum sucks in fresh air from surrounding areas, making the fire even hotter and creating blowtorch-like winds. In 1871, what local people called "Judgment Day" struck near Peshtigo, Wisconsin. A slash fire near a sawmill exploded into a firestorm that spread to a

Pacific Coast lumberjacks taking a break, 1908. Intensive logging operations threatened to destroy the nation's forests within a generation, laying the land bare and open to erosion.

The results of a buffalo hunt, Montana, 1879. Once numbered in the tens of millions, by 1900, fewer than one thousand wild buffalo remained in the United States.

million acres of nearby woodland and farms. The heat grew so intense that trees burst into flame at once, and wind-driven flames leaped across the treetops. Flocks of birds fell dead from the sky. Taken by surprise, perhaps 1,500 people died in the flames or suffocated in the smoke, making Peshtigo the deadliest forest fire in American history. In 1881, a fire in Michigan killed 169 people. The Hinckley fire of 1894 claimed 418 lives in Minnesota. Theodore Roosevelt would have to face the economic, environmental, and safety concerns facing America's forests at the turn of the twentieth century.[10]

Americans waged war on wildlife, too. Since colonial times, frontiersmen had shot game for food and to get rid of dangerous animals. Whenever settlers arrived in an area, dangerous animals quickly disappeared as a result of hunting. Other animals were worth money. Thus, in the Northwest, fur trappers nearly exterminated the beaver.

Yet nothing compared to the slaughter of the buffalo. For Plains Indian tribes, this animal supplied everything they needed except drinking water and wood for tepee poles. In 1870, a Pennsylvania tannery discovered how to turn buffalo hide into leather for use in drive belts; that is, belts that connect the stream engines that drive factory machinery. Buffalo hides, thicker than cowhides, made stronger, more long-lasting belts; nowadays we use rubberized belting. Overnight, the suddenly valuable buffalo hides brought $3.50 apiece, more than a factory worker earned in a day. White hunters wiped out entire herds, skinning the bodies and leaving the plains littered with rotting carcasses. To open the land for settlement, the army encouraged the slaughter. When the tribes resisted, starvation and repeating rifles drove them onto reservations. A Sioux leader, Sitting Bull, called the slaughter "a death-wind for my people," killing not only buffalo but ending a way of life.[11]

Americans killed birds for fun and profit. Shooters, out for a day in the country or by the seashore, bet on how many they could kill within a set time. Some brought down birds one by one, as dogs flushed them from cover or they glided on the water. Killing a swan, a hunter reported, "is like shooting an angel." Others opened up on flocks with shotguns, which scattered pellets, striking many birds with one shot. A lighthouse keeper on an island off the Maine coast described the effect on tiny sandpipers: "They form flocks and sit on the shore. Gunners come here and slaughter them awfully, for it is no trick to fire into a big flock of them and wound a large number. After the gunners have been there, my children bring in many wounded ones, some with broken wings or legs shot off, or eyes shot out. . . ."[12]

A feather for my lady's hat. Driven by the demands of women's fashions, by the early twentieth century, hunters threatened to wipe out whole species of birds for their colorful feathers.

Professional hunters made a living from wild birds. During the nesting season, they collected eggs, destroying entire flocks by killing the next generation. Strings of robins, priced at five cents a dozen, hung in food markets; ladies baked them into pies. Worse, by the 1880s, some five million birds were dying each year in the name of "fashion." Women adorned their hair, hats, and dresses with feathers, even entire birds. "Miss———," a newspaper noted, "looked extremely well in white, with a whole nest of sparkling, scintillating birds in her hair. . . ." Although any colorful bird would do, ladies favored the long white plumes of herons and snowy egrets. At thirty-five dollars an ounce, egret plumes were worth twice as much as an ounce of gold.[13]

Incredibly, the most plentiful bird, the passenger pigeon, suffered the most. Hunters took its eggs by the bushel and pillaged its nests for squabs. These young, unfledged pigeons were considered a gourmet delicacy. They netted adults by the hundreds at a time for food or fat, which manufacturers melted down to make an oil used in soap. The all-time record was 3,500 pigeons caught in a single spring of a net. In Michigan, netters sold 1,107,800,066 pigeons within a few weeks. By 1871, the once-great flocks were rapidly disappearing. The last passenger pigeon, Martha, died of old age in the Cincinnati, Ohio, zoo in 1914.[14]

Theodore Roosevelt's interest in conservation grew out of his experiences in the Dakota Bad Lands. When he moved to Elkhorn Ranch after Alice Lee's death in 1884, he found evidence of the recent buffalo slaughter everywhere. He wrote:

After the hunt. A mound of buffalo skulls at the railway depot in Denver, Colorado. These skulls were shipped east and ground into bonemeal for fertilizer.

> No sight is more common on the plains than that of a bleached buffalo skull; and their countless numbers attest the abundance of the animal at a time not so very long past. On those portions where the herds made their last stand, the carcasses, dried in the clear, high air, or the mouldering skeletons, abound. . . . These carcasses were in sight from every hillock, often lying over the ground so thickly that several score could be seen at once. A ranchman who . . . had made a journey of a thousand miles across northern Montana, along the Milk River, told me that, to use his own expression, during the whole distance he was never out of sight of a dead buffalo, and never in sight of a live one.

Yet Roosevelt called the

slaughter "a blessing," because it was "the only way of solving the Indian question." Without killing off the buffalo, it would have been impossible to force Native Americans onto reservations. Anyhow, animals such as elk and grizzlies were still plentiful.[15]

When Roosevelt returned for a short stay after the birth of Ted Jr. in 1887, he was shocked at what he found—or did *not* find. In less than three years, the big-game animals had nearly vanished from the Badlands. Overgrazing, pasturing more cattle than the land could support, had removed the carpet of grass in many places, leaving the ground bare and ripe for dust storms. Cow dung had so poisoned the roots of the wild plum bushes that they no longer bore fruit. Mud and manure clogged once-sparkling streams. Clearly, our natural heritage was not limitless. It was disappearing fast, thanks to human greed and stupidity. Unless something was done to save it, this heritage would be lost forever.[16]

People hunt for the same reason they climb mountains, walk tightropes, or skydive. Hunting is a personal challenge, a way of testing one's skill and courage. The true hunter, Roosevelt said, knows that, by going after, say, grizzly bear with a rifle, he is going into harm's way. In doing so, he must obey certain rules, such as following a wounded animal to end its suffering. Yet those he branded "swinish game-butchers" killed any animals they safely could, including the young. Finally, Roosevelt thought, the true hunter's joy came not from killing, but from the total wilderness experience. The hunter felt "the joy of the horse well ridden and the rifle well held; for him the long hours of toil and hardship, resolutely endured, and well crowned at the end with triumph." Still, some modern readers may wonder how a person who loved animals, as Roosevelt did, could enjoy shooting them.[17]

Back in New York, Roosevelt met with a few like-minded friends, "sportsmen" who enjoyed hunting as he did. Together they formed the Boone and Crockett Club, named for two of Roosevelt's frontier heroes, Daniel Boone and Davy Crockett. He was elected club president, and under his leadership the club attracted influential men in business, politics, and science. Its list of honorary members included the most honored military men of the day. Generals William Tecumseh Sherman and Philip Sheridan had led Union armies during the Civil War and, later, during the Indian wars. Men like these had "pull"; that is, they knew people in high places, people who could get things done.

At first, the club aimed only at preserving big-game animals for hunting. But then club members became equally concerned with habitat, the environment in which animals live. Experience had taught them that each type of habitat—forest, plain, mountain, marsh, seashore, desert—is a unique world in which everything depends on everything else. Disturb one element, such as the trees, and all suffer. Roosevelt practically worshiped trees. Walking alone in a forest, silent save for the calls of unseen birds and the wind rustling the leaves, felt like a religious experience to him. Like the Native American, he might have said that a forest brought him closer to the Master of Life than anything else.

Starting in the 1870s, as the giant corporations took shape, naturalists', hunters', and fishermen's clubs urged state and local governments to protect the environment. Unlike these clubs, however, the Boone and Crockett had friends in Washington. Early in his political career, Roosevelt took time out from his duties at the Civil Service Commission to lead its lobbying campaign. Thus, in 1891 Congress passed the Forest Reserve Act, allowing the president to set aside forest reserves from public lands. Reserves were just that, areas that the government could never sell or allow logging in. Three years later, with Roosevelt again taking the lead, the club got Congress to pass the Park Protection Act. Created in 1872, Yellowstone National Park in Wyoming, the nation's first, was being trashed by preparations to build a railroad through its most scenic areas. By halting these activities, the act saved a national treasure for future generations.

Later, as governor of New York, Roosevelt made important environmental reforms. For starters, he gave the legislature a lesson in ecology. Every New Yorker, even city folk, had a stake in the state's forests, he said. Comparing them to immense sponges, he described how their loss would dry up the sources of the rivers, and with them wells and reservoirs. To avoid such disasters, he banned logging in certain parts of the Adirondack and Catskill mountains. To safeguard wildlife, he got the legislature to pass a law against jacklighting, or shooting animals blinded by artificial light at night. The law also banned deer hounding; that is, driving deer into water so hunters could shoot them from boats. The thought of destroying an entire species saddened Roosevelt. "When I hear of the destruction of a species," he wrote, "I feel just as if the works of some great writer had perished."[18]

When Roosevelt became president, for the only time in its history America had a naturalist in the White House. Despite his love of big-game hunting, the leading naturalists of the day saw Roosevelt as one of their own. They dedicated their books to him, and he invited them to come to the White House to talk about animals. If he could not do that now and then, he said through clenched teeth, "I-SHOULD-DIE!!" Naturalists regarded him as an authority on North American big-game animals, even named a newly discovered type of elk—*Cervus roosevelti*—in his honor. Always interested in birds, he wrote magazine articles on those of the Washington, D.C., area. The president once burst into a cabinet meeting with wonderful news: "Gentlemen, do you know what happened this morning? I just saw a chestnut-sided warbler, and this is only February!" Another time, he claimed to have seen passenger pigeons. If so, it was probably the last of them in the wild.[19]

Roosevelt tied the protection of our natural heritage to safeguarding democracy itself. Now and in the future, he insisted, natural resources were the basis of the nation's wealth and position in the world. Roosevelt believed that those resources belong to all Americans, not to the "special interests." Just as the people, through their government, must control big business for the common good, so must they control the nation's natural resources. As he explained: "The rights of the public to the natural resources outweigh private rights, and must be given first consideration."[20]

Guided by this belief, Roosevelt did more to defend America's natural heritage than all the earlier presidents combined. Within days of taking office, he advanced a bold four-part program. That program involved land reclamation, forest preservation, wildlife protection, and safeguarding historic sites.

Shortly before Roosevelt became president, Nevada Representative (later Senator) Francis G. Newlands urged Congress to help the Southwest. In this most thinly settled part of the country, the problem was lack of water. For much of the year, rain did not fall; Arizona, after all, is Spanish for "dry region." But when the rains did come, much of the water quickly evaporated or ran off into streams. The result was millions of acres of barren, unproductive land. Newlands sponsored a Reclamation Act allowing the federal government to fund irrigation projects on public lands, then sell the reclaimed lands to farmers and ranchers. Congress, however, had little interest in the scheme.

The new president was *very* interested in it. With superb political skill, he persuaded the Republican leadership not to oppose the Reclamation Act. In June 1902, it became law. Thirty reclamation projects got under way almost immediately in the West. Construction crews built dams across rivers, capturing their waters in artificial lakes; hundreds of miles of irrigation ditches and tunnels then brought water to parched fields. Even by today's standards, these dams are marvels of engineering. At 280 feet high, Roosevelt Dam on the Salt River in Arizona was the largest ever built in America until then; Lake Roosevelt extends twenty-five miles behind it. These projects turned wastelands into farmlands, growing alfalfa, sugar beets, and fruits. By the end of Roosevelt's second term, the acreage under irrigation in the United States had gone from little more than twenty thousand to over three million.[21]

Since pioneer days, said Roosevelt, "the American had but one thought about a tree, and that was to cut it down." To change that attitude, he used the bully pulpit to preach against deforestation. The president laced his annual messages to Congress with warnings about cutting down trees as if there were no tomorrow. Tomorrow is only a day away; it always comes! It came to China, North Africa, and the Mediterranean countries of Europe. There, over centuries, he noted, deforestation exposed the land to the ravages of wind and rain, heat and cold. It was no accident that people there were among the poorest on Earth.[22]

In his crusade to save the forests, Roosevelt had a brilliant ally. Born to a wealthy Connecticut family in 1865, Gifford Pinchot was a tall noodle of a man with a bushy mustache and a high-pitched voice. Like the president, he practically worshiped trees. Since America had no school of forestry, as a young man he studied in France, where government schools treated forests as a scientific subject. In 1898, while the war in Cuba raged, Pinchot became head of the Division of Forestry, a branch of the Department of Agriculture. To manage the nation's forest reserves, he recruited the first federal forest rangers. Pinchot had a golden rule: prevent fires at all costs. Thus, rangers put out fires, cut down dead trees, and planted seedlings to replace losses and absorb rainwater.

Pinchot thought the Forest Reserve Act of 1891 had not gone far enough. Under it, Presidents Harrison, Cleveland, and McKinley had placed fifty million acres of timberland in the reserves. Now Roosevelt went further. By executive order, he added millions more acres, largely in the West. His actions, however, angered the timber barons' friends in Congress. In the House of Representatives, "Uncle Joe" Cannon declared Congress would not spend another penny "for scenery." In 1907, Cannon slyly tacked an amendment to an appropriation bill for the Department of Agriculture. Although the amendment prevented the president from enlarging the forest reserves in six Western states, he knew

Roosevelt dared not veto the entire bill. The president knew it, too. But he had no intention of giving in, either.[23]

Secretly, Roosevelt had Pinchot make a quick survey of lands best suited to become forest reserves. Two days before signing the appropriation bill, he signed executive orders adding a further 16 million acres to the reserves. He had tricked the tricksters, and they were furious. "When the friends of the special interests in the Senate . . . woke up," the president wrote, "they . . . did handsprings in their wrath." During his seven years in office, Roosevelt added a total of 150 million acres of timberland to the reserves, tripling the area set aside by all previous presidents. It was an area larger than France, Belgium, and the Netherlands combined.[24]

The president made his first move to protect wildlife in 1903, after ornithologist Frank M. Chapman told him about Pelican Island. A tiny sliver of land in Florida's Indian River, it had large colonies of pelican, egret, heron, and other waterbirds. Plume hunters had invaded the island, slaughtering birds by the thousands. The federal government seemed powerless to stop them. Apart from the national parks, it did not protect wildlife anywhere in the country. Roosevelt, however, was eager to turn the island into the nation's first wildlife refuge. So, when congressional penny-pinchers balked, he went ahead anyhow. "Is there any law that will prevent me from declaring Pelican Island a Federal Bird Reservation?" he asked aides. Told there was not, he replied, "Very well, then I so declare it." And that was that! By the time he left office, Roosevelt had created another fifty wildlife refuges scattered across the country, even in Puerto Rico, Alaska, and Hawaii.[25]

What about the buffalo? By 1902, wild buffalo had disappeared everywhere in the United States except for fifty in Colorado and twenty-two in Yellowstone

TR and Gifford Pinchot inspect the Mississippi River shoreline from a boat, October 1907. Thanks to their commitment and drive, millions of acres of timberland were spared from lumberjacks' axes and saws.

Paul Kroegel, the first game warden of Pelican Island, Florida, and a friend.

National Park. Fewer than nine hundred others were in private animal collections and in the New York Zoological Gardens, also called the Bronx Zoo. Three years later, members of Roosevelt's old Boone and Crockett Club, wealthy Easterners all, organized the American Bison Society with Roosevelt as its honorary president. Attitudes toward the buffalo had changed since the mass killings began thirty years before. Most Easterners now lived in crowded cities, often working at dull, tedious jobs. Even the wealthy, said a friend of Roosevelt's, were "bored to death with rank luxuries and soft living." Thus, society members believed, saving the buffalo would encourage city folk to go west as tourists. Seeing the lord of the plains in its natural habitat, as the pioneers had done, would renew their zest for life, making them better people and truer patriots.[26]

At the society's urging, the Bronx Zoo gave fifteen buffalo to the federal government. Placed on the Wichita Mountains Wildlife Refuge in Oklahoma, these multiplied rapidly, proving that an animal could return from the brink of extinction. Native Americans were jubilant. When the buffalo arrived by train, Quanah Parker, a famous Comanche chief, welcomed them at the depot. Mounted braves pointed out the animals to their children, who until then had only heard about them but never seen one in the flesh. Soon afterward, the government created the National Bison Range in Montana and buffalo refuges in South Dakota and Nebraska. In the year 2000, roughly 11,000 buffalo lived on government lands. Ranchers had around 200,000 more, with about 40,000 slaughtered each year for the meat industry. Although coarser and darker than beef, buffalo meat is healthier for humans, with far less cholesterol and fat than beef.[27]

The United States had five national parks when Roosevelt took office: Yellowstone, Yosemite, Sequoia, Mount Rainier, General Grant. He persuaded

Congress to add five more. Today, there are fifty-two national parks. Each year, millions of American and foreign visitors marvel at the glories of nature in these parks. Created in 1948, and located in the North Dakota Bad Lands, Theodore Roosevelt National Park honors the memory of the area's best-known citizen.

By establishing the first national monuments, Roosevelt helped save places of unique historical or cultural value. In the late 1800s, Native American relics became highly valued "collectibles." Some people had large collections of their jewelry, pottery, costumes, and tools. To get these relics, dealers dug up sacred burial grounds and looted prehistoric sites such as the cliff dwellings at Mesa Verde, Colorado. Others scoured Revolutionary and Civil War battlefields for rusting weapons, spent bullets, and discarded equipment. Denouncing these "vandals," in 1906 the president persuaded Congress to pass the National Monuments Act to protect historic sites. The act also included natural wonders, such as caves, cactus deserts, and sand dunes. Among these are the Devil's Tower in Wyoming, Arizona's Petrified Forest, and California's Muir Woods, a stand of ancient redwoods named for Roosevelt's friend and naturalist John Muir.

The Grand Canyon, in Arizona, is high on the list of the world's natural wonders. Flowing at speeds of up to twenty miles an hour, the Colorado River carries masses of stone and earth through the canyon every day. Over the ages, this immense "grinding machine" has scoured a gash in the earth a mile deep in places, over 10 miles across, and 280 miles in length. Early in the twentieth century, developers planned to build huge hotels along the canyon's south rim, the most scenic area.

The president had nothing against hotel keepers as such. What troubled him was the way they meant to deface a natural marvel for private

To boost the cause of conservation, TR visited national parks accompanied by photographers. Here, he poses at the rim of a cliff overlooking a valley in Yosemite National Park in the Sierra Nevada Mountains east of San Francisco, California.

TR and friends stand before one of the giant sequoia trees, the oldest living things on Earth, in Yosemite National Park, 1903. The famous naturalist John Muir stands on the president's left.

gain. In May 1903, he spoke out against this special interest. Standing on the south rim, he said:

> I hope you will not have a building of any kind . . . to mar the wonderful grandeur, the sublimity, the great loneliness and beauty of the canyon. Leave it as it is. You can not improve on it. The ages have been at work on it, and man can only mar it. What you can do is to keep it for your children, your children's children, and for all who come after you, as one of the great sights which every American . . . should see. We have gotten past the stage, my fel-

low citizens, when we are to be pardoned if we treat any part of our country as something to be skinned for two or three years for the use of the present generation, whether it is the forest, the water, the scenery. Whatever it is, handle it so that your children's children will get the benefit of it.

Yet, when he asked Congress to make the canyon a national park, it refused. The president would not take no for an answer. Defiantly, he declared 800,000 acres of canyon land a national monument. In all, he was the driving force behind the creation of eighteen national monuments. We have over a hundred today.[28]

Roosevelt had every reason to be proud of his achievements. When he took office, there was a real chance that we would lose our natural heritage. His main accomplishment lay not in the acres of woodland or the number of animals he saved, but in the way he used the bully pulpit to persuade fellow Americans to rise above the interests of the moment for the sake of future generations. Gifford Pinchot said it best: "The greatest work that Theodore Roosevelt did for the United States, the great fact which will give his influence vitality and power long after we shall have gone to our reward . . . is the fact that he changed the attitude of the American people toward conserving the natural resources."[29]

8

THE YOUNG GIANT
OF THE WEST

Is America a weakling, to shrink from the world work of the great powers? No. The young giant of the West stands on a continent and clasps the crest of an ocean in either hand. Our nation, glorious in youth and strength, looks into the future with eager eyes and rejoices as a strong man to run a race.

—THEODORE ROOSEVELT

Our presidents play two roles, each defined by the U.S. Constitution. As chief executive, they "execute"—enforce—federal law and shape domestic policy together with Congress, the lawmaking branch of government. In their second role, they manage the nation's relations with foreign countries. Presidents set foreign policy, appoint ambassadors, and make treaties with the advice and consent of the Senate. To defend the nation, they are commander in chief of the armed forces. Although only Congress may declare war, often presidents have ordered military action with its approval, but without a formal declaration of war. In emergencies, they have sent American forces into action first, asking for congressional approval afterward. Congress always has the final say, since it alone can vote to spend tax money for the military.

At the time of President McKinley's death, America still followed the first president's ideas on foreign relations. Before retiring in 1796, George Washington issued his Farewell Address. In it, he urged Americans "to steer clear of permanent Alliances with any part of the foreign world." We should trade with foreign nations, of course, but not meddle in their internal affairs or take sides in their quarrels. Yet the Industrial Revolution changed not only America, but also its place in the world. Overseas trade had skyrocketed since Washington's day. Theodore Roosevelt, we recall, wanted a larger navy to protect the nation's overseas markets and sources of raw materials. Already faced with unrest at home, the new president also had to define the nation's role in a world very different from Washington's.

Europe's "Great Powers," rich, modern nations with large armed forces, were carving out empires in the world's underdeveloped areas. In Asia, France had seized Vietnam and Cambodia. Great Britain ruled India, Burma, and Malaya. The Dutch held the East Indies, today's Indonesia. In China, England, Germany, and Russia held "spheres of influence," entire provinces controlled by their settlers, merchants, officials, soldiers, and police. This meant, for example, that a European charged with a crime against a Chinese was tried in a European court under European laws, but on Chinese soil. Meanwhile, the "Scramble for Africa" raged, as nearly the entire continent became European colonies. Still dissatisfied, the Great Powers constantly sought more overseas territory, often at one another's expense. Sometimes colonial disputes brought them to the brink of war.

That the world was becoming more dangerous did not surprise Roosevelt, who had always been keenly interested in foreign affairs. Yet, however dangerous the world, the president believed America could not retreat into isolation. For Roosevelt, peace and prosperity at home went hand in hand with moral obligation to the larger world. Nevertheless, that did not mean Roosevelt wanted a European-style empire. He saw no reason for Americans to have large, permanent colonies in foreign lands; their own country, in 1900, still had plenty of room for settlers in the West. Nor did he want to keep Cuba and the Philippines, which Spain had been forced to give up to the United States in 1898. What Roosevelt wanted was naval bases, places where the warships that protected American trade could stop for fuel and repairs. Moreover, Roosevelt insisted, "civilized" nations like America had a duty to the less fortunate. Certain peoples and regions of the world were "backward" by American standards, he noted. America must educate the "backward" peoples, improve their education systems, and give them law and order. He explained that "we should train them for self-government as rapidly as possible, and then leave them free to decide their own fate."[1] Yet, until backward peoples proved able to stand by themselves, they must be "uplifted" whether they liked it or not. Yes, uplifted even if it meant shooting some of them in the process.

In dealing with foreign powers, Roosevelt aimed at keeping the peace. This may seem odd, given his enthusiasm for the Spanish-American War and the popular image of him as a chest-pounding bully. While Roosevelt often praised the "virtues" of fighting in a good cause, his actions as president were always more cautious than his words. Roosevelt was a gifted diplomat, able to bring opponents together, as he did during the coal strike. It was the same with foreign powers. In one crisis after another, he tried to get them to settle their differences without bloodshed. For as a practical man, he wanted to get things done as efficiently as possible, and that meant avoiding costly wars.

By the time Roosevelt moved into the White House, he had matured as a man. Through his experiences in Cuba and the responsibilities of the presidency, he came to realize that war is a messy way of solving problems. "I abhor unjust war," Roosevelt would write in his *Autobiography*. "I abhor injustice and bullying by the strong at the expense of the weak, whether among nations or individuals. I abhor violence and bloodshed. I believe that war should never be resorted to when, or so long as, it is honorably possible to avoid it." No responsible leader of today would question this view of war.[2]

President Roosevelt spoke softly in public, even cautioned aides about talking disrespectfully of foreign powers, so as not to give offense. However, he insisted, weakness encouraged attack rather than avoided it. If pushed, he made it clear that he would push back harder; Roosevelt never bluffed about using the big stick of military force. Although keeping the military strong was expensive, he thought it a bargain if it avoided war while protecting American interests. Roosevelt aimed, he said, "to keep America in trim, so that fighting her shall be too expensive and dangerous a task to likely be undertaken by anybody." Nowadays we would say that he believed in "deterrence."[3] Despite his abhorrence of violence, Roosevelt would take out his big stick to pursue a costly war in the Philippines.

For all that most Americans knew about the Philippine Islands, they could have been on another planet. When the war with Spain over Cuba began, President McKinley himself had trouble finding them on a map. Some Americans imagined that "spotted people" and "striped people with zebra signs upon them" inhabited these distant islands. Yet, in their desire for freedom, Filipinos were no different from Americans. Conquered by Spain three centuries earlier, they had always resented foreign rule. Demanding independence, patriots led by Emilio Aguinaldo, the son of a wealthy landed family, rebelled against Spain. Defeated time and again, Aguinaldo believed that Commodore Dewey's victory at Manila Bay (see Chapter 4) would lead to his country's freedom.[4]

He was wrong. Like Roosevelt, McKinley believed "backward" peoples must eventually rule themselves. But until that time came, perhaps in fifty years or a

Emilio Aguinaldo (seated third from right) and other Filipino insurgent leaders, 1900.

century, he insisted that America must govern Filipinos "as our fellow-men for whom Christ also died." Besides, if American forces just sailed away after defeating Spain, he feared the islands would fall to Germany or Japan, growing military and industrial powers that also wanted them. The Philippines, finally, would provide naval bases from which to protect America's growing trade with Asia.[5]

Diplomats signed the Treaty of Paris ending the Spanish-American War on December 10, 1898, a month after Roosevelt won the governorship of New York. By its terms, Spain ceded Puerto Rico and Guam, a tiny Pacific island, to the United States. Cuba became independent, but American troops would remain there until it had a stable government. In return for $20 million, the Philippine Islands became the property of the United States.

The Treaty of Paris stunned Filipinos. By it, they said, America had betrayed its own ideals. Once ruled by a foreign power, Great Britain, the American colonies had waged a brutal war for independence. America's struggle had come to embody the yearnings for freedom of oppressed peoples the world over. Now it had "bought" an entire nation thousands of miles from its shores.

Another war began. For Filipinos, it remains their war for independence, a

Dead Filipino insurgents lay in the trench where they fell, killed by American artillery and rifle fire, 1899.

sacred struggle for liberty. In America, as it raged, imperialists called it the Philippine Insurrection; that is, a legal struggle against rebels and bandits. Today, most historians blame the war on McKinley and his advisers. Aguinaldo had begun by loving the United States, they note. Before the shooting began, he showed that love in his design for his nation's flag. Its colors are still red, white, and blue.

Although Aguinaldo's army was no match for the Americans in open battle, this was no "splendid little war," as Secretary of State John Hay described the struggle with Spain. In the early battles, American artillery slaughtered the poorly armed Filipinos. As the fighting continued, both sides showed a streak of cruelty. Filipinos took little mercy on captured Americans, killing some outright and mutilating their bodies in horrifying ways. Yet these were the "lucky" ones, if that is the right word. The unlucky ones faced torture before finding release in death. Captives had their ears, noses, and other body parts cut off. Buried up to their necks, their faces smeared with honey, they became food for ferocious jungle ants.

American troops were not angels either. Under military law, certain actions are never allowed. Even under severe battle conditions, soldiers cannot deliberately attack civilians. Wounded enemy fighters must get the same medical attention as Americans; prisoners must have proper food and shelter. Yet there is another principle of war, something written not in books, but in human emotions. It is: hatred breeds hatred, and cruelty breeds cruelty. Although people must always guard against cruelty and hatred, it is hardest to do so in war, where the issue is life and death, and raw emotion can easily overcome reason.

While we have no way of knowing how many Americans committed atrocities in the Philippines, soldiers' letters home tell shameful stories. Finding the mutilated bodies of Americans made their comrades wild for revenge, sometimes prodded by officers who should have known better. For example, A. A. Barnes, Battery G, Third United States Artillery, wrote: "Last night one of our boys was found shot and his stomach cut open. Immediately orders were received . . . to burn the town and kill every native in sight, which was done to a finish. About one thousand men, women, and children were reported killed. . . . Tell all my inquiring friends that I am doing everything I can for Old Glory and for America I love so well."[6] Faced with what we would call "terrorism" today, a traditional rule of warfare, which spared civilians, was breaking down among American troops to the Philippines.

By 1900, Filipino losses were fifteen men killed for each one wounded. During the American Civil War, the number was one soldier killed for every five wounded, the usual proportion in modern warfare. Private Arthur Minkler explained why: "We do not take prisoners. At least the Twentieth Kansas [Regiment] do not."[7]

Prominent Americans opposed the war as costly and immoral. Early in 1899, the Anti-Imperialist League was formed to turn public opinion against the so-called Philippine adventure. League members included former Presidents Benjamin Harrison and Grover Cleveland, labor leader Samuel Gompers, and the presidents of Harvard and Stanford universities. Andrew Carnegie showed more concern for Filipinos than for workers at his Homestead works. The steel tycoon offered to write a personal check for $20 million to buy the islands' independence. As to the claim that America must civilize the Filipinos, Carnegie said many thousands had already "been completely civilized and sent to Heaven."[8]

The humorist and author Mark Twain saw nothing funny about the war. Perhaps the Anti-Imperialist League's most outspoken member, the creator of Tom Sawyer and Huckleberry Finn said America should hide its head in shame. "We have crushed and deceived a confiding people; we have turned against the weak and the friendless who trusted us . . . we have stabbed an ally in the back . . . we have robbed a trusting friend of his land and his liberty . . . we have debauched America's honor and blackened her face before the world. . . ." The humorist was so bitter that he wished to tear off Old Glory's stars and stripes, replacing them with the pirate's skull and crossbones.[9]

Those who favored the war branded its opponents as traitors. Roosevelt, in particular, lashed out at them during the 1900 presidential campaign. For his antiwar stand, Roosevelt attacked William Jennings Bryan, the Democratic

Entrenched American soldiers take aim on Filipino insurgents.

candidate, for giving aid and comfort to the enemy. Not taking the islands, he insisted, would have been "a crime not only against America but against civilization." The rebellion, he added, "must be stamped out as mercifully as possible, but it must be stamped out." Condemning Filipino "savagery," he dismissed charges of American atrocities as "utterly baseless slanders."[10] This was nonsense, and Roosevelt should have known better. This suggests that he, too, allowed his emotions to get the better of his good sense.

Gradually, American forces occupied all the Philippines' major islands and many smaller ones. On Luzon, the largest island, the survivors of Aguinaldo's army fled into the jungle. Yet, far from the war ending, the hardest fighting lay ahead. From his hidden camp, the Filipino leader took a hard look at the war so far. Clearly, he could not defeat the Americans in open battle. They were too strong, too serious about keeping his country. Very well; he must change their minds by changing his strategy. No longer would Filipinos fight in large units, but as guerrillas in small, highly mobile bands. After Americans had bled enough, they would be happy to leave, he believed.

It began in the summer of 1900. When least expected, Filipino guerrillas attacked supply columns, cut telegraph lines, overran outposts, and set booby traps. If an American commander tried to strike back, fighting the Filipinos was like lunging at moving shadows. The occupied areas swarmed with Aguinaldo's spies. Whenever they saw an American column set out, they notified the nearest guerrilla band. The guerrillas either went deeper into the jungle or set an ambush.

After his reelection, McKinley gave orders to smash the guerrillas at any cost. The plan combined both gentle and harsh methods. Gentle methods aimed at winning the Filipinos' loyalty by improving their lives with schools, hospitals, roads, and clean-water projects. Millions of people would benefit from these improvements, and countless lives would be saved as a result of campaigns against tropical disease. On the other hand, harsh methods were aimed at frightening Filipinos into refusing to aid the guerrillas, or punishing them if they did. To carry out each part of the plan, McKinley appointed a civilian governor, William Howard Taft, and a military governor, Major General Arthur MacArthur. An Ohio judge, Taft was a brilliant administrator. A Civil War hero, MacArthur was a tough, smart soldier. So was his famous son, Douglas MacArthur, who liberated the Philippines from Japanese occupation during the Second World War.

American reinforcements poured into the Philippines. While MacArthur sent the bulk of these to keep order in the villages, he formed the rest into "flying columns" to track down the guerrillas. Information provided by the Macabebe Scouts, Filipinos paid by Americans to gather intelligence, allowed the flying columns to hound the guerrillas without letup. Troops raided their camps, seized their weapons, and destroyed their food stocks. In March 1901, an American patrol captured a messenger carrying letters from Aguinaldo to his commanders in central Luzon. After some hardfisted "persuasion," the messenger gave the location of his chief's camp. Captured and brought to MacArthur's headquarters in Manila, Aguinaldo realized that his cause was lost. On April 19, he took an oath of loyalty to the United States and asked Filipinos to stop fighting. The resistance collapsed, as twenty thousand guerrillas surrendered within three months.

Apart from some holdouts on Samar, the Philippines' third-largest island, American forces were victorious everywhere. In the village of Balangiga on Samar's southern coast, the seventy-four officers and men of Company C, Ninth U.S. Infantry Regiment, felt safe. On the evening of September 27, 1901, a ship brought supplies, mail, and newspapers telling of McKinley's death thirteen days earlier. After saying prayers for his soul, the soldiers went about their daily chores. Next morning, guerrillas dressed as women attacked as Company C sat down to breakfast. Caught without their weapons, within minutes forty-eight soldiers died; twenty-six survivors, all wounded, escaped in outrigger canoes to an army outpost on a neighboring island. The victorious guerrillas mutilated the American dead in nauseating ways.[11]

Brigadier General Jacob W. Smith visited Balangiga after the guerrillas fled. Nicknamed "Hell Roaring Jake" because of his booming voice and fierce temper, Smith, sixty-two, had spent forty years in the army, mostly fighting Indians in the

West. Astonished at the mutilations, he gave one of the most brutal (and criminal) orders ever issued by an American commander. All Filipinos on Samar were guilty! Spare no one! "I want no prisoners," Smith barked to his officers. "I wish you to kill and burn; the more you kill and burn the better you will please me. I want all persons killed who are capable of bearing arms . . . against the United States."

What, if any, age limit was there for Filipinos? an officer asked. "Ten years," the general replied, adding that Samar "must be made a howling wilderness."[12]

American soldiers did *not* kill everyone over ten on Samar. But they devastated the island. As "Butcher" Weyler had done in Cuba, they built concentration camps, ordering those living in suspected guerrilla areas to report to them within a given time. Anyone who failed to appear risked being shot on sight. Flying columns burned abandoned villages and tossed dead farm animals into wells to contaminate the guerrillas' water supply. Villagers caught with possessions of Company C members faced death at the hands of their vengeful comrades.

When Hell Roaring Jake's orders leaked to the press, they caused an uproar at home. In April 1902, the army court-martialed him on a minor charge—violating military discipline—not for ordering troops to commit murder. A panel of fellow officers found Smith guilty and ordered a letter of reprimand placed in his personnel file. Nothing else.

The new president approved the court's decision. Privately, however, Roosevelt was furious. Hell Roaring Jake had acted correctly, he thought, given what Roosevelt called the enemy's "cruelty, treachery, and total disregard for the rules and customs of civilized warfare." Smith's real offense, in the president's eyes, was his "loose and violent talk." By it, he embarrassed America overseas and gave ammunition to war critics at home. Rather than punish an officer with such "a long career distinguished for gallantry . . . and good conduct," he allowed him to retire with his general's rank and full pension. Four years later, Roosevelt would show the innocent Brownsville soldiers no such consideration.[13]

Although a handful of guerrillas held out for a few more years, America had conquered the Philippines. On July 4, 1902, Roosevelt officially declared the insurrection over. Congress then passed the Philippine Government Act promising Filipinos self-government under American supervision, leading to eventual independence. All told, some 125,000 American troops served in the Philippines. Of these, 4,234 died and 2,818 were wounded; the fighting in Cuba had claimed

460 American lives. America spent $400 million to subdue the Filipinos, or roughly $8.3 billion in 2005 money. Some 18,000 Filipino soldiers had died in combat; perhaps 200,000 civilians (a fifth of the population) died of disease and starvation directly related to the war.[14]

Yet that was not the end of the story. America built naval, and later air bases, in the Philippines to protect the islands themselves, as well as American trade and investments in Asia. Early in the Second World War (1941–45), what Theodore Roosevelt had feared came to pass. Japanese armed forces conquered the Philippines, starting a reign of torture, terror, and murder that would claim an estimated 1.2 million Filipino lives. Throughout the occupation, American commandos helped the Filipino people fight a guerrilla war against the Japanese. Greeted as liberators, American forces led by General Douglas MacArthur drove out the Japanese in July of 1945. A year later, on July 4, 1946, America kept its promise. With General MacArthur as guest of honor, the Philippines gained its independence.

In the arena of international politics, Roosevelt also faced problems closer to home, in Latin America. During the early 1800s, Spanish colonies from Mexico to Chile had won wars of independence. Yet Spain's friends in Europe, particularly France, spoke of recapturing these countries to control their natural resources and markets. The United States, however, felt threatened by having European forces nearby. So, in December 1823, President James Monroe declared a policy that still bears his name. The Monroe Doctrine said that America would view any effort to crush the young republics as "unfriendly" acts. Translation: Leave them alone or we will fight you. Still, America lacked a strong navy to back up its threat. Great Britain had the Royal Navy, the most powerful force on the high seas. To safeguard its own Latin American trade, Britain said it would support its former enemy, the United States, with steel and gunpowder. Spain's friends backed off.

By the end of the century, America had become a naval power in its own right. After forcing Spain out of Cuba, it set up a military government under General Leonard Wood. Within two years, President McKinley allowed Cubans to draw up a constitution as the first step to independence. Concerned about American property after the army left, in March 1901 Congress passed the Platt Amendment to the Cuban constitution. The work of Connecticut Senator

Orville H. Platt, this forbade Cuba from making any agreement with a foreign power that might later justify intervention in its affairs. However, the United States could intervene at any time to protect Cuban independence. Finally, Cuba had to grant the United States two bases; the navy had already selected one site, Guantánamo Bay on the island's south coast.[15]

Cubans resented the Platt Amendment. In Havana, they held mass demonstrations against it. Yet, if Cubans wanted the Americans out, they had to put the amendment into their constitution. They did, and in 1902, McKinley's successor ordered the army home. Cuba became an American protectorate, a country protected and partially controlled by a stronger nation. Roosevelt left no doubt about what that meant. "Cuba," he said, "must always be peculiarly related to us in international politics. . . . *We expect her to accept a political attitude toward us which we think wisest both for her and for us.*" In other words, Americans, not Cubans, would make key decisions affecting the island.[16] President Franklin D. Roosevelt abrogated—canceled—the Platt Amendment in 1934 as part of his Good Neighbor Policy toward Latin America.

Meanwhile, Theodore Roosevelt turned to a favorite subject of his. He and Captain Mahan, we recall, had agreed that their country needed a canal across Central America to cut ships' travel time between the Atlantic and Pacific oceans. The war with Spain dramatized that need as no speeches and books could. When it began, the navy's finest battleship, the U.S.S. *Oregon,* got orders to sail from the Pacific coast to the waters off Florida. This involved a voyage of 14,700 miles around South America through the stormy Strait of Magellan. Steaming at top speed all the way, *Oregon* still needed sixty-seven days to reach her station. When Roosevelt took office, he persuaded Congress to vote money to build a total of twenty battleships, increasing the size of the navy from fifth in the world to second only to the British Royal Navy. In the future, should a crisis arise in the Atlantic or Pacific waters, the canal would be absolutely necessary for quickly concentrating U.S. naval forces at the trouble spot.[17]

Where to build it? Engineers suggested two routes, each with its own benefits and drawbacks. Nicaragua offered a long—two hundred miles—but easy route over flat ground with deep waterways. A sea-level canal across Nicaragua would be cheaper and easier to build than one along the other route, the Isthmus of Panama. An isthmus is a narrow strip of land connecting two large landmasses bordered on either side by water; the Isthmus of Panama has the Caribbean Sea on the east and the Pacific Ocean on the west. Although only twenty miles at its narrowest point, the isthmus had dense jungles, vast swamps, and steep hills. This meant that a canal would need an intricate series of dams and locks to lift and lower ships mechanically.

Selecting the route was more a matter of moneymaking than engineering. Nicaraguans would do well if the canal crossed their country. It was the same in Panama, then a province of Colombia. A French company had once tried to build a canal across the isthmus, but failed miserably; its rusting equipment still littered the jungle. Should America choose that route, it must buy the company's lease, giving investors a hefty profit. Because Congress favored the longer but easier route, investors in the French company set out to change its mind. Nicaragua was a dangerous place studded with volcanoes that might erupt at any moment, they said. To prove their point, they sent lawmakers Nicaraguan postage stamps picturing a long-silent volcano, a scenic attraction.

Congress still favored the Nicaraguan route. Then, on May 8, 1902, Mount Pelée, a volcano on the Caribbean island of Martinique, erupted. Pelée's was among the most powerful, and deadly, eruptions ever recorded. In under three minutes, clouds of searing gases and ash destroyed the city of Saint-Pierre, killing 29,933 people; there were only two survivors. When news of the disaster reached the White House, Roosevelt wanted to send food and medical supplies to the island's other inhabitants. His advisers liked his idea. But at an emergency cabinet meeting, they reminded him that the president could not spend tax money without the approval of Congress.

"Those people will die of starvation if we lose a minute," said Roosevelt.

"That does not alter the law," replied Secretary of State John Hay. "You should get the consent of Congress." The president did just that. Urgent calls to lawmakers persuaded them to appropriate aid money.[18]

The disaster turned Congress against building the canal anywhere near an active volcano. In 1903, it voted $40 million to buy the rights of the French company. Soon afterward, Colombian diplomats agreed to accept $10 million for a six-mile-wide strip of land, called the Canal Zone, across the Isthmus of Panama. All seemed well, until the Colombian congress turned down the agreement. The deal seemed so unfair. Not only must the United States pay more for the land, members insisted, it must give Colombia the money pledged to the French company. The company had failed to build the canal, so why should it get anything?

Yet there was a strong suspicion in Latin America that, should the United States give in to their demands, most of the money would go into the pockets of corrupt Columbian legislators.

Roosevelt did not take the rejection calmly. He railed against "the blackmailers of Bogotá," criminals bent upon stealing any money the United States paid Colombia. Why, he said, sneering, "You could no more make an agreement with the Colombian rulers than you could nail currant jelly to a wall. . . ."[19]

What to do? The president knew Americans would not support his using force so soon after the Philippine war. Yet there might be another way to persuade the Colombians, a way to use force but keep his hands clean. Philippe Bunau-Varilla, a director of the French company, thought so. On October 9,

Philippe Bunau-Varilla convinced American leaders that Nicaragua's volcanoes presented the danger of earthquakes, and that it was safer to build the canal through Panama.

1903, he told Roosevelt that Panama was ripe for revolution. It was true; Panamanians despised Colombia and had staged fifty-three unsuccessful rebellions in as many years. Should another succeed, he said, America would get its canal. Roosevelt knew he could not tell his guest to stage a revolution against a country at peace with the United States. Yet he did not forbid him from doing so either. At the end of their meeting, the Frenchman felt he had the president's approval. Something in Roosevelt's tone and manner showed that he had given the go-ahead, though without saying it in so many words.

Bunau-Varilla plotted his revolution in Room 1162 of the Waldorf-Astoria Hotel in New York. On November 3, 1903, it came off without a hitch. Some five hundred Panamanian rebels, railway workers, and paid fighters seized the province. The only dead were an innocent bystander and a donkey. As "luck" would have it, an American navy cruiser, the U.S.S. *Nashville,* stood off the coast to turn back Colombian troopships. Next day, crowds surged through the streets of Panama City chanting, "Long live the Republic of Panama! Long live President

Roosevelt! Long live the American Government!" Roosevelt immediately recognized the new nation. Less than a week later, the Hay-Bunau-Varilla Treaty gave the French company its $40 million; Panama received $10 million for allowing the United States to build and use the canal and a "bonus" of $250,000 a year. Colombia got nothing.[20]

Critics denounced Roosevelt's "rape of Panama" as a crime against humanity. Mark Twain called the president a brute and a bully who would not dare confront a real power such as France, Germany, or Russia. The famous writer was unfair, as the president did not want to fight anyone unless he had to. Indeed, in 1906, when France and Germany seemed on the brink of war over a colonial dispute in Africa, Roosevelt worked behind the scenes to negotiate a peaceful settlement. He never claimed credit for this achievement, telling a friend his role was "a deep secret." For he wanted both countries to trust him the next time they had a dispute that threatened to explode into war.[21]

As for Panama, Roosevelt talked from both sides of the mouth, as politicians sometimes do. "I took the Canal Zone," he boasted. Yet he was sensitive to charges that he had done wrong. Once, at a cabinet meeting, he asked the attorney general to build a legal defense against the charges. "Oh, Mr. President," said Mr. Knox jokingly, "do not let so great an achievement suffer from any taint of legality." Roosevelt did not smile. Still, nothing succeeds like success. Panama's (nearly) bloodless revolution won wide public support in America. People applauded the president for bringing independence to a small nation that had struggled for liberty for generations. Americans also saw the benefit to world trade of Roosevelt's "path between the seas." Even South American countries approved of his action, saying Colombia deserved to lose Panama.[22]

In the spring of 1904, work began on the Panama Canal. Had it not been for Roosevelt, that work would have soon ground to a halt, as it had for the French company. The problem was not geography, but yellow fever, the disease that had tormented the American army in Cuba. In the early stages of yellow fever, victims run a high fever and develop jaundice, a yellowish discoloration of the skin. As death nears, they vomit mouthfuls of dark blood, hence the disease's Spanish name, *el vómito negro,* the black vomit. Scientists disagreed about the disease's cause and how it spread. One school of thought blamed bacteria that lived in dirt. Proper sanitation, therefore, would prevent it. Army doctor Walter Reed and Carlos J. Finlay, a Havana physician, denied that dirt had anything to do with yellow fever. Their experiments suggested that a certain type of mosquito carried a virus that caused the disease. The female mosquito needed human blood to mature her eggs. As she sucked a person's blood, the virus entered the bloodstream. So, to prevent yellow fever, they argued, you must erase its mosquito carriers.

Major William C. Gorgas of the Army Medical Corps had the job of conquering the disease in Cuba. Convinced that mosquitoes carried yellow fever, Gorgas set out to destroy their breeding places in water. To prevent female mosquitoes from laying their eggs, Gorgas ordered Cubans to cover their barrels of drinking water with wire mesh. If eggs had already been laid, the oil his men spread on pools of stagnant water smothered the larvae; that is, the newly hatched wormlike creatures that lived in water before changing into winged mosquitoes. General Leonard Wood, the military governor, supported Gorgas's efforts; he had Cubans publicly whipped for leaving water jars uncovered. It worked! After nearly four centuries of terror, yellow fever vanished from Havana in just eight months. So did malaria, another disease carried by mosquitoes.

When work began on the canal, yellow fever spread through the workers' encampments. Every day, fresh victims flooded the tent hospitals while earlier victims went to the undertakers. After his success in Cuba, the army sent Gorgas to Panama, where he ran into a stone wall of ignorance. The Panama Canal Commission, the body in charge of construction, had its own medical advisers. Although Gorgas had already shown how to conquer the disease, the commission's medical advisers insisted yellow fever had nothing to do with mosquitoes. Dirt! Rid the encampments of dirt and end the plague, they insisted. The commissioners agreed, urging Gorgas's dismissal.

Roosevelt was no medical researcher. The doctors' claims and counterclaims only confused him. Yet he knew one thing: no disease control, no canal. He also had sense enough not to argue with success. Gorgas's methods had worked in Cuba. Well, "By George, I'll back up Gorgas and we will see it through." And so he did. By December 1905, Gorgas had eradicated yellow fever in the isthmus. Equally important, public-health officials adopted his methods in the United States. Since colonial days, in summertime yellow fever had ravaged cities such as New York, Baltimore, and Philadelphia. In 1853, an epidemic in New Orleans killed nine thousand people. Gorgas's triumph against mosquitoes, thanks to Roosevelt's support, saved countless lives at home.[23]

In November 1906, the president and his wife visited the Canal Zone to see how the work was going. It was the first time a president had ever traveled outside the country while in office. At a total cost of $223 million, the Panama Canal opened to ship traffic on August 15, 1914. In high-flown language, speakers praised the waterway as an instrument of human progress. The conqueror of yellow fever, William Gorgas, and the canal's chief engineer, George Washington Goethals, got their share of praise, too. A modest man, Goethals gave credit to the man who had made it all possible. "The real builder of the Panama Canal," he said, "was Theodore Roosevelt."[24]

Even before the steam shovels tore into the ground, Roosevelt wondered how to protect the canal, a U.S. investment, from attack by would-be enemies of Amer-

President Roosevelt, dressed in a spotless white suit, poses on a giant steam shovel during the building of the Panama Canal, November 1906.

ica. The best way, he thought, was by enforcing the Monroe Doctrine. Several Latin American nations had borrowed heavily in Europe. In 1902, Venezuela failed to repay loans to German bankers. The bankers turned to their government, which sent a naval squadron to collect the debts. When the Venezuelans said they could not pay, German warships shelled two seaports and landed troops at another.

Roosevelt had no sympathy for Venezuelan dictator Cipriano Castro, calling him "an unspeakably villainous little monkey." Still, he feared Germany would use debt collection as an excuse for seizing a naval base in Venezuela. He dealt with the supposed threat by speaking softy; that is, with secret messages telling Germany to back off. If it refused, he threatened to send an American battle fleet under George Dewey, now an admiral, to protect Venezuela. Germany withdrew. So as not to embarrass the German government, Roosevelt kept the incident hush-hush.[25]

"The Big Stick in the Caribbean," by William A. Rogers in the New York Herald. *TR left no doubt that he would use American power, in the form of marines and battleships, to maintain "peace" and "order" in the New World.*

Two years later, the Dominican Republic went bankrupt. Germany, France, and Italy threatened to collect their debts by force. Asked if America should head them off by annexing the country, Roosevelt said he would rather "swallow a porcupine [by] the wrong end." Although he had no intention of taking over the country, he did not want anyone else doing so, either.[26]

He met the European threat by issuing the "Roosevelt Corollary," or addition, to the Monroe Doctrine. Should any nation in the Western Hemisphere do anything to provoke foreign intervention, he declared, the United States would act as an "international police power." It would step in to set things right, by force if necessary. As for the Dominican Republic, he offered the Europeans his "good offices" in collecting their debts. Yet behind his polite words lay the big stick in the shape of American battleships. Meanwhile, he pressured the Dominicans into allowing the Marine Corps in to keep order. American officials then took over the customs, the taxes paid on imported goods, and used the money to repay the debts. In later years, other presidents would use the Roosevelt Corollary to intervene in Cuba, the Dominican Republic (again), Haiti, and Nicaragua.[27]

The harshest test of Roosevelt's diplomatic skill came in the Far East. For centuries, China had been a center of science and culture. To mention just a few of their achievements, the Chinese invented paper, printing, and gunpowder. Chinese doctors were the first to use inoculation to immunize people against smallpox. By the mid-1800s, however, China had grown weak as droughts, floods, rebellions, and civil wars claimed millions of lives. Seeing their chance, more powerful European countries carved out spheres of influence in various parts of the country. Russia occupied Manchuria in the northeast, a territory rich in coal and iron ore. Japan, however, wanted the natural resources of Manchuria for its developing industries. In February 1904, Japan launched a surprise attack on the Russian naval base at Port Arthur. Moving quickly, Japanese forces occupied Korea, then sank a Russian fleet sent to retake Port Arthur.

Roosevelt was glad to see Russia get a whipping. Like the Russian Jews who fled the land of their birth, Roosevelt thought Russia's rulers corrupt, ignorant, hateful, and horrid. Although he never met Czar Nicholas II, he believed from the accounts of those who had that Nicholas was a royal ignoramus lacking any political ability. Cecil Spring-Rice, a British diplomat in Russia and a close Roosevelt family friend, wrote Edith: "The Emperor lives quietly . . . in his palace and plays with his baby and will hear nothing but baby talk. . . . His ideas, if he has any, are . . . to continue the war until he has gained 'the mastery of the Pacific.'" Edith's husband called His Majesty "a preposterous little creature." Theodore also saw into the future with stunning clarity. Czarist Russia was doomed to die by revolution, he felt. The president expected the revolution to result in "a red terror" that would make America's labor violence seem like child's play. His prediction proved only too accurate in the Russian Revolution of 1917, which toppled the czar and brought communists to power.[28]

Japan, however, was "a great civilized nation," a nation after Roosevelt's own heart. He liked the Japanese, admired and respected them. "The Japs [sic] are a wonderful people," he said, "natural fighters" with age-old traditions of honor, service, and loyalty. Sometimes President Roosevelt paraded around the White House in the armor of a samurai, a warrior of old Japan. Japan's bold moves thrilled the warrior in him; he even approved of the surprise attack on Port Arthur. If Germany and France helped Russia, he secretly warned, the United States would help Japan.[29]

Before long, Roosevelt had second thoughts, as the war became a disaster for Russia. Its humiliating defeats weakened the czar's authority, which set off a revolution. On January 9, 1905, "Bloody Sunday," workers marched through St. Petersburg, the capital, demanding reforms. Nicholas II ordered soldiers to open fire, killing hundreds. That did it. Across Russia, in response to the massacre, workers rose against the government. Although troops eventually smashed the rebellion, Russia was in no shape to continue fighting Japan. The Japanese also had troubles, for the war was bankrupting them. Both sides needed peace. Yet each was too proud to take the first step. Meanwhile, soldiers died and money vanished like water in the desert sands.

Roosevelt wanted Russia humbled, but not crippled. By weakening Russia, Japan would upset the balance of power in the Far East, threatening America's growing interests there, particularly in the Philippines. The only way to avoid disaster, he thought, was to help the warring sides do what they could not bring themselves to do alone. In August 1905, he invited their representatives to begin peace talks at Sagamore Hill. To escape the summer heat, the talks were moved to the naval base at Portsmouth, New Hampshire.

The president found the Russians boorish, "corrupt," and "stupid." He detested their chief negotiator, Count Sergei Witte, who "talked like a fool," jabbering about those awful "Jews swarming in New York." However, Roosevelt found Japan's chief negotiator, Baron Jutarō Komura, a soft-spoken gentleman with a steel rod for a backbone.[30]

Both sides haggled constantly. As Japan's price for peace, Baron Komura demanded that Russia pay a $600 million indemnity for injuries suffered by Japan during the war. Count Witte demanded control of Manchuria, rejecting the indemnity. Roosevelt feared the negotiators would go home without accomplishing anything. Yet he refused to give up, repeatedly coaxing them to try again. Finally, on September 5, they signed the Treaty of Portsmouth. Both sides agreed to leave Manchuria. In exchange for giving up on the indemnity, Japan got half of Sakhalin, an important island north of Japan; Russia kept the other half. Roosevelt also worked out a separate deal with the Japanese. In it, he recognized their control of Korea in return for a promise, eventually broken, to leave the Philippines alone. Korean people regarded the deal as a sellout. No Korean had been present at the negotiation or consented to surrender of Korean independence to Japan.

For his efforts, in 1906 Roosevelt received the Nobel Prize for Peace, the first Nobel Prize in any category won by an American. The awards committee saw nothing odd about honoring a man famous for being a warrior, but who also proved willing to take the lead in ending a war in progress. No Peace Prize winner has done that since. The prize consisted of a gold medal, an engraved diploma, and nearly $37,000 in cash. Roosevelt felt he could not accept a reward for something he did as part of his presidential duty to look after U.S. interests. Instead, he set it aside for donations

Portraits of the envoys at the Portsmouth Conference to end the Russo-Japanese War in 1905. Baron Komura and Kogoro Takahira (left) represented Japan. Count Witte and Baron Rosen (right) represented Russia. TR (center) kept pressing until they agreed to a deal.

to worthy causes. "To receive money for making peace," he wrote Kermit, "would in any event be a little too much like being given money for rescuing a man from drowning. . . ."[31]

The peace treaty did not satisfy the Japanese public. Most civilians had no idea that the war had brought their country to the brink of bankruptcy. All they knew was that their forces were clobbering the Russians. In their eyes, then, leaving Manchuria and giving up on the indemnity was a betrayal by inept diplomats and by that crafty American with the big teeth. Protests rocked Tokyo, killing seventeen and injuring five hundred. Some Japanese suggested that, to erase their shame, the treaty negotiators should commit hara-kiri—ritual suicide—by slicing open their bellies.[32]

Americans made matters worse. California had been a magnet for Asian immigrants for over fifty years. The first arrivals, from China, called it the "Land of the Golden Mountain." During the Gold Rush, they came to work in the mines. After the Civil War, still more came to build the transcontinental railroads. No warm welcome awaited them. While blacks battled Jim Crow, some 200,000 Chinese battled discrimination, too. Racists called them the "Yellow Peril," a tide of "inferior beings" that would take white men's jobs by working for less. Unions refused to have Chinese members. Racist mobs rampaged through Chinatown, the center of the Chinese community in San Francisco, beating people and destroying property. Finally, in 1882, Congress passed the Chinese Exclusion Act, banning more Chinese laborers from entering the country. In April 1906, a massive earthquake struck San Francisco, killing more than 4,000 people and leaving the city in ruins. Amid this horror, the Red Cross refused to aid the city's Chinese. News of that, Roosevelt said, made his "blood boil."[33]

While China was too weak to retaliate for racism in America, Japan had just whipped the mighty "Russian bear." Over 150,000 Japanese had come to California by way of Hawaii, an American possession acquired in 1898. In California, many Japanese became farmers, artisans, and shopkeepers. Soon after the earthquake, the San Francisco Board of Education ordered Asian children to attend segregated schools. Coming so soon after the Portsmouth treaty, the order was like rubbing salt in an open wound. By segregating Japanese children, all Japanese "lost face," or respect. Tokyo's leading newspaper said in bold print:

Stand up, Japanese nation! Our countrymen have been HUMILIATED on the other side of the Pacific. Our poor boys and girls have been expelled from the public schools by the rascals of the United States, cruel and merciless like demons. . . . We should be ready to give a blow to the United States. Yes, we should be ready to strike the devil's head with the iron hammer. . . .

Anti-American riots swept Japan. In Washington, Japan's ambassador handed his government's official protest to the State Department. Meanwhile, the Japanese imperial navy held battle exercises—just in case. Some naval officers spoke of repeating the surprise attack on Port Arthur, this time against the United States.[34]

Roosevelt was flabbergasted. "The infernal fools in California, and especially in San Francisco," he growled, had triggered an international crisis that might ignite a war. To avoid this calamity, the president promised Japan he would use his full power to protect the rights of Japanese immigrants. Should mobs threaten the Japanese with violence, he would send federal troops to protect them, something he never did for African-Americans attacked by lynch mobs. At a White House meeting, he persuaded San Francisco leaders to cancel the segregation order. In return, they won a concession from him. The president agreed to restrict Japanese immigration.[35]

How to save face for the Japanese government? Roosevelt knew it could not publicly agree to such a restriction without appearing to cave in to American prejudices. To spare it any embarrassment, he worked out the "Gentlemen's Agreement" in private. Thus, America would not bar Japanese immigrants or legally discriminate against Japanese already living in the country, while Japan voluntarily restricted immigration to the United States.

This compromise did not satisfy certain Japanese military men, nor the Black Dragon Society, fanatics who wanted to kick all white people out of Asia. Rumors reached the White House that these people wanted not only a surprise attack on the United States, but also an invasion of the Pacific Coast. Roosevelt took the rumors seriously. Secretly, he ordered the navy to draw up War Plan

In 1906, TR won a Nobel Peace Prize for negotiating an end to the Russo-Japanese War. But when California passed laws against Japanese immigrants, Japan threatened war with the United States. In this cartoon, titled "Friction between Japan and California," the president tries to cool tempers on both sides, saying: "Be quiet! Youngsters! Have you forgotten my Nobel Prize?"

Orange in case Japan acted. Publicly, he showed that America could repel any attack. To make his point, he asked Congress to vote money to make Pearl Harbor, in Hawaii, the center of American defenses in the Pacific.[36]

Since it would take years to prepare the Pearl Harbor base, Roosevelt decided to send a naval squadron on a voyage around the world. For Americans, he meant the voyage to "educate" on the importance of sea power. For the Japanese, it would show the big stick. The squadron included sixteen battleships, six torpedo boats, and four supply ships. All had fresh coats of white paint to show their peaceful intentions; in wartime these ships had gray coats ("battleship gray") to make them less visible to the enemy. Seeing the "Great White Fleet" in their home waters would also remind the Japanese that America would not be a pushover. Next to Britain's Royal Navy, the U.S. Navy was the most powerful in the world.

President Roosevelt and friends, Uncle Sam and George Washington, greet the Great White Fleet upon its return, in Hampton Roads, Virginia, February 22, 1909. Originally published in the New York Herald.

Before the fleet left, the president took the fleet's commander, Admiral Robley "Fighting Bob" Evans, aside. "Now, then, Admiral, one word before you go," he said. "Your cruise is a peaceful one, but you realize your responsibility if it should turn out otherwise." *Otherwise* meant that if Japan made trouble, Evans must fight fire with fire.[37]

On December 12, 1907, the Great White Fleet sailed from Hampton Roads, Virginia. With work on the Panama Canal in full swing, a Chilean warship had to lead it through the Strait of Magellan and into the Pacific. Meanwhile, Japan prepared to receive the gleaming battleships. No matter what a few military men might say, the Japanese people wanted good relations with the United States. Upon entering Tokyo Bay, the fleet headed for the port of Yokohama and anchored. Thousands of ordinary citizens greeted it at dockside. Children waved American flags and sang "The Star-Spangled Banner." Nobody could have known that other disagreements would later dash their hopes for peace. Japan's militarists would start a war with America as they had started the war with Russia. On December 7, 1941, Japanese naval and air forces launched a surprise attack on Pearl Harbor.[38]

Standing on the deck of the presidential yacht *Mayflower,* on February 22, 1909, Roosevelt saluted the Great White Fleet's return to Hampton Roads from its fourteen-month voyage. By then, his presidency was in its final days. Yet, looking back on his two terms, he took pride in what he had done in foreign affairs. Although some might disapprove, Americans knew that, for better or worse, Roosevelt had raised their country to a new importance in world affairs.

9

THE MOST DIFFICULT TASK

I do not fear for you in the presidency, Theodore. Your most difficult task will come when you leave the White House. . . . It will be a lot harder for you, Theodore, to be an ex-President than President.

—Columbia University President Nicholas Murray Butler, 1901

What should I do when I leave office? All presidents ask themselves this question. The presidency is the highest office in the land. Its holders command enormous respect. Always on view, their actions and sayings make headlines. Then it all ends, as it must. Becoming an ex-president requires adjustments, which are easier or harder to make, depending on the individual's personality. George Washington and Andrew Jackson eagerly returned to private life. Although free from the burdens of office, they continued to influence national affairs. John Quincy Adams followed a different course. He won election to the House of Representatives, where he led campaigns for free speech and against slavery. Other former presidents become "elder statesmen," giving successors the benefit of their experience and advice. The majority simply fade away, doing little, if anything, that is memorable for the rest of their lives.

We recall that after his victory in 1904, Roosevelt said he would not run for a third term. Edith, standing by his side, winced as she heard his words. She knew her husband was a "political animal," one who relished politics and power. Although he might busy himself with other things, she knew he could not stand to be away from politics, or out of the public spotlight, for very long. As his second term wound down, Theodore was frustrated. His Square Deal reforms had not gone far enough, he thought. His proposals for federal laws on the eight-hour workday and other issues were meeting increasing opposition, particularly from within his own Republican Party. Its Old Guard, allies of big business, insisted he had already done too much. It was time for Roosevelt to go, they felt, time to let someone else run the country.

Roosevelt knew the kind of person he wanted to take his place. That person must have wide experience in government. Above all, he would have to advance his, Roosevelt's, ideas and programs. William Howard Taft seemed to fit the bill. Not only had Taft served as a judge and civilian governor of the Philippines, he was an able secretary of war under Roosevelt.

Taft stood six feet one inch in his socks and weighed 326 pounds. "How is the horse?" friends joked when he returned from the long horseback rides he so enjoyed. Despite his weight, ladies found him "a lovely dancer," graceful and charming. Roosevelt liked Taft's good nature and easy laughter. "When Secretary Taft comes in," said a newspaper reporter, "there isn't room in the White House for any sound other than the chortling laughter of two big men. The Secretary's laugh is a 'Ha! ha! ha! ha!'. . . . The President's is a succession of chuckles—

William Howard Taft in defeat. Taft was furious at TR for running in the 1912 presidential race as a third-party candidate, thus splitting the Republican vote and allowing the Democrats to capture the White House.

a sort of mitrailleuse [machine gun] discharge of laughs. The fun engulfs his whole face; his eyes close, and speech expires in a silent gasp of joy. It is clear that both men get a lot of fun out of life."[1]

Roosevelt worked hard to secure the Republican presidential nomination for Taft. The campaign of 1908 was a walkover. As if determined to stick with a proven loser, the Democrats nominated William Jennings Bryan for the third and last time. The Socialists chose Eugene Debs. Not only did Taft win by over a million votes, the Republicans kept control of Congress.[2]

Although resented by the Old Guard, Roosevelt was still popular with the Republican progressives in Congress, and with the American people. That loyalty might be a problem. For if Roosevelt stayed around, it would be harder for Taft to organize his own administration. Theodore recognized this, so he decided to go away—and the farther, the better. He would go to Africa.

Since childhood, Roosevelt had wanted to hunt big game in Africa. To avoid charges of leading "a game butchering trip," he announced that the expedition would collect specimens for scientific study. To pay expenses, he signed a

President-elect Woodrow Wilson and outgoing president William Howard Taft pose for a picture on Wilson's Inauguration Day, March 4, 1913.

contract with *Scribner's Magazine* for $50,000 for a series of articles it would later publish in book form as *African Game Trails.* The magazine's editors expected the articles to boost circulation, as the material would meet a real need. Africa was still the "Dark Continent," a land of mystery and danger. In those first years of the twentieth century, outsiders still believed ancient myths about it. For example, some believed that elephants stirred up water with their trunks before drinking, since they could not stand to see the reflection of their ugly faces. Rhinoceroses knocked people down and licked off their flesh with sandpaper-rough tongues. Man-apes (gorillas) kidnapped women for mates.[3]

Roosevelt planned his expedition with care. Its destination, British East Africa, today's Republic of Kenya, was a British colony on the continent's east coast. His son Kermit, twenty, took a year off from Harvard to serve as companion, assistant, and "keeper"; Edith wanted him to keep Father from taking foolish risks. Roosevelt also recruited three naturalists from the Smithsonian Institution to study wildlife and preserve specimens. Besides gathering supplies—tents, cots, lamps, medicine, canned food—Roosevelt took the "Pigskin Library," thirty-seven of his favorite books specially bound in pigskin to protect them against rough handling. To learn more about Africa, he met with experts from the American Museum of Natural History and read explorers' accounts. A favorite was Colonel J. H. Patterson's *The Man-Eaters of Tsavo* (1907). The author, a British army engineer, had shot two lions that killed and ate workers building a bridge across the Tsavo River.

Lions fascinated Roosevelt, and he talked about them to anyone who would listen. In his last days as president, he said he wished he could send lions to eat his opponents in Congress. Asked if the big cats might eat the wrong people, Roosevelt replied, "Not if they stayed long enough." Before he sailed from New

York, J. P. Morgan attended a banquet. Raising his champagne glass, the financier declared, "America expects that every lion will do his duty." Washington, D.C., restaurants echoed to another toast: "Health to the lions!"[4]

In April 1909, Colonel Roosevelt, as the ex-president preferred to be called, arrived at Mombasa, a port on the Indian Ocean once favored by Arab slave traders. Countless shops crowded the bazaar, a vast open-air market where the languages of Africa, Asia, and Europe blended in an endless babble. Eager to get going, he left on an old wood-burning train of the Kenya-Uganda Railway. His destination, Nairobi, lay 334 miles to the north. The town would be his jump-off point for the interior.

At night, while passengers slept, the train climbed through a tropical forest to a grassy plateau, or tableland, three thousand feet above sea level. By day, the Colonel and his son had seats over the cowcatcher, a metal frame at the front of the locomotive used to clear obstacles from the track. The plateau teemed with wildlife. Wherever they turned, they saw elephant, rhinoceros, zebra, ostrich, giraffe, and antelope. To scare animals off the tracks, the engineer kept blowing the train's whistle. Yet some animals did not scare easily. Once, Roosevelt learned, a huge rhinoceros had butted the engine with its head. The engine stood its ground; the animal trotted away, dazed but full of fight. At other times, a frightened giraffe might gallop toward the telegraph line that ran beside the track. Unable to see the thin wire, and too tall to pass beneath, the giraffe wound up with a broken neck.[5]

Barely ten years old, Nairobi was still a frontier town. Zebra herds might gallop down its main street in broad daylight. Hyenas killed wandering pets at night. You never knew what to expect once darkness fell. Occasionally, a lion or leopard came in from the surrounding plains. "Father, there's a leopard under my bed," said a little English girl. Sure enough, he saw a leopard's tail swishing back

In this Homer Davenport cartoon, African animals tremble with fear at the approach of the mighty white hunter Theodore Roosevelt. New York Evening Mail, March 23, 1909.

"HIST! SEE WHO'S COMING!"

and forth from under her bed. In a local churchyard, the Colonel saw the graves of seven men recently killed by lions on Nairobi's outskirts. Roosevelt already loved Africa. "I speak of Africa and golden joys," he wrote, "the joy of wandering through lonely lands, the joy of hunting the mighty and terrible lords of the wilderness. . . ."[6]

Of course, he did not go about the "lonely lands" alone. His party left Nairobi with 275 porters to carry its gear and 15 armed native guards for protection. Yet this *safari,* Swahili for a journey into the interior of Africa, was no picnic. The Americans roasted by day and shivered by night. Crawling, buzzing, biting, sucking, stinging insects plagued them. The Colonel seemed tireless. After a grueling day's march, led by a porter carrying the Stars and Stripes, he would sit at a collapsible table with a kerosene lamp. Shrouded in mosquito netting, his hands in thick gloves, he wrote his articles for *Scribner's Magazine.* When he finished an article, a runner took it to an aide in Nairobi. The aide's job was to forward the articles to *Scribner's* and issue bulletins about his chief's progress. Although far from the United States, Roosevelt did not want the American public to forget him.

Bully! Every moment spent on safari was bully, absolutely wonderful. After an early breakfast of, say, crocodile eggs and coffee, the Colonel left camp just as sunrise purpled the eastern sky. Still a keen naturalist, he observed animals as eagerly as he shot them. In a small notebook, he recorded facts about their numbers, coloration, distribution, and mating habits. Yet nothing compared to the hunt. That was a thrill a minute. When he shot his first elephant, a bull with huge tusks, he roasted its heart over an open fire and ate it. Roosevelt celebrated his first lion with a whooping, hollering victory dance around the campfire.[7]

A high point came when the safari met a Nandi hunting party. Expert hunters, the Nandi killed lion not for sport or science, but to protect their cattle herds and prove their manhood. The Colonel wrote:

They were . . . stark naked, lithe as panthers, the muscles rippling under their smooth dark skins. . . . As they ran they moved with long springy strides. Their head-dresses were fantastic; they carried ox-hide shields painted with strange devices; and each bore in his hand a formidable war spear. . . . Suddenly, a maned lion rose . . . a magnificent beast with a dark and tawny mane; in his prime, teeth and claws perfect. . . . One by one the spearmen came up, at the run, and gradually began to form a ring around him. . . . [A]

warrior threw his spear. . . . Rearing, the lion struck the man, bearing down his shield. . . . But on the instant I saw another spear driven clear through his body from side to side; and as the lion turned again the bright spear blades darting toward him were flashes of white flame. The end had come. He seized another man, who stabbed him and wrenched loose. As he fell he gripped a spear-head in his jaws with such tremendous force that he bent it double. Then the warriors were round and over him, stabbing and shouting, wild with furious exultation. From the moment when he charged until his death I doubt whether ten seconds had elapsed, perhaps less; but what a ten seconds![8]

In all, the expedition collected 11,788 mammals, birds, and reptiles, besides thousands of fish, insects, plants, and human skulls from ancient graves; no one

TR poses with his latest kill, a bull rhinoceros, in this photo from his African Game Trails.

196 - THE GREAT ADVENTURE

on Theodore's safari asked the Africans' permission to dig up their ancestors. Among the larger specimens were eight elephants, seventeen lions, two rhinoceroses, eight hippopotamuses, and twenty zebra. Of the smaller creatures, many were new to science. Scientists named one, a variety of Grant's gazelle, *Gazella granti roosevelti* in the Colonel's honor. Most specimens, stuffed for display, went to the Smithsonian Institution and the American Museum of Natural History. Roosevelt kept a score of the best ones as trophies, whose heads visitors can still see on the walls of Sagamore Hill. At his desk, Roosevelt kept a hollowed-out elephant's foot as a wastepaper basket and a rhinoceros foot as an inkwell.[9]

Gradually, the safari moved north, descending the Nile River to Khartoum in the Sudan, where Edith and Ethel met their mighty hunters. There, after eleven months, the safari broke up. The Roosevelts went on to tour Egypt, then sailed across the Mediterranean Sea to Europe.

Europe treated the old Rough Rider like royalty. Wherever he went, cities greeted the man who had ended the Russo-Japanese War with parades and long-winded speeches. Universities gave him honorary degrees. Yet, even for one who loved attention as Theodore did, it became too much when kings and queens fawned on him. These were generally nice people, he thought, but poorly educated and not very bright. He would not change places with them for anything. Although they lived in magnificent palaces, surrounded by flunkies who never dreamed of offending their ears with an unpleasant word, Roosevelt thought that European royalty led such empty lives. On the one hand, he pitied "the tedium, the dull, narrow routine of their lives." On the other hand, he moaned, "Confound these kings! Will they never leave me alone!" Things got so bad that he was tempted to bite the next royal who bothered him.[10]

On June 18, 1910, the Roosevelts returned to an old-fashioned New York welcome. People appreciated what he had done for the country, and his "electric" personality still fascinated them. In the harbor, a swarm of ships and private yachts tooted their whistles, blew their horns, and rang their bells. Fireboats sprayed geysers of water into the air. Tugboat sirens screeched. At the Battery, the Roosevelts stepped into a carriage for the parade up Broadway, surrounded by former Rough Riders on horseback. For five miles, a solid line of cheering humanity lined each side of the road. Bands blared. Blizzards of paper flew from open windows and rooftops. Amid the commotion, the Colonel may have read a little poem in *Life,* a humor magazine:

> Teddy, come home and blow your horn,
> The sheep's in the meadow, the cow's in the corn.
> The boy you left behind to tend the sheep
> Is under the haystack fast asleep.

The sleeper was none other than Big Bill Taft.[11]

Taft was not the sort of president the Colonel expected he would be. To begin with, Taft had not been eager to become president; until he won the election, he had never held elective office. Taft loved the law, and would have preferred a seat on the Supreme Court; he took the presidency at his wife's and Roosevelt's urging. However, once in office, he did not seem "presidential." Should someone say "Mr. President," Taft, startled, would look around for his former chief. After nearly eight years of the energetic Roosevelt, the public found the big fellow boring. Stressed by his duties, Taft had trouble sleeping. At night, the president wandered about the White House in his size-fifty-four pajamas; overtired, he once dozed off at a funeral. He seldom laughed now.[12]

Progressives accused Taft of selling out to big business, although he had brought more antitrust suits than "trust-buster" Roosevelt. Nevertheless, Taft had grown more conservative, more inclined to see things from the big-business point of view. His cabinet, progressives muttered, looked like a board of directors handpicked by J. P. Morgan. When forestry chief Gifford Pinchot quarreled with Secretary of the Interior Richard A. Ballinger over conservation policy, Taft fired Pinchot. Colonel Roosevelt felt betrayed.[13]

That feeling of betrayal deepened as he read the newspapers and spoke to former supporters. The Colonel returned to a nation racked by bitter strikes. State governments often replied with court injunctions halting the strike and ordering the strikers back to work. Defiant union leaders went to jail. Defiant strikers fought strikebreakers, police, state militia, and federal troops. Blood flowed. People, mostly strikers, died. While Roosevelt shot lions, his hometown experienced a strike unmatched for its drama and human interest. We call it the Uprising of the Twenty Thousand.

New York was the center of the women's clothing industry. The manufacture of shirtwaists, an early form of blouse, was the worst-paid branch of an industry noted for its low wages, often seven dollars for an eighty-four-hour week. Bosses charged workers for the needles and thread they used, even for the chairs they sat on. In November 1909, shirtwaist workers held a mass meeting to decide what to do. Most were Jewish and Italian girls, recent immigrants, the poorest of New York's working poor. To speak to one another, Jews learned a little Italian and Italians a little Yiddish, a language similar to German.

Union leaders debated back and forth without deciding anything. Suddenly Clara Lemlich ran onto the platform. At nineteen, Clara had already been arrested a dozen times for union-organizing activities. "I am a working girl, one of those [protesting] against intolerable conditions," she said in Yiddish, her voice rising. "I am tired of listening to speakers who talk in generalities. What we are here for is to decide whether or not to strike. I offer a resolution that a general strike be declared—now."

Pandemonium broke loose as others translated Clara's words into Italian. Cheering, stamping, and waving handkerchiefs, the crowd voted to strike—now. "Do you mean it in good faith?" a union official asked. "Will you take the old

Ladies tailors, or shirtwaist workers, take time off from the picket line to have their picture taken during the Uprising of the Twenty Thousand.

Jewish oath?" Thousands raised their hands, pledging: "If I turn traitor to the cause I now pledge, may this hand wither from the arm I raise!"[14]

Twenty thousand shirtwaist workers walked off the job. For four months the strike dragged on. It continued despite frigid winds and soaking rains. "Gorillas," thugs hired to break it, beat up girls on the picket lines, Clara included. The police made mass arrests, jailing many for "streetwalking"—prostitution—a move to smear the strikers' morals. Still, the strike continued. Before long, it became something more than a struggle for workers' rights. It became a fight for basic human decency. Wealthy Fifth Avenue society ladies understood this; some appeared at union headquarters with money for the strike fund and bail for jailed strikers. Among them was J. P. Morgan's daughter, Anne. Finally, in February 1910, employers agreed to a modest pay raise and some improvements in working conditions.

Events like the Uprising of the Twenty Thousand affected Roosevelt deeply. When he left the White House, his ideas about labor unions and working people were still not fully developed. After he returned from Africa, they took final shape in a program he called the New Nationalism. That program aimed at empowering

Conditions in the New York garment industry were so harsh that workers condemned them as slavery.

the national government, giving it the ability to protect the welfare of the nation as a whole. The New Nationalism drew Roosevelt away from Taft and his Old Guard allies, and closer to the progressives. Eventually, it shattered the Republican Party.

Hoping to benefit from his popularity, party officials asked the Colonel to campaign for Republican candidates in the 1910 congressional elections. He agreed, but gave them a lot more than they expected. The progressive ideas put forth in Roosevelt's speeches had been circulating for years among reformers, union people, and socialists. Yet, until then, no towering political figure, least of all a Republican, had ever brought them together and set them out so forcefully as Roosevelt.

That summer, he went on a speaking tour through sixteen states. If you want to save American democracy and avoid bloody revolution, you'd better listen to me, he seemed to say. The high point came on August 31 at Osawatomie, Kansas. With thirty thousand people looking on, Roosevelt spoke for an hour while standing on a kitchen table. Although he had no mechanical aids, his voice reached every corner of the crowd.

Titled "The New Nationalism," this was perhaps the best speech he ever gave. It brought together all the influences that had shaped his life: his father's "troublesome conscience," *noblesse oblige,* the desire for justice, the need to prevent revolution through reform. The speech began with a call to end the political power of big business, the "special interests" that threatened American democracy.

> The essence of any struggle for healthy liberty has always been . . . to take from some one man or class of men the right to enjoy power, or wealth, or position, or immunity, which has not been earned by service to his or their fellows. . . . In our day it appears as the struggle of free men to gain and hold the right of self-government as against the special interests, who twist the methods of free government into machinery for defeating the popular will. . . . Our government, national and state, must be freed from the sinister influence and control of special interests. . . . The great special business interests too often control and corrupt the men and methods of government for their own profit. We must drive the special interests out of politics. . . .[15]

Roosevelt went on to urge reforms that would set the American agenda for the rest of twentieth century, and beyond. To curb the special interests, he demanded laws banning the use of corporate funds for political purposes. Political parties must make public the amounts, sources, and uses of campaign contributions. Should a firm break the law, government must hold its directors personally responsible, fining them and, in severe cases, jailing them. To reduce the appeal of anarchists and Wobblies, he urged the passage of laws specially designed to benefit working people. These included workmen's compensation for injuries on the job, abolishing child labor, the eight-hour day for all workers, and guaranteeing their right to form and join unions. As to conditions in the workplace, he asked for laws to improve sanitary conditions and provide safety equipment.[16]

The New Nationalism thrilled progressives. A personal triumph for the Colonel, it boosted his reputation among voters in general. Yet it did little for Republican candidates, as Democrats won control of the House of Representatives for the first time in sixteen years.

Events pushed Roosevelt into demanding yet more reforms. On March 25, 1911, a fire roared through the Triangle Shirtwaist Company on Washington Square in New York, a short walk from his birthplace. The building was a death trap. It had no fire extinguishers, no fire hoses, and no fire escapes. Locked stairway doors trapped the mostly Jewish and Italian employees. James McCadeen, a worker in a building across the way, "saw a girl come to the edge of the roof and stand for a minute. Her hair was in flames. I couldn't look any more." Within eighteen minutes, of 500 workers, 146 burned alive or jumped to their deaths to escape the inferno.[17]

The Triangle tragedy sent shock waves of grief and outrage across the nation. It enabled Eugene Debs to convert more workers to socialism. Big Bill Haywood's organizers began to unionize the New England textile mills. A desperate strike gripped the mills in Lawrence, Massachusetts. Fearing violence, strikers decided to send their children to safety in other towns. As the children boarded a train, the police clubbed them and their mothers. The strikers' anger grew.[18]

These events angered the Colonel, too. Following the Triangle fire, he scolded state legislators who tried to block improved fire-safety measures. He visited Pennsylvania's coal country, writing articles about miners' families living in shacks without heat, running water, and sanitation. In speeches, he told of little girls who had lost hands and arms to dangerous machinery. Audiences applauded when he said he stood for "using the collective power of the people [the government] to build up the weak." At Harvard, he had written his senior essay on "the

THE NEW YORK HERALD.

****c   NEW YORK, SUNDAY, MARCH 26, 1911.—112 PAGES.— by the new york herald company.]   PRICE FIVE CENTS.

ONE HUNDRED AND FIFTY PERISH IN FACTORY FIRE;
WOMEN AND GIRLS, TRAPPED IN TEN STORY BUILDING,
LOST IN FLAMES OR HURL THEMSELVES TO DEATH

IDENTIFYING BODIES OF THOSE WHO JUMPED TO THE SIDEWALK.

BUILDING AT NORTHWEST CORNER OF EAST WASHINGTON PLACE AND GREENE STREET, THE THREE TOP FLOORS IN WHICH LOSS OF LIFE OCCURRED, WERE COMPLETELY DESTROYED.

The Triangle Fire as headlined in the New York Herald, March 26, 1911.

practicability of equalizing men and women before the law." In it, he said that American women should have the same rights as their menfolk. Now, in 1911, he decided that women could never better their lot without political power. So he backed a constitutional amendment to give them the right to vote. As for the courts, he attacked their use of injunctions to end strikes, and what he called the Supreme Court's "do-nothing philosophy." The High Court, he said, seemed less interested in human rights than in property rights.[19]

The Republican Party began to split. To save the country, its progressive wing urged Roosevelt to challenge Taft for the presidential nomination. Although he had promised not to seek a third term, Roosevelt easily wriggled out of that pledge. What he "really" meant, he said, was not three terms one after the other. Roosevelt expected the fight of his life. Yet it would be a bully fight, and he would enjoy every moment of it. On February 21, 1912, he announced, "My hat is in the ring, the fight is on, and I am stripped to the buff."[20]

The fight began with an effort to win delegates to the nominating convention, to be held in Chicago in June 1912. Republican voters chose convention delegates in two ways. In some states, they elected delegates in primary elections. In others, politicians chose delegates in state nominating conventions, often in crooked ways. The struggle quickly became personal—and poisonous. Roosevelt lashed out at Taft, calling him a "fathead," a "puzzlewit," a "scoundrel," and a "fool." Taft gave as good as he got, branding his opponent an "egoist," a "demagogue," and "a freak, almost, in the zoological garden, a kind of animal not often found."[21]

That "freak" swept the primaries. Learning that he had lost the Ohio primary, Taft buried his head in his hands and moaned, "Roosevelt was my closest friend." Then he burst into tears. Yet he did not cry for long. Taft's advisers thought they could set aside the primaries. As president, Taft controlled the Republican Party organization, which controlled the convention. When Roosevelt supporters tried to disqualify several Taft delegates, party officials ignored them. With Taft sure to get the nomination, the Roosevelt forces shouted, "Thou Shalt Not Steal!" Tempers flared. Fists flew. Elderly men pulled one another's white beards. But nothing could stop the Taft steamroller.[22]

What next for Roosevelt? Ever since he had backed the corrupt James G. Blaine in 1884, he had been a loyal Republican. Not anymore. Claiming that Taft had "stolen" the nomination, Roosevelt led his supporters out of the convention hall. "The parting of the ways has come," he said, adding that the Republican Party must stand for human rights "or else it must stand for special privilege." Meeting in another building, he announced that he would accept the nomination of a new party, should they decide to form one. They did, calling it the Progressive Party. Asked if he felt up to the job of running for the presidency, the Colonel declared, "I feel as fit as a bull moose!" The name stuck, and the bull moose became the party's symbol and nickname.[23]

Held in Chicago in August 1912, the Progressive convention seemed more like a religious revival than a political gathering. Calling themselves "Bull Moosers," the party faithful believed they were doing God's work, fighting in the holy cause of social justice. Unable to contain their enthusiasm, ten thousand voices would burst into soul-stirring hymns like "The Battle Hymn of the Republic" and "Onward, Christian Soldiers." In accepting the nomination, Roosevelt struck a religious note, too. "We stand at Armageddon, and we battle for the Lord," he said, his voice filling the hall. In the Bible, Armageddon is the scene of the final conflict between the forces of good and evil at the end of time.

Battling for the Lord. During the 1912 presidential election campaign, TR harangued crowds, demanding a broad program of economic and social reforms. The men sitting in front are newspaper stenographers, taking down the former president's remarks word for word in shorthand.

Delegates also sang new songs like "Oh, You Beautiful Moose" and "Roosevelt, My Roosevelt," which had this verse:

Follow, follow,
We will follow Roosevelt
Anywhere, everywhere,
We will follow on![24]

The Progressive platform included Roosevelt's New Nationalism program and other measures, such as increasing citizen participation in local and state government. Among these, the *initiative* would allow citizens to propose laws by gathering enough signatures on a petition. In a *referendum,* voters would accept or reject the proposal. The *recall* would allow voters to remove an elected official by means of a special election. In addition, the platform called for limitations on campaign spending and further conservation measures.

Despite their zeal for reform, Bull Moosers fell short when it came to racial justice. Although the convention seated black delegates from Northern states, it adopted a "lily-white" policy for Southern delegates. Civil-rights leader W.E.B. Du Bois, of the NAACP, asked the party's support for federal bans on lynching and Jim Crow voting laws. Roosevelt, however, would not hear of it. The uproar over his dinner with Booker T. Washington in 1901 had made him wary of provoking Southern voters, especially in the close election he expected. His refusal left an opening for Woodrow Wilson, the Democratic candidate. When Wilson promised blacks "absolute fair dealing," many blacks turned to the Democrats. Yet time would show Wilson to be no friend of theirs.[25]

Although they did not meet face-to-face, Roosevelt and Wilson held one of the greatest political debates in American history. Speaking from the rear platforms of railroad trains and from stages in vast halls, they appealed to voters across the country. While agreeing on most things, they strongly disagreed about the role of government, the key issue in the 1912 campaign. The Colonel preached that big business was here to stay, which was all to the good, because it produced things cheaply and created jobs. Thus, government must control "bad trusts" and monitor "good trusts," while protecting the rights of workers and consumers. Wilson, however, wanted government to promote competition and discourage all trusts. Stronger antitrust laws would allow new businesses to flourish, raising living standards for all Americans, he reasoned. "I do not want a government that will take care of me," said the Democrat. "I want a government that will make other men take their hands off so I can take care of myself."[26]

Everyone, it seemed, was ganging up on Roosevelt. Democrats called him wrongheaded, his support of "good trusts" not what America needed. Socialists called him a secret ally of big business. Republican loyalists branded him a "shameless," "shabby" hypocrite, "a half-mad genius" who dreamed of becoming King Theodore I of America. To the tune of the era's national anthem, they put these words in his mouth:

During the first half of the twentieth century, the historian and sociologist W.E.B. Du Bois was a leading African-American opponent of racial discrimination.

> My country 'tis of me,
> Sweet land of mostly me,
> Of me I yell.
> Land to which I am sent
> Beyond all argument,
> Choose me for president
> Or go to hell.

Heckled at a rally, the Colonel leaped onto a chair and shook his fist at his tormentors. Theodore's fury only served to embarrass him and strengthen the competition. "Good old Teddy," said Wilson. "What a help he is."[27]

On October 14, as Roosevelt left his hotel in Milwaukee, Wisconsin, to give

An eyeglass case and the folded pages of his speech slowed the assassin's bullet, saving TR's life.

a speech, a lunatic named John F. Schrank shot him in the chest at point-blank range. The force of the bullet knocked Roosevelt down, but he sprang to his feet, stunned and pale. Bystanders grabbed Schrank, and would have lynched him had Roosevelt not shouted, "Don't hurt the poor creature." Schrank later told police that President McKinley had come to him in a dream, demanding revenge for Roosevelt's having killed *him*.[28]

Schrank's victim put his hand to his mouth and coughed. No blood! Luckily, the bullet had passed through his eyeglass case and a fifty-page speech, folded double, before striking a rib and stopping a hairbreadth from his right lung. Doctors urged Roosevelt to go to the hospital immediately, but he waved them aside. "I will make this speech or die," he snapped.

Arriving at the hall, the Colonel mounted the platform. Since the audience knew nothing of the shooting, he told them. "Friends," he said, "I shall have to ask you to be as quiet as possible. . . . I have been shot, but it takes more than that to kill a Bull Moose. . . . The bullet is in me now so that I cannot make a very long speech. . . . I do not care a rap about being shot, not a rap. . . . What I do care about is my country." Although aides begged him to cut the speech short, as he had promised, he kept going. Finally, after nearly an hour and a half, he allowed them to take him to the hospital. After seeing the X-rays, doctors announced that he would recover. However, the bullet was too close to the lung to remove. He would carry it to the end of his days. At last, he had a real "war" wound.[29]

The shooting won public sympathy, but not enough votes to return Theodore to the White House. Wilson won the election with 6.3 million votes; the Democrats also captured both houses of Congress. Roosevelt came in second, with 4.1 million votes. Taft ran a poor third, finishing with under 3.5 million votes. Eugene Debs more than doubled his vote in the 1908 election.

The Socialist leader's 900,000 votes, 6 percent of the total, proved that more Americans were dissatisfied with their lives than ever.

The disaster of having a Congress and White House controlled by the Democrats was all Roosevelt's fault, Republicans insisted. For had he not turned against them, or at least kept out of the race, Taft would probably have gotten most of Roosevelt's votes. For their part, the Roosevelt family took defeat hard. The Colonel's sons had campaigned for him. The youngest, Quentin, fifteen, had an awful time at Groton School in Massachusetts, where most of his schoolmates' families favored Taft. To show their dislike of Quentin's father, the boys tormented the youngster, even tricked him into running naked in front of lady visitors. At breakfast the morning after the election, Edith and Ethel cried. The Colonel described himself as "unspeakably lonely," a man "shunned by old friends and neighbors, treated like an outcast." In their eyes, he had become a low-down traitor to the Republican Party.[30]

As always after a setback, Roosevelt tried to pull himself together by keeping busy. Early in 1913, he wrote *An Autobiography,* the story of his life, the first ever by a former president. Despite defeat at the polls, he championed the cause of reform more than ever. When garment workers struck in New York, he visited their picket lines, his way of supporting them without saying it in so many words. He wrote public letters defending workers' right to join unions without fear of being fired. When a West Virginia coal strike turned ugly, he looked beyond the violence of the strikers. In the old days, he would have demanded that the authorities shoot to kill. Now he blamed the mine owners for provoking the trouble by exploiting their workers. Yet, deep down, he was restless. The Colonel needed a change of scene, a new adventure. He needed wilderness.[31]

Roosevelt arranged to give a series of lectures in Brazil and to do some hunting there. With the backing of the American Museum of Natural History, in October 1913, he, Kermit, and two museum naturalists sailed from New York. It was a risky adventure, because he was not the same man who had trekked across Africa. At fifty-five, he was overweight, carrying a bullet in the chest, and exhausted from his failed presidential bid. Yet there was no holding him back. "I have to go," he said. "It's my last chance to be a boy!"[32]

While in Brazil, he heard about the Rio da Dúvida, or the River of Doubt.

This mysterious stream flowed northward toward the Amazon, the world's largest river. Where did it really go? Nobody knew, because no white person had ever traveled its entire length or mapped its course. Roosevelt decided to do just that. In February 1914, his party set out with Colonel Candido Rondon of the Brazilian army and twenty-two paddlers for their seven dugout canoes.

Africa was a lark compared to what Roosevelt and Kermit faced as they hauled the canoes overland, toward the River of Doubt. Tropical heat. Deadly coral snakes. Vampire bats. It was terrible. "We were drenched with sweat," the Colonel wrote. "We were torn by the spines of the innumerable clusters of small pines with thorns like needles. We were bitten by hosts of fire-ants and by the mosquitoes, which we scarcely noticed when the fire-ants were found, exactly as all dread of the latter vanished when we were menaced by the big red wasps, of which a dozen stings will disable a man. . . ." Tents and cots, boots and clothes, rotted in the humidity. Men awoke in the morning to find that termites had eaten their underwear.[33]

Things did not improve. Indian arrows killed a paddler. Another man, driven insane by heat and insect bites, murdered a fellow paddler and ran into the jungle to meet certain death. The jungle was so thick in places that everyone had to pitch in with machetes to cut a path. After reaching the River of Doubt, the party launched the canoes and began its journey downstream. It was the roughest going yet. Rapids shot the dugouts past jagged rocks. In calmer stretches, nobody with the tiniest scratch on a hand dared put it into the river. It swarmed with

TR and Colonel Rondon pose with a bush deer during their search for the mysterious River of Doubt. This photo is from Roosevelt's book Through the Brazilian Wilderness.

piranhas, small fish that seemed all mouth and teeth. Traveling in schools, "they will rend and devour alive any wounded man or beast, for blood excites them to madness," the Colonel noted.[34]

While Theodore struggled on the river, closer to home, a new man took control of the White House. Woodrow Wilson took the oath of office as president a month before Roosevelt's party plunged into the jungle. A former president of Princeton University and governor of New Jersey, Wilson was the Colonel's total opposite. Although a trained historian, unlike Theodore he had no interest in science or the arts, such as literature, painting, or music. No gusts of hearty laughter came from the serious, high-strung Wilson. While his few friends found him pleasant enough, in public he was stuffy. His handshake, a reporter wrote, "felt like a ten-cent pickled mackerel in brown paper." Wilson admitted, "I *am* cold. . . . Were I a judge and my own son should be convicted of murder . . . I would do my duty to the point of sentencing him to death." Smug and arrogant, he lectured fellow politicians as if they were schoolboys. Nor did he show much gratitude for their help.[35]

During his first months in office, Wilson steered several important measures through Congress. His legislation created the Federal Trade Commission (FTC) to investigate unfair business practices, while the Clayton Antitrust Act made it harder for big business to form monopolies. Both measures were good for America, and Roosevelt had called for similar action during his presidency. But when it came to race relations, Wilson was a disaster.

Wilson believed without question that black people were inferior to whites. A confirmed racist and bigot, he described African-Americans as "ignorant and inferior" by nature. All his historical research, apparently, had taught him nothing about the reality of Southern slavery before the Civil War. Slavery, he wrote, had benefited blacks, because it put them on the path to civilization, guided by kindly "masters who had the sensibility and breeding of gentlemen." Nor did Wilson see anything wrong with Jim Crow laws passed in the South after the Confederate defeat. He even told demeaning "darky" stories at cabinet meetings.[36]

Not only did Wilson fail to promote civil rights, he wished to deprive blacks of a right they still had. Ever since the end of the Civil War, blacks had held jobs in the federal civil service. In Washington, D.C., they worked in government offices as managers, clerks, bookkeepers, and secretaries. That a white woman secretary, for example, should take orders from a black man infuriated racists like

Senator "Pitchfork" Ben Tillman. The president agreed with Tillman's racist views. Soon after taking office, he allowed some department heads to fire black employees not covered by the civil-service laws, while segregating the rest from white workers. Thus, segregation became the official policy of the United States government. As in any Jim Crow state, black employees had to use separate cafeterias and toilets from whites, and work in screened-off areas. Segregation, said Wilson, without explaining why, was "in the interest of the Negroes." So much for his campaign pledge to treat African-Americans fairly![37]

African-Americans did not take presidential bigotry lying down. Black church groups collected tens of thousands of signatures on protest petitions. Individuals flooded the White House with protest letters. Northern cities saw mass meetings to denounce "Jim Crowism" in the federal government. Stung by the outcry, Wilson canceled the segregation orders, but never apologized for their issue in the first place.[38]

Meanwhile, in Brazil, things got worse for Roosevelt's exploration party. Food ran short. Five dugouts shattered against the rocks. In trying to save another dugout, Roosevelt gashed his leg. The wound became infected. The next day, a raging fever and malaria laid him low. "The fever was high and father was out of his head," Kermit wrote afterward. Theodore began to recite poetry, then babbled nonsense. In a clearheaded moment, he told Kermit to go ahead and leave him behind alone, as he did not want to be a burden. Kermit, of course, would do no such thing. On they went, jammed into the two remaining dugouts, for they had no choice but to follow the river to its mouth. At last, after forty-eight days, they met a party of rubber gatherers. After traveling 1,500 miles by water, they had reached the junction of the River of Doubt and the Amazon.[39]

The Colonel's expedition had charted the mysterious river's entire course. Impressed by his success, the Brazilians renamed it the Río Roosevelt in his honor. The American Museum of Natural History got some three thousand bird and mammal specimens, not to mention many reptiles, fish, and insects, of which several were new to science.[40]

Roosevelt returned to New York on May 19, 1914. It was not the sort of homecoming he had grown used to during his glory years. Next to losing Alice Lee and his mother on the same day, this was the worst time of his life. No ships' whistles welcomed him now, only his family. No longer a boy, he was a rapidly aging man who needed a cane to walk. Losing fifty-seven pounds on his Brazilian voyage left him exhausted, worn out, a shadow of the rugged outdoorsman he had been. He was a has-been now, an ex-president whose political career seemed over. "I am practically through," he told a doctor. "I am not a man . . . who keeps his youth almost to the end; and I am now pretty nearly done out."[41]

Back at Sagamore Hill, Theodore mended slowly. When thinking about the future, he decided that he had one more fight left in him. That fight would be for his favorite cause now, social reform. Yet it was not to be. A month after his return, a Serbian terrorist assassinated Archduke Franz Ferdinand, heir to the throne of Austria-Hungary. The killing was like a torch plunged into a barrel of gunpowder. In July 1914, war exploded across Europe, then spread worldwide, as one country after another joined in. That war would be the old Rough Rider's last.

10

THE ROUGH RIDER'S LAST FIGHT

I wish I were President at this moment! . . . The first thing I would do . . . would be to interfere in the world war on the side of justice and honesty. . . . I do not believe in neutrality between right and wrong. I believe in justice.

—THEODORE ROOSEVELT, 1915

At the time, people called the war by various names: World War, Great War, First World War. Not that anyone imagined, in that summer of 1914, that there would be a Second World War. They used the term *First World War* because this was the first war fought on a worldwide scale and in every element: on land, on the sea, under the sea, in the air. Simply put, it was a struggle for power in Europe and for colonies in Asia and Africa. On one side stood the Central Powers: Germany, Austria-Hungary, Bulgaria, Turkey. Their opponents, known as the Allies, were France, Belgium, Russia, Italy, Japan, and the British Empire—Great Britain, Canada, Australia, New Zealand, South Africa, India. Humanity had never experienced such a calamity. In certain ways, we still feel its effects today.

In the early days of the war, the British sent an army across the English Channel to help France. Meanwhile, Germany invaded Belgium, a tiny kingdom that lay across the best invasion route into France. This action violated a treaty in which the major powers had promised to respect Belgian neutrality in any war. In the light of military necessity, Germany called the treaty simply a worthless "scrap of paper." The Allies called the invasion the "rape of Belgium."

To succeed, the German plan depended on speed and timing. Yet, in driving across Belgium, the invaders met unexpected resistance. Ordinary Belgians rose against them, launching guerrilla attacks. Operating in small bands, as the Filipinos had done, they ambushed German units and dynamited vital bridges, stalling the advance. In return, German commanders terrorized civilians, largely innocents who had the bad luck to be at the wrong place at the wrong time. The orders for these measures still exist; they are part of the historical record.

Moreover, diaries taken from the bodies of dead Germans describe their own methods in horrific detail. If, for example, civilian snipers fired at passing troops from houses in a village, the German troops burned the village. At Dinant, troops shot six hundred hostages when townspeople failed to hand over snipers. In all, Germans murdered some 5,500 Belgian civilians during the summer of 1914. At least that many French civilians also died when German forces finally plowed into France.[1]

After overrunning much of Belgium, the German army advanced on Paris. In desperate fighting, the French pushed them back, saving the city, but leaving large parts of their country in enemy hands. Unable to strike the knockout blow, each side dug into trench lines stretching for five hundred miles across France, from Switzerland to the North Sea. Massed artillery shelled both the French and German trenches day and night. In charging enemy trenches, artillery, rifles, and machine guns tore the attackers to shreds. Poison gas blinded men and brought death by slow strangulation. Bodies lay unburied or in shallow graves, soon uncovered by exploding shells, then reburied by other shells. The stench of death

Unidentified soldiers slaughtered by artillery fire along a country lane in 1916. These were probably Germans, because the helmet near the feet of the body on the left is the kind worn by German combat troops. Scenes like this were common during the First World War.

filled the air, even filled men's mouths with every bite of food they took. Blue and green flies, smelling of corpses, rose in clouds that momentarily hid the sun. Rats, millions of them, grew fat and sleek on human flesh. "Huge rats. So big they would eat a wounded man if he couldn't defend himself," a horrified Canadian scrawled in his diary.[2]

Americans watched the war with disgust and dismay, and were thankful to have the broad Atlantic between it and them. None was more thankful than President Wilson. Woodrow Wilson, a Southerner, was born in 1856. Some of his most vivid memories were of the Civil War. As a child in Georgia, he knew how the Union Army had burned a wide path across the state on its march to the sea. Now he would do everything in his power to keep another war from America. Also, with one-third of its 100 million citizens born in Europe, or having at least one parent born there, he feared for the unity of the United States. Irish and English, French and German, Italian and Austrian, Jew and Russian—all had long-standing grievances, carryovers from the old world, which might tear America apart if it took sides in the war. So, when the fighting began in Europe, Wilson officially declared neutrality and urged Americans to be neutral "in thought as well as in action."[3]

What if America were threatened? Wilson said he believed that would not happen if the United States remained strictly neutral. Neutrality meant not only not taking sides, but not passing judgment on the conduct of the war. Thus, he never criticized Germany for breaking its pledged word and invading Belgium. Neutrality also meant avoiding any large-scale military preparations like increasing the army's size. The warring nations might take such measures as provocations rather than defensive acts. What is most important, Wilson, a deeply religious man, believed that God had

President Woodrow Wilson throws out the first ball of the 1916 baseball season.

chosen America to be a force for good in the world, guiding and helping less fortunate nations. In keeping with that mission, he hoped that neutrality might allow him to bring the warring nations to their senses by a negotiated peace. Where Roosevelt had succeeded with Russia and Japan in 1905, Wilson hoped to do the same in a far more terrible war.

The Colonel disagreed. Although he liked individual Germans and spoke their language fluently, he distrusted their rulers. During his presidency, their meddling in Latin America had made him wary of Germany. Later, on his return trip from Africa, Roosevelt visited Germany. There

TR and Kaiser Wilhelm II during German army maneuvers, 1910. The former president feared that Germany's growing military power, combined with the emperor's recklessness, would plunge the world into a horrific war.

he met Kaiser Wilhelm II, the emperor, whom he thought "vain as a peacock." A fierce-looking man with a walrus mustache, His Imperial Majesty was a loudmouth who liked parading in military uniform and making threats. Roosevelt worried that, one day, the emperor and his military would ignite "a world conflagration."[4]

Although the Kaiser did not bear sole responsibility for the war, his army's behavior in Belgium infuriated the Colonel. "Germany is absolutely wrong," he told friends. The Allies were in a "grand and noble" struggle, a moral struggle that America dared not allow them to lose. Should Germany win, he feared it only a matter of time before America would have to fight her. Emboldened by victory, German forces could easily menace the Panama Canal, even seize bases in Latin America. Should Germany and Japan join hands, "which . . . is entirely a possibility," they could threaten the American homeland itself, a fear that became reality during the Second World War a generation later. At the very least, then, America must prepare to fight on the Allied side if necessary. If the United States were strong, he reasoned, Germany would not threaten its vital interests.[5]

Despite Wilson's caution, it grew harder to remain neutral. The trouble lay at sea. Wilson did not expect Americans to cut themselves off from the rest of the world. Neutrality, as he saw it, meant they could trade with all countries. True, international law banned neutral ships from carrying war materials to either side. Still, American firms could sell these to anyone, if they took them away in their own ships. Once those ships put to sea, America had no responsibility for them or for how their cargoes were used. The war had disrupted the economies of the fighting nations, causing critical shortages of raw materials and manufactured goods. Thus the conflict became a gold mine for Americans. Farmers sold anything they grew at record-high prices. Factory orders skyrocketed. Profits soared, and unemployment vanished.

Yet there was danger. England, the world's leading naval power, clamped a blockade on Germany, sending swift destroyers to sweep German merchantmen from the high seas. Before long, England tightened the blockade by declaring a long list of items contraband, illegal for any ship to bring to Germany. Besides weapons, the list included anything that might help the enemy: machinery, chemicals, metals, cloth, leather, oil, even food. Germany retaliated against the "hunger blockade" by unleashing its submarines. Each month, these "U-boats," or undersea raiders, sank thousands of tons of Allied shipping. If citizens of neutral countries sailed aboard Allied ships, Germany announced, they did so at their own risk. It also declared a "war zone" around the British Isles, promising to torpedo any vessel sighted in these waters. This was no bluff, as several American crews learned when torpedoes slammed into their ships.

On May 7, 1915, a U-boat sank the British liner *Lusitania* in the Irish Sea. Of the 1,965 people aboard this floating hotel, 1,201 drowned, including 94 children, among them 35 babies; 128 Americans lost their lives. The German press greeted the disaster "with joyful pride," while the government gave German schoolchildren a day's holiday. Three days later, Wilson spoke in Philadelphia. He spoke with emotion about America's devotion to peace and how it must set an example to the world. We are neutral. Neutrality is so right, so moral, we do not have to use force to persuade others of its rightness. He closed with an unforgettable phrase: "There is such a thing as being too proud to fight."[6]

America should be too proud *not* to fight, snapped Roosevelt. He saw the sinkings, especially that of the *Lusitania,* as acts of savagery, crimes against humanity. In an article titled "Murder on the High Seas," he argued that nothing ever excused the deliberate murder of innocent men, women, and children. Torpedoing the liner was no legitimate act of war, "but piracy on a vaster scale of murder than old-time pirates ever practiced." He called Wilson and those who thought like him "flubdubs and mollycoddles," spineless creatures unworthy of the name American. Again the Colonel warned that war was coming; Americans could not wish it away. We must prepare for it with a crash program to expand the army, train officers, and build more fighting ships. We must gear up American industry for an all-out war, not just to meet the Allies' immediate needs, but as their comrades in arms.[7]

Germany's actions made Wilson more determined than ever to remain neutral. Learning that army planners were studying how to fight in Europe if necessary, an aide noted, he turned "trembling and white with passion." The president canceled the exercise. Yet that was just the beginning. Franklin D. Roosevelt had become assistant secretary of the navy, "Uncle Ted's" old post. Franklin wanted to refit the fleet for possible action in European waters. Wilson refused. The president also kept German activities in America under wraps, as the publicity might spur demands for action. British intelligence officers and U.S. Secret Service wiretaps on the German embassy's telephones revealed disturbing information. German agents were trying to disrupt American production for the Allies by stirring up strikes and sabotage. Wilson knew this, but said nothing, until the press broke the story.[8]

The president limited himself to writing protest letters to the German government. If Germany continued sinking American ships in Allied waters, or Allied ships with Americans aboard, he threatened to break relations, a diplomatic term for war. Kaiser Wilhelm had no great fear of America; its military was in no shape to give real trouble. However, Germany did not need another enemy just then. So, in April 1916, the U-boats got orders not to sink merchantmen without warning and to rescue crews and passengers if possible.

The Kaiser's change of mind came just in time for the presidential election. Roosevelt had abandoned the Progressives, hoping to gain the Republican nomination. But when the party easily chose a conservative, Supreme Court Justice Charles Evans Hughes, Roosevelt pledged his support. Even if Hughes lost, he reckoned, supporting Hughes would put him back in the party's good graces, perhaps even win Roosevelt the nomination four years later. For now, however, Wilson was unbeatable. While most Americans hated German atrocities at sea,

Since the start of the First World War, Roosevelt demanded that the United States join the Allies. Most Americans, however, wanted to help the Allies with money and weapons but not soldiers. In this 1915 cartoon by Ding in the Des Moines Register & Mail, Uncle Sam urges a hysterical TR to calm down, saying, "Tut, tut! Theodore!"

they did not want war either. In November, they reelected Wilson on the slogan "He Kept Us Out of War." And so he had, for the moment.

Roosevelt was furious. Furious at the American people—"our foolish, foolish people." Their ignorance and timidity kept them from seeing things as Roosevelt thought they should. Yet the president infuriated him most of all. "I despise Wilson," he snarled. Germany, he insisted, was fighting an unjust war—the most unjust war ever. Its atrocities in Belgium and the sinking of a passenger liner were acts of criminals gone mad, Roosevelt thundered. Seen in this light, Wilson stood for everything weak, meek, corrupt, and cowardly. Roosevelt went overboard in his insults, calling the Democrat (among other things) an "abject coward," a "wretched creature," and a "sissie." In denouncing Wilson so, Roosevelt dismissed all his efforts to keep the peace, or the genuine desire of millions of Americans to stay out of the war. For the Colonel believed absolutely that he was right, that the Allies' war was right, and that anyone who thought differently was a fool or a traitor.[9]

Yet Roosevelt was right about the big issue. War was coming to America. Early in 1917, battlefield losses forced Czar Nicholas II to step aside in favor of a democratic socialist republic. Another revolution, led by Nikolai Lenin, would soon trigger a Russian civil war ending in a communist dictatorship. With Russia near collapse, the German military finally saw a chance for the knockout blow. The Allies were in bad shape on the Western Front. When British troops got orders for an assault, marching columns bleated "Baaa, Baaa, Baaa," knowing they were going to almost certain death. Entire French divisions, thousands of troops, had mutinied, refusing to go like sheep to the slaughter. French commanders decimated whole units; that is, shot every tenth man who refused to go into action.

Secretly, the Germans transferred troops from the Russian front for a massive offensive aimed at winning the war. To succeed, however, Germany also had to cut the Allied supply lines to America. Again they must unleash the U-boats, even if it resulted in America joining the Allies. No matter. Wilson's failure to prepare properly meant that American forces would not reach Europe in time to halt their offensive, German leaders thought. Within days of announcing "unrestricted submarine warfare," U-boats sank five American ships in British waters.

No longer too proud to fight, on April 2, 1917, Wilson addressed a joint session of Congress. Since Germany had become the "natural foe of liberty," now, he said, "the world must be made safe for democracy." With that, he asked Congress to do its duty under the Constitution. Returning to the White House, Joe Tumulty, a top aide, noted in his dairy, "the President . . . sobbed as if he had been a child." Wilson wept because he knew the terrible sacrifices Americans would have to make for victory. Four days later, Congress declared war on Germany.[10]

On the day Congress voted for war, the U.S. Army numbered 127,000 officers and men, about enough, experts figured, to last a month in the trenches. To have a real impact in the war, America would need millions of troops. Although Wilson signed a draft law, it would take months to raise, organize, train, equip, and send the first units overseas. But with the Allies under growing pressure, speed was urgent. Knowing this, the Colonel wanted to raise a volunteer division of 20,000 to 25,000 men under his command, as he had done with the Rough Riders. His idea was to get this "Roosevelt Division" into action quickly, before the main force arrived. "The appearance of an ex-President of the United States carrying the Star-Spangled Banner over a body of American soldiers to the battle front would glorify us as will nothing else," he wrote. "It will electrify the world." Better still, it would encourage the Allies, raising their spirits.[11]

Roosevelt opened a private recruiting station in New York. The old magic was still there. Attracted by his fame, on some days over two thousand men applied for the division. The problem was not finding volunteers, but getting permission for him to lead them. When the War Department balked, he decided to go to the top. "I will promise Wilson," he said, "that if he will send me to France, I will not come home alive." Franklin D. Roosevelt arranged a private White House meeting, but the president had not forgotten the Colonel's insults. Icily, he listened to his proposal, then refused, saying modern war was for professionals, not aging amateurs. Disappointed, from then on the old Rough Rider

Though ailing, TR not only welcomed the declaration of war against Germany, but volunteered to organize and personally lead a regiment into battle.

called him "Wilson—that skunk in the White House."[12]

Several Allied leaders later told Wilson they approved of the Colonel's plan. French premier Georges Clemenceau, nicknamed "The Tiger," said in an open letter that French soldiers called to the president to "Send them Roosevelt—it will gladden their hearts." British fighting men echoed their French comrades; some outfits put a bull-moose insignia on their battle flags. When the first American troops landed in France, crowds cheered "Les Teddies."[13]

Wilson may later have regretted turning down the Roosevelt Division. Before long, the Colonel became a thorn in his side, all the more painful because he spoke the truth. For while draftees poured into the training camps, the war materials they needed did not.

Although American industry was able to fill Allied orders, now it must also produce for a vast new American war machine. This required a complicated system of collecting raw materials, transporting them to factories with specially built assembly lines, and getting the finished products to the fighting men. However, since industry and government were not used to working together, there were massive delays and foul-ups. Eventually, many problems were solved, but others were not. As a result, the AEF (American Expeditionary Force) had to depend on the Allies for gear once it arrived in Europe. Heavy artillery, tanks, machine guns— it had to borrow nearly all of these. While Americans Orville and Wilbur Wright had invented the airplane, the American aircraft industry was backward compared to Europe's. Thus, Americans flew only British and French combat planes.

Adding to the confusion, Wilson was no war manager, nor were most of his aides. The Colonel learned this from various sources, including Franklin D. Roosevelt. Franklin's position in the Navy Department gave him the opportunity to pass inside information to his most "affectionate Uncle," especially about crew shortages that prevented warships from putting to sea. Other informants were army officers, among them an unnamed major general, who told the Colonel about the goings-on in the training camps. Soldiers lacked winter overcoats, warm underwear, and heavy socks. They trained with wooden machine guns and log cannons. During a visit to one camp, Roosevelt saw with his own eyes units drilling with broomstick rifles.[14]

Roosevelt became the administration's leading critic. "Speed up the war," he demanded. Cut through the red tape and nonsense that slowed war production and training! Do it now, or you will have blood—young Americans' blood—on your hands!

Others, however, had different reasons for scolding Wilson. These were the dissenters, those who saw nothing just or noble in this war. For them, the conflict was about European countries grabbing one another's empires, not making the world safe for democracy. Senator Robert M. La Follette, Democrat of Wisconsin, and Senator George W. Norris, Republican of Nebraska, agreed with socialists like Eugene Debs in denouncing the "capitalist" war—a war promoted by bankers and munitions makers on both sides. "War brings prosperity to the stock [market] gambler on Wall Street," Norris told the Senate. "We are going into war upon the command of gold. We are going to run the risk of sacrificing millions of our countrymen's lives in order that other countrymen may coin their lifeblood into money."[15]

Battered by those who favored stronger actions as well as those who opposed the war, Wilson asked Congress to pass a law limiting freedom of speech. Congress gave him two laws. The Espionage Act banned spying, but also saying or writing anything harmful to the war effort. The Sedition Act made it a crime to use "abusive language" toward the government, government policy, or the military. Violators faced $10,000 fines and twenty years in a federal prison.

Even though the Sedition Act made criticisms of Wilson's war effort illegal, the Colonel would not keep quiet. Rather than frighten him, the Sedition Act emboldened Roosevelt. Angered by his criticisms, Wilson supporters urged action against this pesky has-been politician. A few even wanted to try him for treason, then have him "shot at sunrise." What they did not realize was that attacking Roosevelt would make bad publicity for Wilson.[16]

Just you try it, just you jail me, Roosevelt shot back. "Whenever the need arises I shall in the future speak truthfully of the President in praise or in blame, exactly as I have done in the past," he wrote. "My loyalty is due to the United States, and therefore it is due to the President, the Senators, the Congressmen, and all other public servants only and to the degree in which they loyally and efficiently serve the United States." Rather than risk bad publicity, the administration decided to leave the Colonel alone.[17]

Yet Roosevelt's was not a blanket defense of free speech, only of the right to criticize failings in the war effort. To him, free speech was not an absolute right to be protected under any circumstances. Instead, it was reserved for "patriotic" Americans like himself. "Unpatriotic" dissenters were something else entirely. The Colonel, like the president, agreed that nobody had the right to question the justice of the Allied cause. Such questioning, they thought, was a slippery slope leading to national disaster. Questioning led to doubt, doubt to disloyalty, disloyalty to the shattering of national unity and to defeat, he insisted.

Only days before delivering his war message, Wilson told a newspaper editor about his fears. "Once lead this people into war," he said, "and they'll forget there ever was such a thing as tolerance. . . . Conformity would be the only virtue, and every man who refused to conform would have to pay the penalty." He was right. Having gone to war to make the world safe for democracy, Americans experienced the cruelest test of their democracy ever. Hysteria swept the nation, infecting even the president, who so feared it. What made this even more tragic was that Wilson did nothing to check the war frenzy.[18]

Millions of Americans supported the war effort with dignity and decency. But millions of others saw anything German as devilish, including fellow Americans who spoke German or whose families came from Germany long ago. Blinded by hatred, they acted in ignorant, hurtful ways. Libraries took German books off their shelves. Orchestras fired German-born conductors and refused to play the music of German composers. Restaurants changed German toast to French toast. Sauerkraut became victory cabbage and dachshunds liberty pups. Colleges canceled courses in German literature. Professors of religion, ignoring the Christian message of love and peace, urged students to "see Jesus Christ Himself sighting down a gun barrel and running a bayonet through an enemy body." Preachers adopted an English war poem:

> Fight for the colors of Christ the King,
> Fight as he fought for you;
> Fight for the right with all your might,
> Fight for the Red, White, and Blue.[19]

As Wilson said he feared, war frenzy proved dangerous to traditional American liberties. The U.S. government prosecuted more than 2,100 people under the Espionage and Sedition Acts, mostly for their words, not their actions. It denied use of the mail to publications critical of the war, shutting down some and jailing their editors. "Patriot" mobs broke windows of stores owned by people with German-sounding names. Teachers who refused to take loyalty oaths were fired. Filmmaker Robert Goldstein got a ten-year jail sentence for *The Spirit of '76,* which dramatized scenes from the American Revolution. Nobody said events like the Boston Massacre had not happened; children read about them in their history books. But portraying them in a movie was a crime because it showed an ally—Great Britain—in a bad light. "Hundred-percent" Americans set out to uproot disloyalty; that is, whatever seemed disloyal to them. Those suspected of sympathizing with the Central Powers had German iron crosses painted on their bodies as signs of disgrace. Mobs stripped some people naked, covering them with boiling tar and feathers.[20]

Eugene Debs, perhaps America's leading war opponent, was branded a traitor. Rather than the war being a crusade against evil, as Roosevelt, Wilson, and others claimed, the Socialist Party leader denied that working people had any stake in the European bloodbath. After all, why should a Philadelphia carpenter want to kill a carpenter from Berlin? Why should he wish to maim another man, a worker like himself, for life? As for the draft, Debs condemned it as nothing but modern-day slavery—a form of slavery far worse than old-time slavery, which merely forced black people to work on cotton plantations. With modern slavery, Debs insisted, the government, in effect, kidnapped a free man solely to turn him into an "automaton," a mindless killing machine. In June 1918, after a blistering antiwar speech in Canton, Ohio, police arrested him for violating the Sedition Act.

Debs admitted to breaking the law, as a truly moral person must occasionally do. Before passing sentence, the judge asked if he had anything to say to the court. In a powerful, emotional speech, Debs refused to plead for mercy. Instead, he described his draft protest as part of the larger crusade for social justice.

> Your Honor, years ago I recognized my kinship with all living beings, and made up my mind that I was not one bit better than the meanest on earth. I said then, and I say now, that while there is a lower class, I am in it, while there is a criminal element, I am of it, and while there is a soul in prison, I am not free. . . . In this country . . . there are still vast numbers of our people who are the victims of poverty and whose lives are an unceasing struggle all the way from youth to old age, until at last death comes to their rescue and stills their aching hearts. . . . It is not the fault of the Almighty: it cannot be charged to nature, but is due entirely to the outgrown social system in which we live that ought to be abolished not only in the interest of the toiling masses but in the higher interest of all humanity. . . .

The judge gave Debs ten years in a federal prison. Good riddance, President Wilson snarled, thinking that this "traitor to his country" got exactly what he deserved. Debs became a prison favorite, beloved by inmates and guards alike. In 1920, he campaigned for the presidency from his jail cell, winning 919,000 votes; President Warren G. Harding, who believed he had been wrongly convicted, pardoned Debs the following year. Meanwhile, federal agents staged raids on IWW offices nationwide, carting off records and membership lists, and jailing leaders on trumped-up charges of disloyalty. Persecution grew so intense that IWW head Big Bill Haywood jumped bail and fled to Russia, where he lived for the rest of his life.[21]

In his response to World War I, Theodore seemed like two different men. At his worst, he appealed to the worst in his fellow Americans. Instead of rising above the war frenzy, he lent his name and prestige to it. If words could leap off the printed page and grab a person by the throat, the Colonel's would have. His writings, such as his 1915 book, *The Foes of Our Own Household,* are lengthy rants against dissenters. In this great world crisis, the ex-president wrote, there can be "no fifty-fifty allegiance." In wartime, the nation demanded absolute, unquestioning loyalty. "Either a man is whole-hearted in his support of America and her allies, and in his hostility to Germany and her allies, or he is not a loyal American at all." At the very least, dissenters should lose the right to vote, he said.[22]

Roosevelt would have forced foreign-language newspapers to switch to English. The government should crush dissent of any kind, he urged. Socialists, Wobblies, draft opponents, pacifists whose religious beliefs forbade military service—all were disloyal. These "half-hidden traitors," he urged, "should be arrested and either shot, hung, or imprisoned for life." Such ranting is always inexcusable, because it substitutes vicious words for careful analysis, but especially so amid the passions of wartime. Yet we must remember that this did not represent the whole man. He had another side, one worthy of America's highest ideals.[23]

At his best, Roosevelt was marvelous. For any American who fit his definition of "loyal," he demanded equality and fair play. "We must give every man a square deal," he said. By all means "shoot the spy or the traitor . . . [but] stand by the good American of any creed, no matter where he was born or whence his parents came." This war was not only against an evil foreign power, but also represented a fight for social justice at home. Nobody should grow rich, or richer, from the war effort; let the government put a heavy tax on war profits. As to workers, they deserved certain benefits, not as favors, but as basic human rights. Roosevelt said workers must have old age pensions and health insurance. If a company did well, its workers should share in the profits. Eventually, these ideas would become reality in our modern Social Security and Medicare systems.[24]

None appreciated the Colonel's call for justice more than black people. In 1917, nine out of ten African-Americans lived in the South, mostly on farms and in small towns, where they held low-wage jobs, often earning only fifty cents a day. The World War I draft, however, created a severe labor shortage. To expand their workforce, Northern factory owners sent agents south to recruit blacks. So began the "Great Migration," as perhaps 750,000 African-Americans boarded northern-bound trains. The Macon, Georgia, *Telegraph* printed a warning about the exodus: "Everybody seems to be asleep to what is going on right under our noses—that is, everybody but those farmers who waked up mornings recently to find every Negro over twenty-one on their places gone—to Cleveland, to Pittsburgh, to Chicago, to Indianapolis." Black people left not only for better wages, but to escape Jim Crow.[25]

Up north, white workers, fearing competition for jobs, resented blacks,

In response to the East St. Louis, Illinois, race riot, African-Americans held a silent protest march along Fifth Avenue in New York City.

especially when some bosses used black laborers as strikebreakers. In two dozen cities, white resentment ignited in race riots. The worst riot occurred on July 2, 1917, in East St. Louis, Illinois. *Riot* is too gentle a term for what happened that day; a Jewish newspaper called it a Russian-style pogrom. "Get the niggers!" mobs shouted. Black people were shot, stabbed, clubbed, scalped, and burned alive. When the smoke cleared, thirty-nine lay dead, including four children. Some six thousand others were driven from their homes. Police officers watched from a safe distance, laughing as fellow Americans fled in terror.[26]

Grief and rage swept black America. What are we fighting for? black soldiers asked. Does the war against Germany mean anything when our families are not safe in their homes? In New York, civil-rights leaders W.E.B. Du Bois and James Weldon Johnson led ten thousand black men, women, and children in a Silent Protest Parade along Fifth Avenue. Children carried signs reading:

MOTHER, DO LYNCHERS GO TO HEAVEN?
MR. PRESIDENT, WHY NOT MAKE AMERICA
SAFE FOR DEMOCRACY?

These were fair questions. But when a delegation of civil-rights leaders asked to discuss the East St. Louis atrocity with President Wilson, he refused, claiming he was too busy with foreign affairs. In public, he said not a word about East St. Louis.[27]

Theodore Roosevelt said plenty. Because of the war, he had matured as a man and a thinker on the subject of race relations. There had been no black men in the Rough Riders. Yet nineteen years later, in 1917, he argued that if black people were good enough to fight for America, then they had earned equality with their blood. "We demand that the Negro submit to the draft and do his share of the fighting exactly as the white man does," he said. "Surely, when such is the case we should give him the same protection, by the law, as we give to the white man." Even before East St. Louis, he tried to make amends for the past by serving as a trustee of the Tuskegee Institute and Howard University. Before black army units shipped out to Europe, he spoke to them, paying his respects and thanking them for their service. Part of his Nobel Prize money went to help families of black soldiers.[28]

President Wilson was a racist who believed black people naturally inferior to whites. In the wake of the East St. Louis race riot, his attitude prompted the figures in this cartoon to ask: "Mr. President, why not make America safe for Democracy?"

Yet nothing showed the change in Roosevelt better than his reaction to East St. Louis. On July 6, four days after the riot, he attended a mass meeting at Carnegie Hall in New York to salute the Allies. After listening to the opening speeches, the Colonel rose to speak himself. There was something he had to get off his chest. Given the "appalling outbreak of savagery" in East St. Louis, he demanded that the federal authorities protect African-Americans when state and local officials either could not or would not.[29]

Samuel Gompers disagreed. As president of the AFL, Gompers saw things through the narrow lens of his members'—nearly all white—interests. He defended the white workers, explaining that they merely wanted to protect their jobs. When he finished, the audience broke into loud applause.

Roosevelt's "troublesome conscience" reacted to the applause as it would to an insult. His face red with rage, the ex-president sprang across the stage and leaned over Gompers, shaking his fist inches from his nose. "Justice with me is not a mere phrase or form of words," he shouted. "In the past I have listened to the same form of excuse advanced on behalf of the Russian autocracy for pogroms of Jews. Not for a moment shall I acquiesce in any apology for the murder of women and children in our country. . . . I will do anything for the laboring man except what is wrong. . . . Never will I sit motionless while directly or indirectly apology is made for the murder of the helpless."[30]

Hissing and hooting rose from the audience. When Roosevelt left the hall, he needed a police escort. Blacks would have given him an honor guard. Overnight, it seemed, the African-American community's bitterness toward him over the Brownsville Affair vanished. For he had shown his "better angel," as Abraham Lincoln might have said, his true self. Later, in a most radical idea for its time, Roosevelt said the country would never truly be a democracy "until we have had both a Negro and a Jewish president of the United States."[31]

The Colonel's support for the war effort revived his popularity. Republicans, who had treated him as an outcast since his Bull Moose days, began to talk about him as their party's candidate to oppose Wilson, should he run in 1920. That talk grew louder when it became known that he asked nothing of any American family that he would not ask of his own first. The old Rough Rider expected family members who could to go into harm's way for their country.

Roosevelt women did their "bit" for the war effort. Daughter Ethel was married to Dr. Richard Derby, a surgeon, and had a young child. She became a nurse in a French army hospital, assisting her husband in the operating room. Like any nurse who worked with seriously wounded men, Ethel knew that talk about the "glories" of war, including her father's, was nonsense. Had she known of it, Ethel would probably have agreed with Dr. LeBrun, a French colleague of her husband's, after a seventy-two-hour shift in the operating room. As he opened the door to leave, LeBrun, exhausted and bleary-eyed, muttered, *"La gloire, la gloire! Bah! C'et de la merde!"* (Glory, glory, it's all shit!)[32]

Ethel's half sister, Alice, married but without children yet, did undercover work. Since she knew everyone who was anyone in Washington, Alice had invitations to countless social events. Sometimes the Secret Service asked her to place listening devices in the homes of suspected German sympathizers. Ted Jr.'s wife, Eleanor, left their three children with her mother to take charge of all YMCA women in France. Cousin Eleanor, Franklin's wife, helped the Red Cross in the states.[33]

The Colonel had never gotten over his father's avoidance of combat during the Civil War. Roosevelt expected his sons to fight, and to the death if need be. "Honor" left them no choice in the matter. *He* left them no choice. "I'd rather none of them came back," Roosevelt would say grimly, "than that one, able to go, had stayed home."[34]

Inspired by patriotism and driven by fatherly pressure, all four sons enlisted. Edith feared for their safety, but she shared her husband's ideals of patriotism, duty, and heroism. Hoping to see action without delay, Kermit joined the British army fighting the Turks in the Middle East. There he won a medal for bravery in the battles of Baghdad and Tikrit, places where other Americans would fight nearly a century later. Kermit's brothers went with the AEF—American Expeditionary Force—to France. There, in the trenches, Archie got the horrible wound his father had yearned for in Cuba. A shell fragment shattered his knee and broke his arm. For that, Archie won the Croix de Guerre (War Cross), the French equivalent of the Medal of Honor awarded by Congress for courageous acts "above and beyond the call of duty." He received it as he lay on the operating table from a whiskered French officer who kissed him on both cheeks. Ted Jr. also fought in the trenches. He was shot in the leg and laid low by German poison gas twice. For these close calls he received the U.S. Distinguished Service Cross and Silver Star. Although eager for his sons to fight, and proud of their deeds, as a father, the Colonel feared for their safety. That fear often woke him at night with his heart racing. "My boys—I am afraid I shall never see them whole again. They are all doing this for my sake," he would say.[35]

Quentin, twenty-one, he never did see again. Airplanes fascinated Theodore's youngest child. Civilians idolized combat pilots as daredevils of the sky, fighting alone, as the knights of old. Although Quentin had poor vision, he so wanted to be like them that he memorized the chart to pass the eye examination. In France, he showed reckless courage. When friends urged him to take care, he dismissed their concerns with a laugh. Quentin would do anything, take any risk, to make his father proud of him.[36]

The Germans had sent the "Flying Circus," their top fighter squadron, to the sector patrolled by Quentin's outfit. On July 6, 1918, he slipped behind a bloodred German plane and shot it down in flames. Eight days later, an enemy pilot did the same to Quentin. While Edith took her son's death hard, she said no one mourned Quentin more than her husband. It nearly broke the Colonel's spirit. Overnight,

Quentin Roosevelt (top left) and his pals. A reckless fighter pilot, Quentin was shot down in flames. TR blamed himself for his son's death. It broke his heart.

it seemed, he had become a wasted old man who blamed himself for his son's death. At Sagamore Hill, servants noticed how the former president, once so outgoing, would sit silently for hours, staring into the distance. Now and then, he murmured, "Poor Quinikins! Poor Quinikins!" A servant once found him in an isolated corner of the house, crying bitterly.[37]

Quentin's death harmed Germany in an unexpected way. When German airmen found his charred body, they buried it with full military honors. Their government, however, had pictures taken of the corpse, then circulated them to boost army morale. The effort backfired. For when German soldiers saw the pictures, they became angry at their royal family. Despite the war, Quentin's father was still much admired in Germany. Everyone knew that he could have found his sons safe posts but did not. Kaiser Wilhelm's six sons, for instance, had cushy jobs at home. German morale sank.[38]

To make matters worse, the grand German offensive had not crushed the Allies before the AEF arrived in strength. By the fall of 1918, 2.3 million "Yanks" were in France. Not only did they play a key role in halting the German drive, the fresh American troops joined a massive Allied counterattack. Outnumbered and outgunned, the Germans began a slow retreat toward the German border. The Germans realized that the Allies, once joined by the United States, were too strong. Faced with certain defeat, Berlin offered to discuss peace. President Wilson wanted a quick end to the bloodshed, too. In his proposal for peace, called the Fourteen Points, he offered generous terms and described an idea for a league of nations, a worldwide organization to prevent future wars. The idea was to avert further grievances and the bitterness that, Wilson believed, would surely lead to another war.

Roosevelt did not want peace just yet. In the ex-president's view, Wilson had called for a "peace without victory," a negotiated peace in which neither side dictated terms to the other. That was unthinkable, said Roosevelt, given Germany's "atrocious" actions. No, Roosevelt said to Wilson's peace terms. The Germans were criminals. You defeat criminals, you punish criminals—you demand their unconditional surrender. If Germany refused to place itself completely in Allied hands, then the Allies should invade. So far Germany had fought only on its neighbors' territory. Now let the war end with its armies defeated on its own soil! Let the German people see their defeat up close, amid the ruins of their own cities! That way Germans would have no illusions about who had won the war.[39]

Beating Germany to its knees, Roosevelt knew, might take many months and claim thousands more Allied lives. "But," he explained, "it is a much worse thing to quit now and have the children growing up to be obliged to do the job all over again, and with ten times more bloodshed and suffering, when their turn comes." A Germany not totally defeated and disarmed would rise again, stronger than ever. Of that Roosevelt was sure. It might take just a few years, or perhaps a generation, but then "our country and the other free countries would have to choose between bowing their necks to the German yoke or going into another war under conditions far more disadvantageous to them." His proposal to invade Germany found little support. Too many had died already, Allied leaders thought. To ask for more dying when the enemy was willing to talk peace, was asking too much.[40]

Meanwhile, Roosevelt's health was failing rapidly. In February 1918, a serious infection put him in the hospital. He left a month later, deaf in one ear and off balance, walking "more like a lunatic

While his daughter Ethel and her husband, Dr. Richard Derby, were tending to wounded American troops in France, the proud grandfather looked after their baby daughter, Edith.

duck than anything else." On November 11, high fever, rheumatism, chest pains, and anemia sent him back to the hospital. As he checked in, the Armistice, or cease-fire, went into effect. The First World War was over! The Allies had won! Outside the hospital, America went wild with joy. In France, soldiers on both sides cheered, hardly believing they were still alive. Some 126,000 Americans had died in the war. Another 234,000 were wounded and 4,526 declared "missing"; most of the missing had been blown to bits, making their remains impossible to find, let alone identify.[41]

Not everyone welcomed the Armistice. That day, General John J. Pershing, commander of the AEF, watched as the guns fell silent. "What I dread is that Germany doesn't know that she was licked," he said, echoing Roosevelt. As the general spoke, a German corporal temporarily blinded by poison gas lay in a German hospital. When doctors announced the Armistice, the corporal, one Adolf Hitler by name, vowed a terrible vow. If he recovered, he swore to avenge the "stab in the back" of Germany's army.

A combat veteran at twenty-seven, Adolf Hitler (seated left, an x over his head) poses with friends and his company's mascot during a lull in fighting on the Western Front.

Hitler thought the German army had been defeated not on the battlefield, but through its "betrayal" by Jewish and socialist traitors at home. Already the seeds of the disaster Roosevelt feared and predicted had taken root in Hitler's warped mind. The Second World War, in which Roosevelt's prediction for another war with Germany became a reality, would be the worst conflict in history.[42]

Theodore Roosevelt would not see that tragedy. After six weeks in the hospital, the former president returned to his beloved Sagamore Hill for Christmas. On the evening of January 5, 1919, he felt strange, as if his heart and breathing were about to "shut down." He was so weak that his African-American butler, James Amos, had to undress him and put him to bed. As Amos left the room, Roosevelt said, "James, will you put out the light?" Those were his last

words. In the early hours of January 6, he died of a blood clot in a coronary artery.[43] He was sixty years old.

Archie, home on leave, cabled his brothers overseas: "The old lion is dead."[44]

Newspapers ran Roosevelt's obituary, along with pictures of him doing his favorite things—speaking, riding, hunting, laughing. Airplanes from nearby Quentin Roosevelt Field flew low, in V formation, to drop flowers on Sagamore Hill. Eulogies poured in, praising the man and his achievements.

No eulogy was so sincere, and so true, as the one by W.E.B. Du Bois. In it, the scholar and civil-rights leader went to the core of Roosevelt the man, revealing the special qualities that formed his very being. Writing in the NAACP's journal *Crisis,* Du Bois noted that the former president was not perfect. But nobody is. Above all, Du Bois wrote, Theodore Roosevelt meant well, doing good as he understood it. For that reason, surely, African-Americans should mourn his passing:

The front page of the New York World, *January 7, 1919, announces Theodore Roosevelt's death in his sleep.*

Take him all in all he was a man, generous, impulsive, fearless, loving the public eye, but intent on achieving the public good. . . . We have lost a friend. That he was our friend proves the justice of our cause, for Roosevelt never championed a cause which was not in essence right. . . . Even in our hot bitterness over the Brownsville affair, we knew that he believed he was right, and he of all men had to act in accordance with his beliefs. It is good to remember that in 1917 he justified our trust when at the time of the East St. Louis riots he alone, of all Americans prating of liberty and democracy, uttered his courageous pronouncement at the meeting in Carnegie Hall. . . . "Justice with me," he had shouted, "is not a mere form of words!"[45]

Can anyone ask more of a fellow human being?

NOTES

PROLOGUE
SEVEN COACHES
ALL DRESSED IN BLACK

1. David McCullough, *The Path Between the Seas: The Creation of the Panama Canal, 1870–1914* (New York: Simon & Schuster, 1971), 249.

2. David McCullough, *Truman* (New York: Simon & Schuster, 1992), 7; Edmund Morris, *The Rise of Theodore Roosevelt* (New York: Coward, McCann & Geoghegan, 1979), 22.

3. John Milton Cooper Jr., *Pivotal Decades: The United States, 1900–1920* (New York: W. W. Norton, 1990), 34.

4. Lawrence F. Abbott, *Impressions of Theodore Roosevelt* (Garden City, N.Y.: Doubleday, Page, 1919), 270.

5. Abbott, *Impressions of Theodore Roosevelt,* 267; Edward Wagenknecht, *The Seven Worlds of Theodore Roosevelt* (New York: Longmans, Green, 1958), 105, 107; Morris, *The Rise of Theodore Roosevelt,* 24, 25.

6. Kathleen Dalton, *Theodore Roosevelt: A Strenuous Life* (New York: Knopf, 2002), 522.

7. H. W. Brands, *The Reckless Decade: America in the 1890s* (New York: St. Martin's Press, 1995), 293.

8. H. W. Brands, *T.R.: The Last Romantic* (New York: Basic Books, 1997), 577; Morris, *The Rise of Theodore Roosevelt,* 24; Peter Collier, *The Roosevelts: An American Saga* (New York: Simon & Schuster, 1994), 76; Dalton,*Theodore Roosevelt: A Strenuous Life,* 291; J. Anthony Lukas, *Big Trouble: A Murder in a Small Town Sets Off a Struggle for the Soul of America* (New York: Simon & Schuster, 1997), 395.

9. William E. Leuchtenberg, "FDR: The First Modern President" in Fred I. Greenstein, ed., *Leadership in the Modern Presidency* (Cambridge, MA: Harvard University Press, 1988), 16.

10. Page Smith, *The Rise of Industrial America* (New York: McGraw-Hill, 1984), 485–486.

11. Morris, *The Rise of Theodore Roosevelt,* 579; Dalton, *Theodore Roosevelt: A Strenuous Life,* 4, 343; Christopher Caldwell, "Tagging After Teddy," The Atlantic Online, March 22, 2000, at www.theatlantic.com/unbound/polipro/pp2000-03-22.htm.

12. Theodore Roosevelt, *An Autobiography* (New York: Da Capo, 1985), 372.

13. Ibid., 372.

14. Dalton, *Theodore Roosevelt: A Strenuous Life,* 7.

15. Elting E. Morison, John Morton Blum, and Alfred Chandler, eds. *The Letters of Theodore Roosevelt* (8 vols., Cambridge, Mass.: Harvard University Press, 1951–54), V, 840.

1
A BOY OF
OLD MANHATTAN

1. Nathan Miller, *Theodore Roosevelt: A Life* (New York: William Morrow, 1992), 28.

2. Stefan Lorant, *The Life and Times of Theodore Roosevelt* (Garden City, N.Y.: Doubleday, 1959), 14.

3. Kathleen Dalton, "Early Life of Theodore Roosevelt," Ph.d. Dissertation, John's Hopkins University, 1979, 84; Brands, *T.R.: The Last Romantic,* 6.

4. Bayrd Still, *Mirror for Gotham: New York as Seen by Contemporaries from the Dutch Days to the Present* (New York: New York University Press, 1956), 138, 143–144 .

5. Miller, *Theodore Roosevelt,* 28; Joseph P. Lash, *Eleanor and Franklin* (New York: W. W. Norton, 1971), 16.

6. Morris, *The Rise of Theodore Roosevelt,* 35; Dalton, "Early Life of Theodore Roosevelt," 56.

7. Lash, *Eleanor and Franklin,* 4; Theodore Roosevelt, *An Autobiography* (New York: Da Capo, 1985), 7–8.

8. Morris, *The Rise of Theodore Roosevelt,* 34.

9. Miller, *Theodore Roosevelt,* 32.

10. Louis Auchincloss, *Theodore Roosevelt* (New York: Henry Holt, 2002), 36.

11. Carleton Putnam,*Theodore Roosevelt: The Formative Years, 1858–1886* (New York: Charles Scribner's Sons, 1958), 48.

12. David McCullough, *Mornings on Horseback* (New York: Simon & Schuster, 1981), 37; Joseph P. Lash, *Eleanor and Franklin,* (New York: W.W. Norton, 1971), 4; Collier, *The Roosevelts,* 31; Dalton, *Theodore Roosevelt: A Strenuous Life,* 34–35.

13. Dalton, "Early Life of Theodore Roosevelt," 112.

14. Miller, *Theodore Roosevelt,* 35–36.

15. Dalton, *Theodore Roosevelt: A Strenuous Life,* 35.

16. Dalton, "Early Life of Theodore Roosevelt," 119; Edward J. Renehan Jr., *The Lion's Pride: Theodore Roosevelt and His Family in Peace and War* (New York: Oxford University Press, 1998), 23.

17. Dalton, *Theodore Roosevelt: A Strenuous Life,* 27.

18. McCullough, *Mornings on Horseback,* 59–60.

19. Joseph Bucklin Bishop, *Theodore Roosevelt and His Time, Shown in His Own Letters* (2 vols., New York: Charles Scribner's Sons, 1920), I, 2; Morris, *The Rise of Theodore Roosevelt,* 53; Miller, *Theodore Roosevelt,* 31; McCullough, *Mornings on Horseback,* 103.

20. McCullough, *Mornings on Horseback,* 92–93.

21. *Ibid.,* 90–93; Lincoln Steffens, *The Autobiography of Lincoln Steffens* (New York: The Literary Guild, 1931), 350.

22. Miller, *Theodore Roosevelt,* 45.

23. Roosevelt, *Autobiography,* 29.

24. Roosevelt, *Autobiography,* 14–15; Dalton, *Theodore Roosevelt: A Strenuous Life,* 42.

25. Hermann Hagdorn, *The Boys' Life of Theodore Roosevelt* (New York: Harper & Brothers, 1918), 28–29.

26. Morris, *The Rise of Theodore Roosevelt,* 47.

27. Brands,*T.R.: The Last Romantic,* 23, 25.

28. Corinne Roosevelt Robinson, *My Brother Theodore Roosevelt* (New York: Charles Scribner's Sons, 1921), 50.

29. Roosevelt, *Autobiography,* 29–30.

30. *Ibid.,* 54.

31. *Ibid.,* 19.

32. McCullough, *Mornings on Horseback,* 118.

33. Richard Hofstadter,*The American Political Tradition: And the Men Who Made It* (New York: Vintage Books, 1948), 210–211.

34. Miller, *Theodore Roosevelt,* 53–54.

35. Wagenknecht,*The Seven Worlds of Theodore Roosevelt,* 247; Dalton, "Early Life of Theodore Roosevelt," 245–247.

36. Dalton, *Theodore Roosevelt: A Strenuous Life,* 55.

37. Morris, *The Rise of Theodore Roosevelt,* 71; Miller, *Theodore Roosevelt,* 60.

38. Roosevelt, *Autobiography,* 23.

39. Morris, *The Rise of Theodore Roosevelt,* 82; McCullough, *Mornings on Horseback,* 189, 198–199.

40. Brands, *T.R.: The Last Romantic,* 58.

41. Morris, *The Rise of Theodore Roosevelt,* 83; Dalton, *Theodore Roosevelt: A Strenuous Life,* 61–62; Miller, *Theodore Roosevelt,* 66–67.

42. Wagenknecht, *The Seven Worlds of Theodore Roosevelt,* 32.

43. Morris, *The Rise of Theodore Roosevelt,* 84; McCullough, *Mornings on Horseback,* 160.

44. Collier, *The Roosevelts,* 45; Miller, *Theodore Roosevelt,* 66, 67.

45. Morison, *Letters of Theodore Roosevelt,* I, 18.

46. McCullough, *Mornings on Horseback,* 512.

47. Morris, *The Rise of Theodore Roosevelt,* 84-85.

48. Miller, *Theodore Roosevelt,* 80; Brands, *T. R.: The Last Romantic,* 80.

49. Miller, *Theodore Roosevelt,* 81; Morris, *The Rise of Theodore Roosevelt,* 95.

50. Morris, *The Rise of Theodore Roosevelt,* 104; McCullough, *Mornings on Horseback,* 220; Putnam, *Theodore Roosevelt,* 71.

51. Dalton, "Early Life of Theodore Roosevelt," 299; Dalton, *Theodore Roosevelt: A Strenuous Life,* 72–73; Miller, *Theodore Roosevelt,* 99.

52. The Inflation Calculator, http:/westegg.com/inflation/infl.cgi

53. Miller, *Theodore Roosevelt,* 113.

54. William Roscoe Thayer, *Theodore Roosevelt: An Intimate Biography* (New York: Grosset & Dunlap, 1919), 21.

55. Miller, *Theodore Roosevelt,* 100–101.

2
THE LIFE OF EFFORT

1. Miller, *Theodore Roosevelt,* 105.

2. Brands, *T.R.: The Last Romantic,* 73; Roosevelt, *Autobiography,* 55.

3. Roosevelt, *Autobiography,* 57–58.

4. Miller, *Theodore Roosevelt,* 76; Roosevelt, *Autobiography,* 57.

5. Abbott, *Impressions of Theodore Roosevelt,* 41–42; Miller, *Theodore Roosevelt,* 117–121.

6. Brands, *T.R.: The Last Romantic,* 131; Dalton, *Theodore Roosevelt: A Strenuous Life,* 81; Thomas G. Dyer, *Theodore Roosevelt and the Idea of Race* (Baton Rouge: Louisiana State University Press, 1980), 127.

7. Brands, *T.R.: The Last Romantic,* 133–134.

8. Miller, *Theodore Roosevelt,* 122, 123; Morris, *The Rise of Theodore Roosevelt,* 161, 170.

9. Morris, *The Rise of Theodore Roosevelt,* 166.

10. McCullough, *Mornings on Horseback,* 258.

11. Jacob Riis, *Theodore Roosevelt, the Citizen* (New York: The Outlook Company, 1904), 57.

12. Roosevelt, *Autobiography,* 28.

13. McCullough, *Mornings on Horseback,* 259.

14. Roosevelt, *Autobiography,* 82.

15. Miller, *Theodore Roosevelt,* 136.

16. *Ibid.,* 141–142.

17. Morris, *The Rise of Theodore Roosevelt,* 198–199.

18. McCullough, *Mornings on Horseback,* 283.

19. Morris, *The Rise of Theodore Roosevelt,* 241.

20. *Ibid.,* 243–244.

21. McCullough, *Mornings on Horseback,* 247.

22. Dalton, *Theodore Roosevelt: A Strenuous Life,* 91–92.

23. Morris, *The Rise of Theodore Roosevelt,* 212; McCullough, *Mornings on Horseback,* 332; Putnam, *Theodore Roosevelt,* 312.

24. Morris, *The Rise of Theodore Roosevelt,* 224; Miller, *Theodore Roosevelt,* 151.

25. Morris, *The Rise of Theodore Roosevelt,* 273.

26. Hermann Hagdorn, *Roosevelt in the Bad Lands* (Boston: Houghton Mifflin Company, 1921), 101.

27. Roosevelt, *Autobiography,* 94–95.

28. Hagdorn, *Roosevelt in the Bad Lands,* 151–153, 284–285.

29. McCullough, *Mornings on Horseback,* 34, 350; Morris, *The Rise of Theodore Roosevelt,* 303.

30. Sylvia Jukes Morris, *Edith Kermit Roosevelt: Portrait of a First Lady* (New York: Coward, McCann & Geoghegan, 1980), 1–2.

31. Robinson, *My Brother Theodore Roosevelt,* 97; Morris, *Edith Kermit Roosevelt,* 59.

32. Miller, *Theodore Roosevelt,* 180–181.

33. Hagdorn, *Roosevelt in the Bad Lands,* 432; McCullough, *Mornings on Horseback,* 344; Miller, *Theodore Roosevelt,* 188.

34. Miller, *Theodore Roosevelt,* 187; Wagenknecht, *The Seven Worlds of Theodore Roosevelt,* 167.

35. Dalton, *Theodore Roosevelt: A Strenuous Life,* 115, 123; Wagenknecht, *The Seven Worlds of Theodore Roosevelt,* 166.

36. Miller, *Theodore Roosevelt,* 190, 192.

37. Dalton, *Theodore Roosevelt: A Strenuous Life,* 134; Hermann Hagdorn, *The Bugle That Woke America: The Saga of Theodore Roosevelt's Last Battle for His Country* (New York: The John Day Company, 1940), 91; Collier, *The Roosevelts,* 124.

38. Collier, *The Roosevelts,* 124; Brands, *T.R.: The Last Romantic,* 380–381.

39. Miller, *Theodore Roosevelt,* 256–257.

40. *Ibid.,* 205.

41. Henry F. Pringle, *Theodore Roosevelt: A Biography* (New York: Harcourt, Brace, 1931), 29.

42. Brands, *T.R.: The Last Romantic,* 240-241.

43. Riis, *Theodore Roosevelt, the Citizen,* 131; Jacob Riis, *The Making of an American* (New York: Macmillan, 1901), chap. XIII, "Roosevelt Comes: Mulberry Street's Golden Age."

44. Steffens, *Autobiography,* 257–258.

45. Morris, *The Rise of Theodore Roosevelt,* 496; Brands, *T.R.: The Last Romantic,* 274.

46. Brands, *T.R.: The Last Romantic,* 284; Dalton, *Theodore Roosevelt: A Strenuous Life,* 157.

47. Riis, *Making of an American,* 330–331; Morris, *The Rise of Theodore Roosevelt,* 289; Miller, *Theodore Roosevelt,* 23.

48. Hagdorn, *Boys' Life of Theodore Roosevelt,* 167–168.

49. Dalton, *Theodore Roosevelt: A Strenuous Life,* 157.

50. Roosevelt, *Autobiography,* 185, 191–192.

51. Brands, *T.R.: The Last Romantic,* 303; Roosevelt, *Autobiography,* 194, 196.

52. Morris, *The Rise of Theodore Roosevelt,* 509.

53. Ferdinand C. Inglehart, *Theodore Roosevelt: The Man as I Knew Him* (New York: The Christian Herald, 1919), 112.

54. Roosevelt, *Autobiography,* 197.

55. Brands, *T.R.: The Last Romantic,* 299.

3
A THUNDERING EXPRESS TRAIN

1. Roy P. Basler, *The Collected Works of Abraham Lincoln* (9 vols., New Brunswick, N.J.: Rutgers University Press, 1953), IV, 240.

2. Crandall Shifflett, *Victorian America, 1876 to 1900* (New York: Facts on File, 1996), 65–66. See also John F. Stover, *American Railroads* (Chicago: University of Chicago Press, 1992).

3. Nell Irvin Painter, *Standing at Armageddon: The United States, 1877–1919* (New York: W. W. Norton, 1987), xix–xx; Page Smith, *America Enters the World: A People's History of the Progressive Era and World War I* (New York: McGraw-Hill, 1985), 9–10.

4. Richard Hofstadter, *Social Darwinism in American Thought* (Boston: The Beacon Press, 1955), 45.

5. Richard Hofstadter, *The Age of Reform: From Bryan to F.D.R.* (New York: Knopf, 1955), 136–137.

6. Frederick Townsend Martin, *The Passing of the Idle Rich* (New York: Arno Press, 1975), 389, 390.

7. Charles A. and Mary Beard, *The Rise of American Civilization,* 2 vols. in 1 (New York: Macmillan, 1930), II, 392; Stewart H. Holbrook, *The Age of the Moguls* (Garden City, N.Y.: Doubleday, 1953), 330–33; Martin, *Passing of the Idle Rich,* 39.

8. Martin, *Passing of the Idle Rich,* 30, 36; Beard, *The Rise of American Civilization,* II, 393.

9. Holbrook, *Age of the Moguls,* 95.

10. Bishop, *Theodore Roosevelt and His Time,* II, 32.

11. William Henry Harbaugh, *Power and Responsibility: The Life and Times of Theodore Roosevelt (New York: Farrar, Straus & Cudahy, 1961),* 152; Steffens, *Autobiography,* 504; Irving Greenberg, *Theodore Roosevelt and Labor, 1900–1918* (New York: Garland Publishing, 1988), 393.

12. U.S. population: 50,155,783 (1880), 62,947,714 (1890), 75,004,575 (1900), 91,972,266 (1910), Shifflett, *Victorian America,* 74; Robert A. Rosenbaum, *The Penguin Encyclopedia of American History* (New York: Penguin Reference, 2003), 168.

13. Irving Howe, *World of Our Fathers* (New York: Harcourt Brace Jovanovich, 1976), 27.

14. *Ibid.,* 39, 40–41.

15. Still, *Mirror for Gotham,* 213–214.

16. Painter, *Standing at Armageddon,* xxiv.

17. Dalton, *Theodore Roosevelt: A Strenuous Life,* 185; Painter, *Standing at Armageddon,* xx; Shifflett, *Victorian America,* 54–55; Greenberg, *Theodore Roosevelt and Labor,* 75.

18. Painter, *Standing at Armageddon,* 206; H. Paul Jeffers, *An Honest President: The Life and Presidencies of Grover Cleveland* (New York: William Morrow, 2000), 194.

19. Smith, *Rise of Industrial America,* 449.

20. *Ibid.,* 168–176.

21. Lukas, *Big Trouble,* 64; Louis Adamic, *Dynamite: The Story of Class Violence in America* (Gloucester, Mass.: Peter Smith, 1960), 48.

22. Smith, *Rise of Industrial America,* 225.

23. Brands, *Reckless Decade,* 160–162, 172–175.

24. Smith, *Rise of Industrial America,* 521; Ray Ginger, *The Bending Cross: A Biography of Eugene Victor Debs* (New Brunswick, N.J.: Rutgers University Press, 1949), 54. The Mercy Seat is also called the Judgment Seat of God.

25. Smith, *Rise of Industrial America,* 619.

26. Jim Crow originated in popular minstrel shows that featured a white man made up as a blackened-face clown dancing to a snappy tune, "Jump Jim Crow." C. Vann Woodward, *The Strange Death of Jim Crow* (New York: Oxford University Press, 1955), 82–84; Thomas F. Gossett, *Race: The History of an Idea in America* (New York: Schocken Books, 1965), 277–278.

27. Brands, *Reckless Decade,* 231–232.

28. Smith, *Rise of Industrial America,* 659; Philip Dray, *At the Hands of Persons Unknown: The Lynching of Black America* (New York: Random House, 2002), 98–100; Gossett, *Race,* 262–263.

29. Shifflett, *Victorian America,* 334.

30. Quoted in NAACP, *Thirty Years of Lynching in the United States, 1889–1918* (New York: NAACP, 1919), 12–13.

31. Dray, *At the Hands of Persons Unknown,* 112; Francis Butler Simkins, *Pitchfork Ben Tillman: South Carolinian* (Baton Rouge: Louisiana State University Press, 1944), 396.

32. Nicholas D. Kristof, "Is Race Real?," *New York Times,* July 11, 2003.

33. Smith, *Rise of Industrial America,* 621.

34. Dray, *At the Hands of Persons Unknown,* 83.

4

FOLLOWING THE DRUM: FROM BATTLEFIELD TO WHITE HOUSE

1. Steffens, *Autobiography,* 258–259.

2. Jay M. Shafritz, ed., *Words on War* (New York: Prentice Hall, 1990), 279.

3. Wagenknecht, *The Seven Worlds of Theodore Roosevelt,* 250; Morris, *The Rise of Theodore Roosevelt,* 598; Miller, *Theodore Roosevelt,* 235.

4. Morris, *The Rise of Theodore Roosevelt,* 569.

5. Brands, *T.R.: The Last Romantic,* 309.

6. Morris, *The Rise of Theodore Roosevelt,* 599.

7. Miller, *Theodore Roosevelt,* 266.

8. *Ibid.,* 267.

9. Morris, *The Rise of Theodore Roosevelt,* 603.

10. Miller, *Theodore Roosevelt,* 271; Morris, *The Rise of Theodore Roosevelt,* 610; Archie Butt, *The Letters of Archie Butt: Personal Aide to President Roosevelt* (Garden City, N.Y.: Doubleday, Page, 1924), 146.

11. Morris, *Edith Kermit Roosevelt,* 172.

12. Renehan, *The Lion's Pride,* 21, 27.

13. Theodore Roosevelt, *The Rough Riders*

and Men of Action (New York: Charles Scribner's Sons, 1926), 12–13.

14. Smith, *Rise of Industrial America,* 875.

15. Brands, *Reckless Decade,* 328.

16. Morris, *The Rise of Theodore Roosevelt,* 641; Wagenknecht, *The Seven Worlds of Theodore Roosevelt,* 250.

17. Morris, *Edith Kermit Roosevelt,* 179–180; Dalton, *Theodore Roosevelt: A Strenuous Life,* 173.

18. Roosevelt, *Rough Riders,* 79–80.

19. *Ibid.,* 81.

20. Roosevelt, *Rough Riders,* 81; Morris, *The Rise of Theodore Roosevelt,* 654.

21. Morris, *The Rise of Theodore Roosevelt,* 655.

22. *Ibid.,* 656.

23. Brands, *T.R.: The Last Romantic,* 359–360; Dalton, *Theodore Roosevelt: A Strenuous Life,* 176.

24. Miller, *Theodore Roosevelt,* 311–312.

25. Auchincloss, *Theodore Roosevelt,* 30.

26. Smith, *America Enters the World,* 12.

27. Brands, *T.R.: The Last Romantic,* 367.

28. William Henry Harbaugh, *Power and Responsibility: The Life and Times of Theodore Roosevelt* (New York: Farrar, Straus and Cudahy, 1961), 113; Miller, *Theodore Roosevelt,* 314, 321.

29. Miller, *Theodore Roosevelt,* 328, 335.

30. *Ibid.,* 338; Brands, *T.R.: The Last Romantic,* 397.

31. Harbaugh, *Power and Responsibility,* 143; Brands, *T.R.: The Last Romantic,* 410.

32. Miller, *Theodore Roosevelt,* 354.

5

AT HOME IN THE WHITE HOUSE

1. Dalton, "Early Life of Theodore Roosevelt," 4.

2. Steffens, *Autobiography,* 503.

3. Alice Roosevelt Longworth, *Crowded Hours: Reminiscences of Alice Roosevelt Longworth* (New York: Charles Scribner's Sons, 1933), 44.

4. Margaret Leech, *In the Days of McKinley,* (New York: Harper & Brothers, 1959), 121; Morris, *Edith Kermit Roosevelt,* 223; Dalton, *Theodore Roosevelt: A Strenuous Life,* 218.

5. Miller, *Theodore Roosevelt,* 416; Morris, *Edith Kermit Roosevelt,* 416; Steffens, *Autobiography,* 512.

6. Miller, *Theodore Roosevelt,* 418; Dalton, *Theodore Roosevelt: A Strenuous Life,* 220.

7. Abbott, *Impressions of Theodore Roosevelt,* 89–90.

8. William Bayard Hale, *A Week in the White House with Theodore Roosevelt* (New York: G. P. Putnam's Sons, 1908), 44.

9. Wister, *Roosevelt,* 238–240.

10. Morris, *Edith Kermit Roosevelt,* 294.

11. Morris, *The Rise of Theodore Roosevelt,* 15.

12. Morton Keller, ed., *Theodore Roosevelt: A Profile* (New York: Hill and Wang, 1967), 95; Morris, *Edith Kermit Roosevelt,* 209.

13. James E. Amos, *Theodore Roosevelt: Hero to His Valet* (New York: John Day, 1927), 43–44. What cost $50,000 in 1900 would have cost $1,037,800 in 2002. The Inflation Calculator, www.westegg.com/inflation.

14. Amos, *Theodore Roosevelt,* 23–24.

15. Dalton, *Theodore Roosevelt: A Strenuous Life,* 213.

16. Morris, *The Rise of Theodore Roosevelt,* 28; Abbott, *Impressions of Theodore Roosevelt,* 184.

17. Hale, *A Week in the White House,* 133; Wagenknecht, *The Seven Worlds of Theodore Roosevelt,* 32, 44.

18. Theodore Roosevelt, *Letters to Kermit from Theodore Roosevelt* (New York: Charles Scribner's Sons, 1946), 22; Brands, *T.R.: The Last Romantic,* 564.

19. Theodore Roosevelt, *Letters to His Children* (New York: Charles Scribner's Sons, 1928), 93; Wagenknecht, *The Seven Worlds of Theodore Roosevelt,* 117.

20. Dalton, *Theodore Roosevelt: A Strenuous Life,* 273; Wagenknecht, *The Seven Worlds of Theodore Roosevelt,* 13, 14; Morris, *The Rise of Theodore Roosevelt,* 18.

21. Miller, *Theodore Roosevelt,* 415-416; Frederick S. Wood, *Theodore Roosevelt as We Knew Him* (Philadelphia: The John C. Winston Company, 1927), 297–298.

22. Morris, *Edith Kermit Roosevelt,* 278.

23. Miller, *Theodore Roosevelt,* 414, Roosevelt, *Letters to His Children,* 153–154.

24. Miller, *Theodore Roosevelt,* 414; Wagenknecht, *The Seven Worlds of Theodore Roosevelt,* 175.

25. Roosevelt, *Letters to His Children,* 199–200.

26. *Ibid.,* 217.

27. Earle Looker, *The White House Gang* (New York: Fleming H. Revell Company, 1929), 16–18; Roosevelt, *Letters to His Children,* 225–226.

28. Looker, *White House Gang,* 45–46; Brands, *T.R.: The Last Romantic,* 562.

29. Sarah Watts, *Rough Rider in the White House: Theodore Roosevelt and the Politics of Desire* (Chicago: University of Chicago Press, 2003), 89; Morris, *Edith Kermit Roosevelt,* 273; Miller, *Theodore Roosevelt,* 376; Dalton, *Theodore Roosevelt: A Strenuous Life,* 218.

30. Brands, *T.R.: The Last Romantic,* 521. Roosevelt got Alice off his hands in 1908, when she married Ohio congressman Nicholas Longworth.

6
"I BELIEVE IN POWER"

1. Wister, *Roosevelt,* 253; William Larry Ziglar, "Negro Opinion of Theodore Roosevelt," Ph.d. Dissertation, University of Maine at Orono, 1972, 54–56; Dyer, *Theodore Roosevelt and the Idea of Race,* 31–32; Dalton, *Theodore Roosevelt: A Strenuous Life,* 126.

2. George Sinkler, *The Racial Attitudes of American Presidents from Abraham Lincoln to Theodore Roosevelt* (Garden City, N.Y.: Doubleday, 1971), 342, 355.

3. Dray, *At the Hands of Persons Unknown,* 161.

4. Thayer, *Theodore Roosevelt,* 283.

5. Brands, *T.R.: The Last Romantic,* 423; Dalton, *Theodore Roosevelt: A Strenuous Life,* 216; Miller, *Theodore Roosevelt,* 362.

6. Ziglar, "Negro Opinion of Theodore Roosevelt," 140–141.

7. Inglehart, *Theodore Roosevelt,* 198.

8. Eric Rauchway, *Murdering McKinley: The Making of Theodore Roosevelt's America* (New York: Hill and Wang, 2003), 93.

9. Dalton, "Early Life of Theodore Roosevelt," 92; Kathleen Dalton, "Theodore Roosevelt, Knickbocker Aristocrat," *New York History,* January 1986, 45.

10. Dalton, *Theodore Roosevelt: A Strenuous Life,* 17; Dalton, "Theodore Roosevelt, Knickbocker Aristocrat," 55; Charles Willis Thompson, *Presidents I've Known and Two Near Presidents* (Philadelphia: Bobbs-Merrill, 1929), 125–126.

11. Dalton, "Early Life of Theodore Roosevelt," 70; Roosevelt, *Autobiography,* 439; Smith, *America Enters the World,* 56; Wagenknecht, *The Seven Worlds of Theodore Roosevelt,* 217; Inglehart, *Theodore Roosevelt,* 197.

12. John Morton Blum, *The Republican Roosevelt* (Cambridge: Harvard University Press, 1961), 60; Roosevelt, *Letters,* I, 101–102; Hofstadter, *The American Political Tradition,* 218; Ray Ginger, *The Bending Cross: A Biography of Eugene Victor Debs* (New Brunswick, NJ: Rutgers University Press, 1949), 191.

13. Roosevelt, *Letters,* II, 1141.

14. The railways were the Great Northern; Northern Pacific; and Chicago, Burlington and Quincy.

15. Theodore Roosevelt, *The Foes of Our Own Household,* in *The Works of Theodore Roosevelt,* National Edition (New York: Charles Scribner's Sons, 1926), XIX, 72.

16. Dalton, *Theodore Roosevelt: A Strenuous Life,* 224.

17. Harbaugh, *Power and Responsibility,* 150.

18. Painter, *Standing at Armageddon,* 185; Harbaugh, *Power and Responsibility,* 169.

19. John Spargo, *The Bitter Cry of the Children* (New York: Macmillan, 1906), 163–164.

20. Painter, *Standing at Armageddon,* 182; Miller, *Theodore Roosevelt,* 371.

21. Greenberg, *Theodore Roosevelt and Labor,* 120–121.

22. Wagenknecht, *The Seven Worlds of Theodore Roosevelt,* 115; Roosevelt, *Letters,* III, 360; Strouse, *Morgan,* 449.

23. Roosevelt, *Letters,* III, 331–332.

24. Greenberg, *Theodore Roosevelt and Labor,* 143; Miller, *Theodore Roosevelt,* 374; Roosevelt, *Letters,* III, 339–340.

25. Harbaugh, *Power and Responsibility,* 177; Wood, *Theodore Roosevelt as We Knew Him,* 111–112.

26. Samuel Gompers, *Seventy Years of Life and Labor, An Autobiography;* 2 vols. (New York: E. P. Dutton, 1925), II, 117.

27. Brands, *T.R.: The Last Romantic,* 513.

28. Lash, *Eleanor and Franklin,* 138.

29. Miller, *Theodore Roosevelt,* 22.

30. Harbaugh, *Power and Responsibility,* 264–265; Cooper, *Pivotal Decades,* 86–87.

31. Edward M. Brecher, *Licit and Illicit Drugs* (Boston: Little, Brown, 1972), 3; David F. Musto, "Opium, Cocaine and Marijuana in American History," *Scientific American,* July 1991, 40–47, 38; John C. Burnham, *Bad Habits: Drinking, Smoking, Taking Drugs, Gambling, Sexual Misbehavior, and Swearing in American History* (New York: New York University Press, 1993), 114; Edward Robb Ellis, *Echoes of Distant Thunder: Life in the United States, 1914–1918* (New York: Coward, McCann & Geoghegan, 1975), 108.

32. Leon Harris, *Upton Sinclair: American Rebel* (New York: Thomas Y. Crowell,

1975), 70; Upton Sinclair, "What Life Means to Me," *Cosmopolitan Magazine,* October 1906), 41; Upton Sinclair, *The Jungle* (New York: Signet Books, 1960), 136–137.

33. Roosevelt, *Letters,* V, 340–341.

34. *Ibid.,* 340–341.

35. Smith, *America Enters the World,* 106; Peter Carlson, *Roughneck: The Life and Times of Big Bill Haywood* (New York: W. W. Norton, 1983), 16–17.

36. Smith, *America Enters the World,* 113.

37. *Ibid.,* 29.

38. Lukas, *Big Trouble,* 387, 460; Greenberg, *Theodore Roosevelt and Labor,* 334–335.

39. Lukas, *Big Trouble,* 461.

40. Eugene V. Debs, *The Letters of Eugene V. Debs,* ed. J. Robert Constantine, 3 vols. (Urbana: University of Illinois Press, 1990), I, 237; Eugene V. Debs, *Writings and Speeches,* ed. Arthur M. Schlesinger Jr. (New York: Hermitage Press, 1948), 268, 271.

41. Lukas, *Big Trouble,* 470; Adamic, *Dynamite,* 148,150; Dalton, *Theodore Roosevelt: A Strenuous Life,* 329.

42. Lukas, *Big Trouble,* 329.

43. Greenberg, *Theodore Roosevelt and Labor,* 304, 337–338.

44. Dray, *At the Hands of Persons Unknown,* 159; Gail Buckley, *American Patriots: The Story of Blacks in the Military from the Revolution to Desert Storm* (New York: Random House, 2001), 160–161.

45. John D. Weaver, *The Senator and the Sharecropper's Son: Exoneration of the Brownsville Soldiers* (College Station: Texas A&M University Press, 1997),106–107.

46. Weaver, *The Senator and the Sharecropper's Son,* 130–131.

47. James A.Tinsley, "Roosevelt, Foraker and the Brownsville Affray," *Journal of Negro History,* January 1956, 48–49; Ziglar, "Negro Opinion of Theodore Roosevelt," 322.

48. Dalton, *Theodore Roosevelt: A Strenuous Life,* 322.

7
"CONSERVATION IS A GREAT MORAL ISSUE"

1. Gordon G. Whitney, *From Coastal Wilderness to Fruited Plain: A History of Environmental Change in Temperate North America, 1500 to the Present* (Cambridge, Eng.: Cambridge University Press, 1994), 53; John Opie, *Nature's Nation: An Environmental History of the United States* (New York: Harcourt Brace College Publishers, 1998), 16; Richard G. Lillard,*The Great Forest* (New York: Knopf, 1948), 4.

2. Lillard, *The Great Forest,* 6.

3. Wayne Gard, *The Great Buffalo Hunt* (New York: Knopf, 1960), 6; Tom McHugh, *The Time of the Buffalo* (New York: Knopf, 1972), 16.

4. Lillard, *The Great Forest,* 6; Opie, *Nature's Nation,* 16; John Bakeless, *Eyes of Discovery: American as Seen by the First Explorers* (Philadelphia: J. B. Lippincott, 1950), 195, 216, 273; Richard A. Bartlett, *The New Country: A Social History of the American Frontier, 1776–1890* (New York: Oxford University Press, 1974), 250; John James Audubon, *Writings and Drawings* (New York: The Library of America, 1999), 265–266.

5. Whitney, *From Coastal Wilderness to Fruited Plain,* 180–181; Ted Steinberg, *Down to Earth: Nature's Role in American History* (New York: Oxford University Press, 2002), 18.

6. Steinberg, *Down to Earth,* 17.

7. Richard Drinnon, *Facing West: Indian Hating and Empire Building* (New York: Schocken Books, 1990), 100.

8. Stephen Bosnal, *When the French Were Here* (New York: Kennikat Press, 1968), 92–93.

9. Steinberg, *Down to Earth,* 142; Lukas, *Big Trouble,* 618.

10. Lillard, *The Great Forest,* 101–107; Frank Graham Jr., *Man's Dominion: The Story of Conservation in America.* Philadelphia (J. B. Lippincott, 1971), 69; Smith, *America Enters the World,* 118.

11. Davis D. Smits, "The Frontier Army and the Destruction of the Buffalo: 1865–1883," *Western Historical Quarterly,* Autumn 1994, 338.

12. Graham, *Man's Dominion,* 20, 24.

13. *Ibid.,* 23, 46–48.

14. James B. Trefethen, *An American Crusade for Wildlife* (New York: Winchester Press and the Boone and Crockett Club, 1975), 64.

15. Theodore Roosevelt, *Hunting Expeditions in the West* (New York: G. P. Putnam's Sons, 1927), 186–187, 191.

16. Morris, *The Rise of Theodore Roosevelt,* 382.

17. Miller, *Theodore Roosevelt,* 168.

18. Paul Russell Cutright, *Theodore Roosevelt: The Making of a Conservationist* (Urbana: University of Illinois Press, 1985),178–179, 203–204; Stephen Fox, *John Muir and His Legacy: The American Conservation Movement* (Boston: Little, Brown), 124.

19. Fox, *John Muir and His Legacy,* 124-125; Graham, *Man's Dominion,* 115; Paul Russell Cutright, *Theodore Roosevelt the Naturalist* (New York: Harper & Brothers, 1956), 152.

20. Filler, Daniel, "Theodore Roosevelt: Conservation as the Guardian of Democracy," www.http//pantheon.cis.yale.edu/-thomast/essays/filler/filler.html.

21. Cutright, *Theodore Roosevelt the Naturalist,* 166–168.

22. *Ibid.,* 168; Cutright, *Theodore Roosevelt: The Making of a Conservationist,* 218–219.

23. Graham, *Man's Dominion,* 109.

24. *Ibid.,* 130; Cutright,*Theodore Roosevelt the Naturalist,* 172–173.

25. Cutright, *Theodore Roosevelt: The Making of a Conservationist,* 223.

26. William Hornaday, *The Man Who Became a Savage* (1896), quoted in Andrew C. Isenberg, *The Destruction of the Bison* (New York: Cambridge University Press, 2000), 172.

27. Isenberg, *The Destruction of the Bison,* 188–189.

28. Theodore Roosevelt, *Presidential Addresses and State Papers; European Addresses,* 8 vols. (New York: The Review of Reviews, 1910), I, 370; Dalton, *Theodore Roosevelt: A Strenuous Life,* 247. The Grand Canyon finally became a national park in 1919, shortly after Roosevelt's death.

29. Cutright, *Theodore Roosevelt the Naturalist,* 183–184.

8
THE YOUNG GIANT OF THE WEST

1. Roosevelt, *Autobiography,* 516.

2. *Ibid.,* 212.

3. Wagenknecht,*The Seven Worlds of Theodore Roosevelt,* 262; Morris, *Edith Kermit Roosevelt,* 287.

4. Brands, *Reckless Decade,* 333.

5. Leech, *In the Days of McKinley,* 345.

6. Philip S. Foner and Richard C. Winchester, *The Anti-Imperialist Reader: A Documentary History of Anti-Imperialism in the United States,* 2 vols. (New York: Holmes & Meier Publishers, 1984, 1986), II, 323.

7. Stuart C. Miller, *"Benevolent Assimilation": The American Conquest of the Philippines, 1899–1903* (New Haven: Yale University Press, 1982), 189; Foner and Winchester, *Anti-Imperialist Reader,* II, 318.

8. Joseph Frazier Wall, *Andrew Carnegie* (New York: Oxford University Press, 1970), 697.

9. Foner and Winchester, *The Anti-Imperialist Reader,* II, 206, 207.

10. Dyer, *Theodore Roosevelt and the Idea of Race,* 140; Dalton, *Theodore Roosevelt: A Strenuous Life,* 228; Brands, *T.R.: The Last Romantic,* 386.

11. Stanley Karnow, *In Our Image: America's Empire in the Philippines* (New York: Random House, 1989), 189–190; Leon Wolff, *Little Brown Brother: How the United States Purchased and Pacified the Philippines at the Century's Turn* (Garden City, N.Y.: Doubleday, 1961), 355–357.

12. Joseph L. Schlott, *The Ordeal of Samar* (Indianapolis: Bobbs-Merrill, 1964), 71; Wolff, *Little Brown Brother,* 357; Karnow, *In Our Image,* 189.

13. Schlott, *The Ordeal of Samar,* 278–279.

14. Karnow, *In Our Image,* 194; Painter, *Standing at Armageddon,* 154.

15. Hugh Thomas, *Cuba: The Pursuit of Freedom* (New York: Harper & Row, 1971), 453–454.

16. Theodore Roosevelt, "The Administration of the Island Possessions," www.english.uiuc.edu/maps/poets/a _f/espada/roosevelt.htm.

17. Miller, *Theodore Roosevelt,* 383–384.

18. Trumbull White, *In the Shadow of Death: Martinique and the World's Great Disaster* (New York: The Publisher's Association, 1902), 81.

19. Miller, *Theodore Roosevelt,* 404; Smith, *America Enters the World,* 53.

20. Harbaugh, *Power and Responsibility,* 209.

21. Dalton, "The Early Life of Theodore Roosevelt," 14; Morris, *The Rise of Theodore Roosevelt,* 12; William G. Gibson, *Theodore Roosevelt Among the Humorists* (Knoxville: University of Tennessee Press, 1980), 25–26; Auchincloss, *Roosevelt,* 76.

22. Smith, *America Enters the World,* 53; Gibson, *Theodore Roosevelt Among the Humorists,* 33–34; Wagenknecht, *The Seven Worlds of Theodore Roosevelt,* 270; Miller, *Theodore Roosevelt,* 408.

23. Cutright, *Theodore Roosevelt the Naturalist,* 124.

24. www.pbs.org/wgbh/amex/tr/panama.html.

25. Miller, *Theodore Roosevelt,* 389–392; Howard K. Beale, *Theodore Roosevelt and the Rise of America to World Power* (Baltimore: The Johns Hopkins Press, 1956), 407.

26. Wagenknecht, *The Seven Worlds of Theodore Roosevelt,* 263.

27. John Milton Cooper, *The Warrior and the Priest: Woodrow Wilson and Theodore Roosevelt,* (Cambridge: The Belknap Press, 1983), 71–72. In 1934, President Franklin D. Roosevelt abandoned the corollary in favor of his Good Neighbor Policy. However, presidents after F.D.R. still used force in places like Panama and Grenada.

28. Morris, *Edith Kermit Roosevelt,* 287; Harbaugh, *Power and Responsibility,* 277; Brands, *T.R.: The Last Romantic,* 319.

29. Smith, *America Enters the World,* 68; Dyer, *Theodore Roosevelt and the Idea of Race,* 136–137; Miller, *Theodore Roosevelt,* 442.

30. Smith, *America Enters the World,* 68; Miller, *Theodore Roosevelt,* 447; Dalton, *Theodore Roosevelt: A Strenuous Life,* 283.

31. Roosevelt, *Letters to Kermit,* 174.

32. Dalton, *Theodore Roosevelt: A Strenuous Life,* 286; Wagenknecht, *The Seven Worlds of Theodore Roosevelt,* 115.

33. Dalton, *Theodore Roosevelt: A Strenuous Life,* 320.

34. Fletcher Pratt, *The Navy: A History* (Garden City, N.Y.: Garden City Publishing Company, 1941), 378–379.

35. Miller, *Theodore Roosevelt,* 479.

36. Dalton, *Theodore Roosevelt: A Strenuous Life,* 333–335.

37. Robert A. Hart, *The Great White Fleet: Its Voyage Around the World, 1907–1909* (Boston: Little, Brown, 1965), 59.

38. Miller, *Theodore Roosevelt,* 481.

9

THE MOST DIFFICULT TASK

1. Thompson, *Presidents I've Known and Two Near Presidents*, 245; Hale, *A Week in the White House,* 57.

2. The total popular vote was: Taft, 7.7 million; Bryan, 6.4 million; Debs, 420,000.

3. Miller, *Theodore Roosevelt,* 490.

4. Cutright, *Theodore Roosevelt the Naturalist,* 195; Brands, *T.R.: The Last Romantic,* 646; Cooper, *Pivotal Decades,* 114.

5. Theodore Roosevelt, *African Game Trails: An Account of the African Wanderings of an American Hunter-Naturalist* (New York: Charles Scribner's Sons, 1910),16–17.

6. Roosevelt, *African Game Trails,* ix, 71, 74.

7. Dalton, *Theodore Roosevelt: A Strenuous Life,* 51; Collier, *The Roosevelts,* 156.

8. Roosevelt, *African Game Trails,* 406–410.

9. Cutright, *Theodore Roosevelt the Naturalist,* 209–210; Miller, *Theodore Roosevelt,* 533.

10. Miller, *Theodore Roosevelt,* 506, 508.

11. *Ibid.,* 511.

12. Dalton, *Theodore Roosevelt: A Strenuous Life,* 356; Miller, *Theodore Roosevelt,* 500, 502.

13. Brands, *T.R.: The Last Romantic,* 666.

14. Howe, *World of Our Fathers,* 297–298; Maxine Schwartz Seller, "The Uprising of the Twenty Thousand," in Dirk Hoerder, ed., *Struggle a Hard Battle: Essays on Working-Class Immigrants* (Dekalb: Northern Illinois University Press, 1986), 254–280. See also Joan Dash, *We Shall Not Be Moved: The Women's Factory Strike of 1909* (New York: Scholastic, 1996).

15. Mario B. DiNunzio, ed., *Theodore Roosevelt: An American Mind, Selected Writings* (New York: Penguin Books, 1994), 141–142.

16. DiNunzio,*Theodore Roosevelt: An American Mind,* 142–146.

17. Leon Steen, *The Triangle Fire* (Philadelphia: Lippincott, 1962), 48. The best recent study is David Van Drehle's, *Triangle: The Fire That Changed America* (New York: Atlantic Monthly Press, 2003).

18. Dalton, *Theodore Roosevelt: A Strenuous Life,* 377.

19. Dalton, *Theodore Roosevelt: A Strenuous Life,* 372–373; Greenberg, *Theodore Roosevelt and Labor,* 416.

20. Dalton, *Theodore Roosevelt: A Strenuous Life,* 370.

21. Cooper, *Pivotal Decades,* 157; Wagenknecht, *The Seven Worlds of Theodore Roosevelt,* 139; Dalton, *Theodore Roosevelt: A Strenuous Life,* 392.

22. Brands, *T.R.: The Last Romantic,* 707; Miller, *Theodore Roosevelt,* 526.

23. James Chace, *1912: Wilson, Roosevelt, Taft and Debs—the Election That Changed the Country* (New York: Simon & Schuster, 2004), 118.

24. DiNunzio, *Theodore Roosevelt: An American Mind,* 160; Smith, *America Enters the World,* 333.

25. Rayford W. Logan, *The Betrayal of the Negro from Rutherford B. Hayes to Woodrow Wilson* (New York: Collier Books, 1965), 361.

26. Cooper, *Pivotal Decades,* 181.

27. Abbott, *Impressions of Theodore Roosevelt,* 280–281; Wood, *Theodore Roosevelt as We Knew Him,* 275–276; William Manners, *TR and Will: A Friendship That Split the Republican Party* (New York: Harcourt Brace Jovanovich, 1969), 266; Chace, *1912,* 205.

28. Abbott, *Impressions of Theodore Roosevelt,* 277; Collier, *The Roosevelts,* 168.

Schrank spent the rest of his life in an asylum.

29. Abbott, *Impressions of Theodore Roosevelt,* 277–278.

30. Dalton, *Theodore Roosevelt: A Strenuous Life,* 406, 408, 411.

31. *Ibid.,* 417–418.

32. Miller, *Theodore Roosevelt,* 535.

33. Miller, *Theodore Roosevelt,* 536–537; Theodore Roosevelt, *Through the Brazilian Wilderness* (New York: Charles Scribner's Sons, 1925), 268.

34. Dalton, *Theodore Roosevelt: A Strenuous Life,* 432.

35. Smith, *America Enters the World,* 312; Ellis, *Echoes of Distant Thunder,* 36.

36. "Woodrow Wilson: The Last Confederate," http://www.pressroom.com/afrimale/wilson.htm; Nancy J. Weiss, "The New Negro and the New Freedom," *Political Science Quarterly,* March 1969, 62.

37. Weiss, "The New Negro and the New Freedom," 67.

38. Kathleen Wolgemuth, "Woodrow Wilson and Federal Segregation," *Journal of Negro History,* April 1959, 166.

39. Brands, *T.R.: The Last Romantic,* 742.

40. Cutright, *Theodore Roosevelt the Naturalist,* 252.

41. *Ibid.*, 254.

10
THE ROUGH RIDER'S LAST FIGHT

1. John Horne, "German 'Atrocities' and Franco-German Opinion, 1914: The Evidence of German Soldiers' Diaries," *Journal of Modern History,* March 1994, 21.

2. John Ellis, *Eye-Deep in Hell: French Warfare in World War* (New York: Pantheon Books, 1976), 54.

3. Cooper, *The Warrior and the Priest,* 273.

4. Wagenknecht, *The Seven Worlds of Theodore Roosevelt,* 245; Brands, *T.R.: The Last Romantic,* 576.

5. Cooper, *The Warrior and the Priest,* 278; Brands, *T.R.: The Last Romantic,* 752; Wagenknecht, *The Seven Worlds of Theodore Roosevelt,* 283; Harbaugh, *Power and Responsibility,* 474.

6. Robert K. Massie, *Castles of Steel: Britain, Germany, and the Winning of the Great War at Sea* (New York: Random House, 2003), 532, 534, 537.

7. Harbaugh, *Power and Responsibility,* 476;

Bishop, *Theodore Roosevelt and His Time,* II, 367, 378, 387.

8. Hagdorn, *The Bugle That Woke America,* 78; Collier, *The Roosevelts,* 193; Dalton, *Theodore Roosevelt: A Strenuous Life,* 456–457.

9. Brands, *T.R.: The Last Romantic,* 773; Wagenknecht, *The Seven Worlds of Theodore Roosevelt,* 142; Dalton, *Theodore Roosevelt: A Strenuous Life,* 469; Collier, *The Roosevelts,* 183.

10. Joseph P. Tumulty, *Woodrow Wilson as I Knew Him* (Garden City, N.Y.: Doubleday, Page, 1921), 259; Woodrow Wilson, *War Messages,* 65th Congress, Senate Document No. 5, Washington, D.C., 1917, 308.

11. Robert H. Ferrell, *Woodrow Wilson and World War I, 1917–1921* (New York: Harper & Row, 1985), 14; Hagdorn, *The Bugle That Woke America,* 36, 131.

12. Mark Sullivan, *Our Times: The United States, 1900–1925,* 5 vols. (New York: Charles Scribner's Sons, 1926–1935), V, 496; Bishop, *Theodore Roosevelt and His Time,* II, 424; Ellis, *Echoes of Distant Thunder,* 337.

13. Sullivan, *Our Times,* V, 497; Longworth, *Crowded Hours,* 245; Dalton, *Theodore Roosevelt: A Strenuous Life,* 481.

14. Dalton, *Theodore Roosevelt: A Strenuous Life,* 447; Renehan, *The Lion's Pride,* 89; Theodore Roosevelt, *Roosevelt in the Kansas City Star: War-Time Editorials* (Boston: Houghton Mifflin, 1921), 97, 100.

15. "Opposition to Wilson's War Message," *www.mtholyoke.edu/acad/intrel/doc19.htm*

16. Hagdorn, *The Bugle That Woke America,* 176.

17. Roosevelt, *Roosevelt in the Kansas City Star,* 132.

18. Cooper, *The Warrior and the Priest,* 320.

19. Ellis, *Echoes of Distant Thunder,* 474; Albert Marrin, *The Last Crusade: The Church of England in the First World War* (Durham, N.C.: Duke University Press, 1974), 182.

20. *Ibid.,* 428–429.

21. Debs, *Writings and Speeches,* 437–439; Tumulty, *Woodrow Wilson as I Knew Him,* 505.

22. Roosevelt, *Foes of Our Own Household,* 33; Roosevelt, *Roosevelt in the Kansas City Star,* 142.

23. Dalton, *Theodore Roosevelt: A Strenuous Life,* 478; H. C. Peterson and Gilbert C. Fite, *Opponents of War, 1917–1918* (Seattle: University of Washington Press, 1968), 14; Roosevelt, *Roosevelt in the Kansas City Star,* 128.

24. Roosevelt, *Roosevelt in the Kansas City Star,* 137; Dalton, *Theodore Roosevelt: A*

Strenuous Life, 493.

25. Sullivan, *Our Times,* V, 486; Ellis, *Echoes of Distant Thunder,* 410–411.

26. Dalton, *Theodore Roosevelt: A Strenuous Life,* 480; Elliott M. Rudwick's *Race Riot at East St. Louis, July 2, 1917* (Carbondale: Southern Illinois University Press, 1964) tells the whole sad story.

27. Lerone Bennett Jr., *Before the Mayflower: A History of Black America* (New York: Penguin Books, 1984), 349–350.

28. Roosevelt, *Letters,* VIII, 1211; Dalton, *Theodore Roosevelt: A Strenuous Life,* 485–486, 509–510.

29. Bishop, *Theodore Roosevelt and His Time,* II, 432.

30. *Ibid.*, II, 433–434.

31. Dalton, *Theodore Roosevelt: A Strenuous Life,* 519.

32. Fleming, *Illusion of Victory,* 210–211.

33. Collier, *The Roosevelts,* 219.

34. Hagdorn, *The Bugle That Woke America,* 140–141.

35. Miller, *Theodore Roosevelt,* 560; Wagenknecht, *The Seven Worlds of Theodore Roosevelt,* 179.

36. Eddie W. Rickenbacker, *Fighting the Flying Circus* (Garden City, N.Y.: Doubleday, 1965), 153.

37. Hagdorn, *The Bugle That Woke America,* 191.

38. Morris, *Edith Kermit Roosevelt,* 429; Dalton, *Theodore Roosevelt: A Strenuous Life,* 511.

39. Harbaugh, *Power and Responsibility,* 495; Hagdorn, *The Bugle That Woke America,* 198.

40. Hagdorn, *The Bugle That Woke America,* 197.

41. Renehan, *The Lion's Pride,* 174; Susan Everett, *The Two World Wars* (London: Bison Books, 1982), 248.

42. Meirion and Susie Harries, *The Last Days of Innocence: America at War, 1917–1918* (New York: Random House, 1997), 421.

43. For Roosevelt's last hours, see Amos, *Theodore Roosevelt: Hero to His Valet,* 153–157.

44. Brands, *T.R.: The Last Romantic,* 811.

45. Dalton, *Theodore Roosevelt: A Strenuous Life,* 523–524.

FOR FURTHER READING

About Theodore Roosevelt and his family

Auchincloss, Louis. *Theodore Roosevelt*, New York: Henry Holt, 2002.

Brands, H.W. *T.R. The Last Romantic*. New York: Basic Books,1997.

Chace, James. *1912: Wilson, Roosevelt, Taft & Debs—the Election That Changed the Country*. New York: Simon & Schuster, 2004.

Collier, Peter. *The Roosevelts: An American Saga*. New York: Simon & Schuster, 1994.

Dalton, Kathleen. *Theodore Roosevelt: A Strenuous Life*. New York: Knopf, 2002.

Dyer, Thomas G. *Theodore Roosevelt and the Idea of Race*. Baton Rouge: Louisiana State University Press, 1980.

Hagdorn, Hermann. *The Boys' Life of Theodore Roosevelt*. New York: Harper & Brothers, 1918. Hagdorn was a close friend of Roosevelt's, so what he says is often based on firsthand information.

McCullough, David. *Mornings on Horseback: The Story of an Extraordinary Family, a Vanished Way of Life and the Unique Child Who Became Theodore Roosevelt*. New York: Simon & Schuster, 1981.

Miller, Nathan. *Theodore Roosevelt: A Life*. New York: William Morrow, 1992.

Morris, Edmund. *The Rise of Theodore Roosevelt*. New York: Coward, McCann & Geoghegan, 1979.

————*Theodore Rex*. New York: Random House, 2001.

Morris, Sylvia Jukes. *Edith Kermit Roosevelt: Portrait of a First Lady*. New York: Coward, McCann & Geoghegan, 1980.

Riis, Jacob A. *Theodore Roosevelt the Citizen*. New York: The Outlook Company, 1904.

Renehan, Edward J., Jr. *The Lion's Pride: Theodore Roosevelt and His Family in Peace and War*. New York: Oxford University Press, 1998.

Roosevelt, Theodore. A Book Lover's Holiday in the Open. New York: Charles Scribner's Sons, 1916.

————*African Game Trails: An Account of the African Wanderings of an American Hunter-Naturalist*. New York: Charles Scribner's Sons, 1910.

————*American Problems*. New York: Charles Scribner's Sons, 1926.

———— *An Autobiography*. New York: Da Capo, 1985. First published in 1913.

————*Diaries of Boyhood and Youth*. New York: Charles Scribner's Sons, 1928.

————*The Foes of Our Own Household, in The Works of Theodore Roosevelt*, National Edition, vol. XIX. New York: Charles Scribner's Sons, 1926.

————*History as Literature and Other Essays*. New York: Charles Scribner's Sons, 1913.

————*Hunting Expeditions in the West*. New York: G. P. Putnam's Sons, 1927. Contains *Hunting Trips of a Ranchman* and *The Wilderness Hunter*.

————*Letters to Kermit from Theodore Roosevelt*. New York: Charles Scribner's Sons, 1946.

————*The Letters of Theodore Roosevelt*, ed. Elting E. Morison, John Morton Blum, and Alfred Chandler. 8 vols. Cambridge, MA.: Harvard University Press, 1951-1954.

————*Roosevelt in the Kansas City Star: War-Time Editorials*. Boston: Houghton Mifflin Company, 1921.

————*The Rough Riders and Men of Action*. New York: Charles Scribner's Sons, 1926.

————*Theodore Roosevelt: An American Mind, Selected Writings*, edited by Mario R. DiNunzio. New York: Penguin Books, 1994.

————*Theodore Roosevelt's Letters to His Children*. New York: Charles Scribner's Sons, 1928.

————*Through the Brazilian Wilderness*. New York: Charles Scribner's Sons, 1925.

————*Presidential Addresses and State Papers; European Addresses*. 8 vols., New York: The Review of Reviews Co., 1910.

————*The Selected letters of Theodore Roosevelt*, New York: Cooper Square Press, 2001.

————*The Works of Theodore Roosevelt*. 20 vols. National Edition, New York: Charles Scribner's Sons, 1926.

Samuels, Peggy. *Teddy Roosevelt at San Juan: The Making of a President*. Texas: Texas A&M University Press, 1997.

Watts, Sarah. *Rough Rider in the White House: Theodore Roosevelt and the Politics of Desire*. Chicago: University of Chicago Press, 2003.

About Theodore Roosevelt's America

Avrich, Paul. *The Haymarket Tragedy*. Princeton: Princeton University Press, 1984.

Bennett, Lerone, Jr. *Before the Mayflower: A History of Black America*. New York: Penguin Books, 1984.

Buckley, Gail. *American Patriots: The Story of Blacks in the Military from the Revolution to Desert Storm*. New York: Random House, 2001.

Dray, Philip. *At the Hands of Persons Unknown: The Lynching of Black America*. New York: Random House, 2002.

Du Bois, W.E.B. *Writings*. New York: The Library of America, 1986.

Franklin, John Hope. *From Slavery to Freedom: A History of American Negroes*. New York: Knopf, 1960.

Gossett, Thomas F. *Race: The History of an Idea in America*. New York: Schocken Books, 1965.

Harlan, Louis R. *Booker T. Washington: The Wizard of Tuskegee, 1901-1915*. New York: Oxford University Press, 1983.

Isenberg, Andrew C. *The Destruction of the Bison*. New York: Cambridge University Press, 2000.

Jackson, Kenneth T., and Dunbar, David S., eds. *Empire City: New York Through the Centuries*. New York: Columbia University Press, 2002.

Karnow, Stanley. *In Our Image: America's Empire in the Philippines*. New York: Random House, 1989.

McCullough, David. *The Path Between the Seas: The Creation of the Panama Canal, 1870–1914*. New York: Simon & Schuster, 1971.

Miller, Char. *Gifford Pinchot and the Making of Modern American Environmentalism*. Washington, D.C.: Island Press, 2001.

O'Toole. *The Spanish War: An American Epic—1898*. New York: W.W. Norton, 1984.

Painter, Nell Irvin. *Standing at Armageddon: The United States, 1877–1919*. New York: W.W. Norton, 1987.

Porter, Glenn. *The Rise of Big Business, 1860–1920*. Arlington Heights, Illinois: Harlan Davidson, Inc., 1992.

Rauchway, Eric. *Murdering McKinley: The Making of Theodore Roosevelt's America*. New York: Hill and Wang, 2003.

Riis, Jacob A. *The Making of an American*. New York: Macmillan, 1901.

———*How the Other Half Lives*. New York: Penguin Classics, 1997.

Smith, Page. *America Enters the World: A People's History of the Progressive Era and World War I*. New York: McGraw-Hill, 1985.

———*The Rise of Industrial America*. New York: McGraw-Hill, 1984.

Steinberg, Ted. *Down to Earth: Nature's Role in American History*. New York: Oxford University Press, 2002.

Strouse, Jean. *Morgan: American Financier*. New York: Random House, 1999.

Wall, Joseph Frazier. *Andrew Carnegie*. New York: Oxford University Press, 1970.

Wells, Ida B. *Southern Horrors and Other Writings: The Anti-Lynching Campaign of Ida B. Wells, 1892–1900*. Bedford Books: Boston: 1997.

Woodward, C. Vann. *The Strange Career of Jim Crow*. New York: Oxford University Press, 1955.

Young, Marguerite. *Harp Song For a Radical: The Life and Times of Eugene Victor Debs*. New York: Alfred A. Knopf, 1999.

Page number in *italics* refer to illustrations.